Sing Along | Sing Together!

The Open Singing Choir Songbook

Edited by
Michael Gohl and Jan Schumacher

Eigentum des Verlegers · Alle Rechte vorbehalten
All rights reserved

C. F. PETERS Ltd & Co. KG, Leipzig
A member of the Edition Peters Group
Leipzig · London · New York
www.editionpeters.com

© 2015 by C. F. Peters Ltd & Co. KG, Leipzig

All rights reserved. No part of this publication may be reproduced, stored in a retrieval system or transmitted in any form or by any means, electronic, mechanical, photocopying, recording or otherwise, without the prior permission of the publisher.

ISMN 979-0-014-11926-3

Translated by Richard George Elliott
Additional translations: Arne Muus, James Phetterplace
Music set by Julia Juraschewski
Cover Design: Goscha Nowak
Layout inside pages: Dominik Joswig
Illustrations: Sabrina Quintero

Printed in England by Halstan & Co, Amersham, Bucks.

THIS BOOK WAS ADAPTED FROM THE ORIGINAL GERMAN EDITION,
"SING ALONG – SINGT MIT. DAS CHOR- UND LIEDERBUCH
ZUM OFFENEN SINGEN" (EP 11400),
UNDER THE AUSPICES OF THE
EUROPEAN CHORAL ASSOCIATION – EUROPA CANTAT (ECA-EC).

Compilations with individually selected titles for specific Open Singing events can be requested from the publisher.

Email: vertrieb@editionpeters.com
Phone: +49 (0) 341 / 98 97 92 - 10
www.edition-peters.de

A Note from the President of the European Choral Association – Europa Cantat

In the late 1950s, a number of choral directors came together to consider how they and their choirs could contribute to peace in Europe. This led to the first EUROPA CANTAT Festival, at which choirs and individual singers from different countries spent ten days living alongside one another and learning new repertoire in internationally constituted *ateliers*. In order to boost the sense of community even further, a daily "open singing" session was held in which all the festival participants took part.

From that time right up to the present day, our number one concern has been to bring together people of different cultures and of all ages through collective singing in order to promote understanding, tolerance and rapprochement between different cultures in Europe and beyond.

Following on in this tradition that stretches back almost 60 years, we now wish to widen the circle of those we are able to reach with this message. Under the motto "Reach Out", a key aspect of our strategy for the forthcoming years is therefore to tap into a new public and to get through to those who have not (yet) had the opportunity to sing in a choir and, based on their initial experiences, develop a taste for singing with others.

In this sense, "open singing" is a fundamental component of our strategy and events. For the participants, it offers a means of connecting with one another and helps them to develop a shared repertoire. Traditionally, open singing events of this kind involved only the festival participants and were often held in closed rooms on the outskirts of a city. Gradually, however, it was discovered that there was an opportunity for open singing to open up further, through the holding of events in public places or by drawing audiences in churches and concert halls into active participation. As a result, the EUROPA CANTAT Festival in Turin in summer 2012 saw several thousand people – festival participants, inhabitants of the city and tourists – congregating each evening in the central Piazza San Carlo to sing and move together. Anyone who experienced the atmosphere in this square knows what a profound effect it had on all concerned.

Other important aims of the European Choral Association – Europa Cantat include the training and development of conductors. Thus our recommending of the open singing masterclass at the European Festival of Youth Choirs in Basel in 2014, under the direction of Michael Gohl, marked the beginning of a cycle of training that will continue at the EUROPA CANTAT Festival in Pécs in 2015 and which is designed to equip more musicians with the necessary tools of the trade. We are therefore delighted by this publication, which will offer an increasing number of choral directors the opportunity to discover, and try out, open singing.

It gives the European Choral Association great pleasure to become patron of the English-language international edition of *Sing Along – Sing Together*!

Gábor Móczár,
President of the European Choral Association – Europa Cantat

The European Choral Association - Europa Cantat came into being as the result of a merger between the European Federation of Young Choirs (later Europa Cantat), founded in 1960/1963, and the Arbeitsgemeinschaft Europäischer Chorverbände (AGEC), founded in 1955.

www.europeanchoralassociation.org

Contents

PREFACE, ACKNOWLEDGEMENTS	6
INTRODUCTION	8
CONTENTS MUSIC	10
I. CANONS, HUMOUR, MOVEMENT	13
II. AROUND THE WORLD	55
III. CLASSICAL AND SACRED	117
IV. ADVENT AND CHRISTMAS	153
V. GOSPEL, BLUES, JAZZ	169
VI. ROCK, POP, EVERGREEN	191
OPEN SINGING – PRINCIPLES AND METHODOLOGY (MICHAEL GOHL)	230
APPENDIX I: ALPHABETICAL INDEX OF TITLES	246
APPENDIX II: INDEX OF TITLES BY CATEGORIES	248
THE EDITORS	255

Torino, Piazza San Carlo, Open Singing at Europa Cantat Festival 2012

Preface

Turin, Piazza San Carlo, in August 2012 – the grand finale of the 13th Europa Cantat Festival sees 4000 singers from all across the world perform Puccini's "Nessun Dorma", and several thousand amazed passers-by, tourists and festival guests join in with the participants. The following year, a similar event concludes the "Choralies" festival in Vaison-la-Romaine, and much the same is to be expected at this year's 14th Europa Cantat Festival in Pécs/Hungary. *Open Singing* of this kind is an extraordinary experience, and has been shared – on a smaller or larger scale – by many people.

Shortly after the Turin Festival, a discussion between Hermann Eckel (Managing Director, Edition Peters Germany) and the editors led to the idea for this book: What exactly is *Open Singing*? How is it characterized? How can a performance bring together singers and "non-singers" (if indeed there such a thing)? By which means will *Open Singing* inspire choirs and audience members in equal measure? When singing together at concerts, festivals or religious services, how do you avoid chaos or boredom? This book sets out to answer these questions!

Open Singing events involving hundreds or thousands of performers formed the cradle of Europa Cantat, a series of large-scale festivals originally organised by the European Federation of Young Choirs, EFYC (now the European Choral Association, ECA). It was created and fostered as a means to build strong bridges between the nations that had been divided by the Second World War, initially between France and Germany. The 1960 founding members of the EFYC were the French organisation "À Chœur Joie" and the German Association "Musik in der Jugend" (AMJ).

Many of the greatest choir directors have since been involved in this way of making music. Figureheads of *Open Singing* in the post-war period included César Geoffray in France, Gottfried Wolters in Germany, and Oriol Martorell in Spain. Its foundations had been laid previously by the "Fathers of Singing", such as Fritz Jöde in Germany, who developed a set of guiding principles for *Open Singing* as early as 1920, and the French humanist and musician César Geoffray, founder of the "À Chœur Joie" movement (1940). Programmes produced by public broadcaster WDR in Germany (from 1958), and by Willi Gohl for DRS, the radio station of the German- and Romansh-speaking parts of Switzerland (starting a few years later), brought *Open Singing* into everyone's home. Hundreds of episodes of long-running series like "Sing mit uns" (WDR) and "Sing mit!" (Radio DRS), accompanied by printed song books, enabled literally thousands of listeners to join in. These programmes were so popular that they continued to be produced and broadcast well into the new millennium.

One aspect that did not form part of the mindset espoused by Fritz Jöde and other members of the pre-war generation has since become a prevalent theme: as the founding fathers of Europa Cantat and their successors have demonstrated time and again, singing together has the power to overcome all cultural and religious borders between the performers, and to create a fresh sense of community through a common repertoire of songs. Their work also shows that singing together does not necessarily take on an ideological dimension – a danger that undeniably lurks behind any collective occasion or mass event.

The end of the 20th century saw a decline in the popularity of traditional *Open Singing*. At the same time, there has been an improvement in the quality of choirs and choral singers worldwide, raising both skills and expectations for *Open Singing* events. The gap between well-trained choral singers and lovers of singing who are not members of a choir has widened – but even greater is now their remove from the vast majority of people from all social backgrounds, who have less and less occasion to sing together spontaneously. The high social prestige accorded to pop and "classical" stars makes singing with others seem rather unappealing at first glance, particularly to young people. Only strong emotional experiences of this kind can reveal the fundamental difference between consuming music, and singing or performing it yourself.

Fortunately, a certain movement in this direction has been evident for some time: singing projects involving people of all ages, and catering for diverse requirements, are springing up in more and more places; and strong-willed, idealistic music educators have created high-profile schemes aimed at schools and at those on the margins of society. Through these projects, many people have been able to experience for the first time that there are no losers in making music, only winners. The popularity of films like "Sister Act", "The Chorus", and "As It Is in Heaven", along with casting shows for choirs, serves to emphasise this trend: in a completely new way, singing is "in" again. Therefore we are confident that a new and fresh kind of *Open Singing* is the order of the day, providing novel fare for those who love singing already, and opening doors for those who are only just beginning to discover their urge to sing.

A crucial element in the success of *Open Singing* is the choice of appropriate repertoire. This book contains more than 150 compositions, which could not be more stylistically diverse. What unites them is the creative potential they offer: most pieces can be sung in unison or in several parts; chord symbols make it easy to accompany them, if desired; and notes on interpretation and movement instructions provide a wealth of further ideas. Additional material for leaders of *Open Singing* sessions is available for download (www.editionpeters.com/singalong). We have deliberately opted for a practical type of notation that is easily accessible for choirs and audiences alike. This book sets out to encourage and enable both young and experienced choral directors to increase the *Open Singing* activities in their community, and to develop them in their own individual way.

Michael Gohl and Jan Schumacher

Acknowledgements

Above all, what is needed is a publisher's heart that beats for the subject in general, and for a book of this kind in particular. First and foremost, we are therefore grateful to Hermann Eckel for his vision and his encouraging ideas. He also made the fortunate decision of teaming us up with Sabrina Quintero, who was equally supportive as an enthusiastic project manager and a discerning editor. Many thanks, Sabrina, for your expert advice and tireless attention to detail! Sincere thanks are due to the wonderful colleagues at Peters who worked on the music setting, layout, corrections etc., and who had to keep up with our frequent changes and new ideas. Thanks to the many fellow choral directors who, directly or indirectly, provided suggestions or critical feedback. The real groundwork for this book, however, was completed by generations of choral directors who ventured into the field of *Open Singing* in the past, and continue to do so today. Many of them have achieved true mastery of this métier, and they serve us as models and infinite sources of inspiration.

Michael Gohl and Jan Schumacher   July 2015

Introduction

 Music: You more than us..., from every wherefore freed...
Rainer Maria Rilke (tr. John L. Mood)

WHAT IS IT THAT MAKES OPEN SINGING SO SPECIAL?

"Singing along" with other people, freely and without any pressure, is possible in a variety of situations today, for example at family, social or religious occasions and even at mass gatherings and sporting events. There is also an increasing number of singing opportunities "for beginners" and within the context of paths to self-awareness and the development of inner equilibrium. The Open Singing that forms the subject of this publication differs from the above in three key respects:
- It is a musical event. In other words the focus is on the singing itself, the songs and the music.
- The event is directed by music professionals.
- The aim is for the participants to be musically inspired and enriched, to make new discoveries and for their musical skills to be fostered and developed.

As a result, the directors and organizers have a threefold task:
- Open Singing must also be open in the sense that it remains independent of religious worship and ideology.
- The participants must be allowed to feel that singing with other people is a natural and existential ability, and their confidence in their own abilities must be fostered on a sustained basis.
- The music must be selected and handled in such a way that the Open Singing event bridges traditions and cultures and enables the participants to widen their horizons and grow as individuals.

THE ESSENTIAL CHARACTERISTICS OF OPEN SINGING TODAY

- All participants are made to feel unconditionally welcome and encouraged in their singing.
- The focus is on music-making, not on delivering or listening to lectures.
- Pieces are only rehearsed for as long as it takes to experience their essence and message.
- Material is only repeated in order to intensify the musical experience.
- Songs are selected on the basis of high quality standards.
- The participants will be introduced to new songs and musical forms.

Within the context of festivals and choral conventions, Open Singing can achieve even more than this:
- The elaboration of a festival repertoire.
- Artistic inspiration from a versatile pilot choir of exemplary quality.
- Encounters with other cultures and musical traditions.
- Encounters with a range of conductors.
- Brief introductions to new songs as a stimulus to singing these pieces at a later date.
- And most importantly: the creation of a festival atmosphere characterized by open-mindedness, mutual respect and a coming together in the act of shared music-making.

THE CHOICE OF REPERTOIRE

"The choice of repertoire determines the quality of the choir". This principle, one well known to choral directors, applies more than ever to Open Singing. Because little is known during the planning stage about the public's expectations and abilities, the selection of songs being made available must be both generous and varied.

An initial selection will be made when drawing up the songs for the song sheet or songbook. A second selection will follow just before, and at times spontaneously during, the Open Singing event itself. Although a methodical approach, attention to detail and communication skills on the part of the leader are crucial, the choice of repertoire is the prerequisite for, and foundation of, a successful Open Singing event. (For more on repertoire see p. 234ff.)

An ideal, well-balanced repertoire of songs will include:
- Songs that can be sung, and that will sound good, quickly in order to encourage people to enter into the spirit of the event and get to know one another.

INTRODUCTION

- Canons of various degrees of difficulty in order to develop and dynamize a shared communicative and sound space among the participants.
- Songs involving movement or body percussion aimed at relaxing and animating the participants and focusing their concentration.
- Forming the heart of the programme, a varied repertoire offering a wide range of character, style, genre and content.
- At international festivals, attention should also be paid to achieving a balance in terms of the country of origin of the songs.

In the Appendix to this book there is a chart giving the authors' recommendations regarding the suitability of the individual pieces for different groups of participants (content by category).

INSTRUMENTAL ACCOMPANIMENT, SONG LEADERS, PILOT CHOIRS

The notion of "singing ALONG" is all very well, but with whom? Who will lead the singing? Who will establish the musical space in which the participants will feel they are in safe hands?

Directing an Open Singing session alone, without piano, so to speak "freehand", is a very great challenge for a choral director, above all when the repertoire includes songs that are not well known and when the participants are not adept at reading music. (The circle song and related forms of song-leading are a useful option at such times.) The bigger the occasion and the greater the need for the Open Singing event to be successful and of high quality, the more it makes sense to provide musical accompaniment and enhancement, for example in the form of a versatile pianist and if need be other instruments as well, song leaders, and ideally a pilot choir.

What Zoltán Kodály called for in music teaching aimed at children applies equally to Open Singing: "Only the best is good enough!".

„DON'T STOP THE FLOW!"

Directing a large-scale Open Singing event is like steering an ocean liner: getting it moving requires an enormous impetus, every instruction or change of direction is magnified many times and braking requires a huge amount of energy.

Successful "steering" of an Open Singing event calls for an alert seizing of the momentum and an ability to assess the potential of the participants quickly and reliably.

The most successful Open Singing directors have always impressed with their outstanding musicality, their talent for communication and their charisma. Skills such as creativity, spontaneity, the courage to experiment and a clear view of the whole cannot be learned from a book. Upon closer inspection, however, a number of recurring musical and methodological organizational principles can be identified that will help an Open Singing event to succeed without hitch and without interruption to the musical flow. The aim of this book is to invite its users to discover such methods for themselves and develop them further.

HINTS AND TIPS

The key factors in directing an Open Singing event are summarized in the chapter "Open Singing - Principles and Methodology" (p. 230ff.).

The advice and suggestions provided in this book do not claim to be complete, scientifically proven or even absolutely new. They are not intended to be regarded as set in stone or as the be-all and end-all of Open Singing. Experienced choir directors will find they are already familiar with many of them. Rather, the statements and recommendations offered here are the result of many years of pedagogical activity in the musical field, and of dealing with and pondering pedagogical issues in general. In particular, however, they are the result of experience acquired and observation and reflections made during the directing of countless Open Singing events. These events have taken place under all imaginable circumstances, involving both complete beginners and proficient choral singers, with participants of all ages, in dozens of schools and on every scale from the small and intimate to the immense, involving thousands of participants. The remarks and explanations offered here represent an attempt to highlight the various factors that will allow the participants to rediscover their own, perhaps buried, pleasure in singing and to regain confidence in their own abilities, but also to learn something new and thrilling within a short space of time and to help to raise each other's game, thereby experiencing exhilarating moments of shared music-making.

Michael Gohl

Contents – Music

I. CANONS, HUMOUR, MOVEMENT

1. All Praise to Thee (Th. Tallis), 4–8 part canon......14
2. Glory, Glory (M. Gohl), 3-part canon............14
3. Réunis Aujourd'hui (C. Geoffray), 3-part canon....15
4. Da pacem, Domine (M. Franck), 4-part canon.....16
5. Da pacem, Domine (P. Petersen), 3 canons........16
6. Jubilate Deo (M. Praetorius), 5-part canon........17
7. Jubilate (M. Praetorius), 6-part canon 17
8. Laudemus Virginem, 3-part canon 18
9. Splendens Ceptigera, 3-part canon..............18
10. Dona nobis pacem, 3-part canon................19
11. Jahreszeiten-Kanon (P. Dubs), 4-part canon.......19
12. Apollo (M. Gohl), 4-part canon 20
13. Give It Up! (M. Gohl), 5-part canon..............21
14. Hello (F. Fluri), 3-part canon 22
15. Goodbye (F. Fluri), 4-part canon 23
16. Good Morning (R. Sund), 5-part canon 24
17. Lai-la (Czech folk tune, M. Gohl)................25
18. Ding dong (M. Gohl), 4-part canon 26
19. Ayelevi (Trad. Ghana) 27
20. Branle du Quercy (French dance music) 28
21. Robinson (German children's song, M. Frey).......29
22. Heigh-Ho! Anybody home?, 3-part canon 30
23. Hine ma tov u'manayim, 2-part canon...........30
24. Frère Jacques, 4-part canon....................31
25. Ja dan duia (S. Perkiö), 8-part canon 32
26. I Like The Flowers, 4-part canon 33
27. Zwei Schritt nach links, 4-part canon............33
28. Move On! (Barkani / Natzchan), 6-part canon.....34
29. Dito (J. Siegrist), 3-part canon...................35
30. Makumaná (J. Debón), 4-part canon.............36
31. Hotaru Koi (Trad. Japan), 3-part (or more) canon ..37
32. The Big Band (J. Fischer), 3 to 6-part canon.......37
33. Fruit canon, 3-part canon 38
34. Calypso (J. Holdstock), 3-part canon.............39
35. Funky Goodbye (M. Detterbeck)................40
36. Me and Jack (J. Rathbone).....................42
37. Vanitas Vanitatum (J. P. Sweelinck), 4-part canon...43
38. Spring (Th. Gummesson), 3-part canon..........43
39. Flying (A. Simmons), 3-part canon 44
40. Sambabrasil (Th. Gummesson), 3-part canon......45
41. Alpen-Rumba (U. Führe), 3-part canon...........46
42. Alpen-Rumba Vocal percussion (M. Gohl)........47

Picture credits:
Front cover: © Festival Europa Cantat Torino 2012.
Pages 5, 90: © Festival Europa Cantat Torino 2012.
Page 15, 93, 146: With kind permission of the European Choral Association – Europa Cantat (ECA-EC).
Page 32: © Michael Gohl
Illustrations pp. 26, 27, 36, 75: © Sabrina Quintero

CONTENTS – MUSIC

43. Goli goggoli!!! (W. Buchenberg).................48
44. Taga del i öst och väst (G. Eriksson), circle song 50
45. A Summer's Over (G. Christensen), 3-part canon....51
46. Polska efter Jon-Sebastian (G. M Hägg) 52
47. The First Commandment of Art (J. Haydn), canon.... 54
48. Von guten Mächten (M. Gohl), 4-part canon......54

II. AROUND THE WORLD

49. Un poquito cantas (Trad. South America).........56
50. Sakura (Trad. Japan, H. Willisegger) 57
51. Evening Rise (Indian folk song) 58
52. Evening Rise (SSAATB, arr. M. Ansohn) 58
53. Let me fish off cape St. Mary's (Kelland/Loomer) .. 60
54. Shenandoah (Trad. USA).......................61
55. La Bamba (Trad. Mexico) 62
56. Janie Mama (Trad. Caribbean), 4-part canon......63
57. Hue Gim Go (Trad. Taiwan)....................63
58. Mo Li Hua (Chinese folk song, arr. A. Merusch) 64
59. Arirang (Korean folk song) 65
60. Arirang (SATB, arr. Young Jo Lee)................66
61. Minoi, Minoi (Trad. Samoan, arr. C. Marshall)......70
62. O-re-mi (Trad. Nigeria, arr. M. Brewer) 72
63. Si ya hamba (Trad. South Africa, arr. F. Gohl) 74
64. Sangena (Trad. Zulu, arr. Prof. M. Khumalo) 75
65. Nginesi Ponono (Trad. South Africa, arr. M. Gohl) ...78
66. Noyana (Trad. South Africa, arr. F. Gohl) 79
67. African Alleluja (M. Detterbeck)..................80
68. Ah ya zein (Trad. Arabic, arr. H. Willisegger).......81
69. Keshet l'vana / A White Rainbow (J. Hadar).......82
70. Samiotissa (Greece, Island Samos) 84
71. El haderech (Trad. Israel, arr. M. Gohl)............84
72. Što mi e milo (Trad. Macedonia) 85
73. Istanbul Kasap Havası (Trad. Turkish-Greek).......86
74. Çayeli'nden öteye (Trad. Turkish, arr. M. Başman)....87
75. Tiliseb (from Estonia, L. Virkhaus) 88
76. Nocturne (E. Taube / A. Öhrwall)................89
77. Dobrú noć (Trad. Czech, arr. Van den Borre) 90
78. Mu Süda, Ärka Üles (from Estonia, C. Kreek) 91
79. Leijoo (Trad. Lapland, S. Valvanne)...............92
80. Flikkain polska (Trad. Finland, K. A. Pöllanen)......93
81. Gamla Moder Jord (Trad. Sweden, M. Detterbeck)... 94
82. Vem kan segla förutan vind (arr. G. Eriksson)......95
83. Kom! (M. Åslund).............................96
84. All through the Night (Trad. Wales, M. Goldring)... 98
85. Autumn Comes (Trad. England, arr. A. Merusch) ...99
86. Greensleeves (Trad. England / Scotland) 100
87. Porompom pón / El Porompompero (Trad. Spain)..101
88. Lili eder bat (Basque Country, arr. J. Busto) 102
89. Santa Lucia (Trad. Italy) 104
90. Sankta Lucia (SAB, arr. C.-B. Agnestig) 105
91. Pique la baleine (P. Denain / L. Guilloré).........106
92. Una mattina (Trad. Italy) 107
93. Ritsch, ratsch fidirullala (Trad. Swiss, M. Gohl) ...108
94. Der Hasbâcher (Trad. Austria)..................109
95. Schläft ein Lied (M. Gohl / J. von Eichendorff)... 110
96. Der Mond ist aufgegangen (J. A. P. Schulz) 110
97. Der Mond ist aufgegangen (SATB, A. Seifert).....111
98. Du fragsch mi, wär i bi (Trad. Switzerland).......112
99. All mein Gedanken, die ich hab (arr. M. Gohl) 113
100. All mein Gedanken, die ich hab (SATB, J. Brahms)..114
101. The River She is Flowing (Trad. Indian, arr. M. Gohl) ..116

III. CLASSICAL AND SACRED

102. Da pacem Introitus (arr. B. Kinzler) 118
103. Miserere mei Domine (J. P. Sweelinck / M. Gohl)...120
104. Canon angelicus – Sanctus (R. Micheli) 121
105. Magnificat (Taizé, J. Berthier) 122
106. Nada te turbe (Taizé, J. Berthier)................123
107. Tebe pojem (St. St. Mokranjak) 124
108. Nun ruhen alle Wälder (H. Isaac / J. S. Bach).....126
109. Alta Trinità Beata (Italian lauda, anonymous) 127
110. Veni Creator Spiritus (P. Esterházy) 128
111. Come Ye Sons of Art (H. Purcell) 129
112. Alleluja (Trad., arr. W. Gohl) 129
113. Stabat Mater (Z. Kodály, arr. I. Sulyok) 130
114. Immortal Bach (J. S. Bach, arr. K. Nystedt) 131
115. Olson III (T. Riley)............................132
116. Breath Soft, Ye Winds (W. Paxton) 134
117. La Nuit (J. Ph. Rameau, arr. J. Noyon) 136
118. Sweet and low (J. Barnby) 140
119. Guten Abend, gut' Nacht (J. Brahms) 142
120. Dindirindin (Cancionero de Palacio) 144

CONTENTS – MUSIC

121. Tuonane Paradiso (Trad. Tansania, arr. A. Schmid) . . . 145
122. An Irish Blessing (Trad. Irland, J. E. Moore Jr.) 146
123. An Irish Blessing (SATB, arr. J. E. Moore Jr.) 147
124. Va, pensiero (from "Nabucco", G. Verdi) 148
125. Tábortűznél (L. Bárdos) 150
126. Jerusalem (C. H. H. Parry) 152

IV. ADVENT AND CHRISTMAS

127. Joy To The World (G. F. Händel, arr. B. Fritschi). . . . 154
128. Halleluja (K. Lafferty), 2-part canon 155
129. Hark! The Herald Angels Sing (W. H. Cummings) . . . 156
130. Hail! Blessed Virgin Mary (Ch. Wood) 157
131. O Little Town of Bethlehem (17th century) 158
132. El cant dels ocells (arr. O. Martorell) 160
133. Cantique de Noël (A. Adam, arr. A. Lindström) 162
134. Feliz Navidad (J. Feliciano) 164
135. Noël, Noël (J. Holdstock), 3-part canon 165
136. Jingle Bells (J. L. Pierpont, arr. M. Detterbeck) 166

V. GOSPEL, BLUES, JAZZ

137. A Loop Song (B. Gröger) 170
138. Everybody Sings (B. Gröger) 171
139. If You're Happy (H. Førde, arr. R. Sund) 172
140. Now Let Us Sing (anonymous) 173
141. C-Jam-Blues (D. Ellington, arr. B. Gröger) 174
142. Give thanks (Trad., arr. M. Gohl) 176
143. Sister, Carry On (C. McDade, arr. F. Gohl) 178
144. My Lord, What a Morning (arr. M. Gohl) 180
145. I Am His Child (M. Hogan) 182
146. Hallelujah Gospel Theme (A. Crouch) 184
147. Hymn to Freedom (O. Peterson) 185

148. Hymn to Freedom (SATB, arr. P. Read) 186
149. Yes, Lord, Yes (A. Crouch) 190

VI. ROCK, POP, EVERGREEN

150. I am Sailing (G. Sutherland) 192
151. Love Me Tender (Presley / Matson, arr. M. Gohl) . . . 192
152. With a Smile (M. Detterbeck) 194
153. Salsa Beach Band (M. Detterbeck) 195
154. Rock 'n' Roll Band (M. Detterbeck) 196
155. Pata Pata (M. Makeba, arr. M. Detterbeck) 198
156. Hit The Road, Jack (P. Mayfield, arr. M. Carbow) . . 200
157. All my Loving (Lennon / McCartney, arr. T. Gohl) . . 202
158. Yesterday (Lennon / McCartney, arr. M. Gohl) 204
159. Aunt Dinah has Blowed de Horn (S. Joplin) 206
160. Tears in Heaven (Clapton / Jennings, arr. J. Høybye) . . 208
161. That Lucky Old Sun (arr. R. Sund) 210
162. Autumn Leaves (J. Kosma / J. Mercer) 213
163. As Tears Go By (arr. W. Hoffmann) 214
164. Lemon Tree (arr. M. Detterbeck) 216
165. Hallelujah, I Just Love Him (Her) So (arr. R. Sund) . . 224
166. Happy (Ph. Williams, arr. B. Gröger) 227

I. Canons, Humour, Movement

Laughter is the dancing of the breath.

Indian saying

Rhythm is order in movement.
Harmony is order in voices.

Plato

I. CANONS, HUMOUR, MOVEMENT

1. All Praise to Thee 4–8-part canon

Music: Thomas Tallis (1505–1585)
Words: Thomas Kern / Goethe

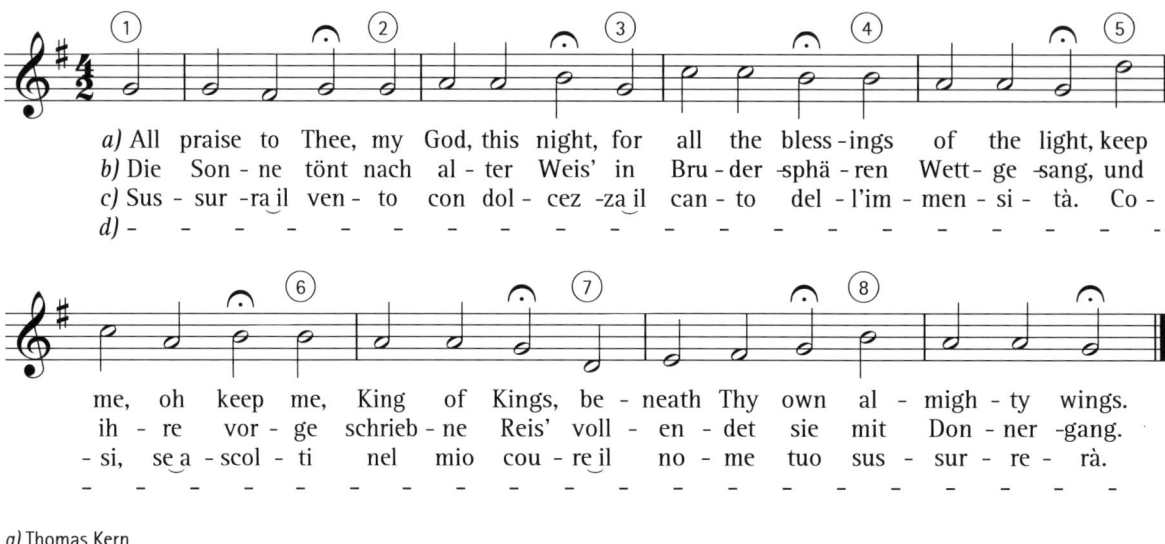

a) Thomas Kern
b) Johann Wolfgang von Goethe (1749–1832)
c) Marco Narduzzi (1986)
d) Create your own words to go with this song!

2. Glory, Glory 3-part canon

Michael Gohl (b 1954)

© Verlag Schweizer Singbuch

I. CANONS, HUMOUR, MOVEMENT

3. Réunis Aujourd'hui 3-part canon

César Geoffray (1901–1972)

Ré - u - nis au-jour-d'hui dans la joie et dans l'ef - fort notre a - mi - tié tou - jours pré - sen - te il - lu - mi - ne nos vi - sa - ges et la mu - si - que, et la mu - si - que en est le lien ma - gi - que.

© ÉDITIONS À CŒUR JOIE, "Les Passerelles", 24 avenue Joannès Masset, F-69009 Lyon.
  Tous droits réservés

Note

César Geoffray (France) and Gottfried Wolters (Germany) were the spiritual fathers of Europa Cantat. The song *Réunis Aujourd'hui* was the first piece in the songbook of the inaugural Europa Cantat, which took place in Passau (Germany) in 1961. (Möseler Verlag M 62.001).

In 1940 César Geoffray founded the French singing movement A Coeur Joie, which met in the Roman amphitheatre at Vaison la Romaine in Provence, an ideal venue for Open Singing. Since 1950, regular Open Singing events involving up to 5,000 participants have been held there within the context of the "Les Choralies" choir festival.

I. CANONS, HUMOUR, MOVEMENT

4. Da pacem, Domine 4-part canon

Melchior Franck (c. 1580–1639)

*) Parts ② and ④ begin a fourth lower

Ending: parts 1 and 2 hold the final note until they have been joined by parts 3 and 4.

5. Da pacem, Domine, triptych Three 4-part canons at the fifth

(Arrangement and combination: Peter Petersen)

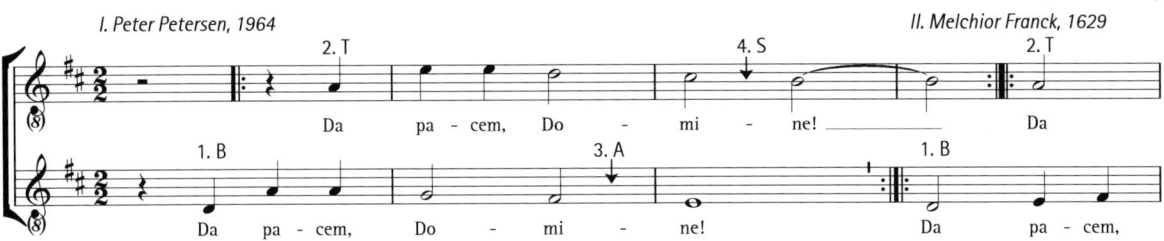

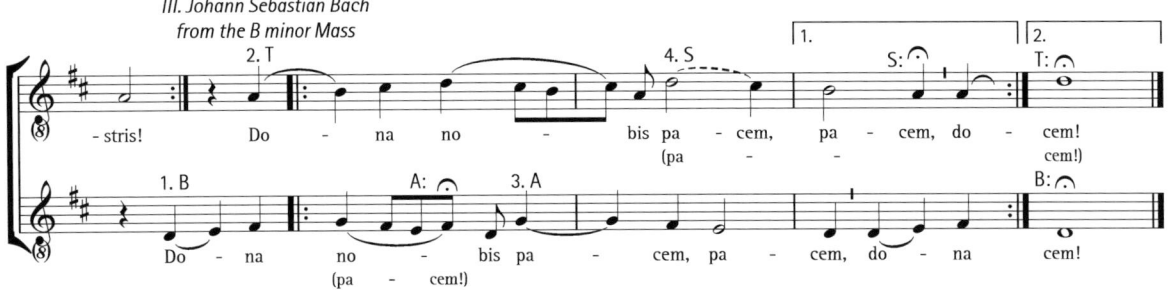

Copyright © by Möseler Verlag, Wolfenbüttel

I. CANONS, HUMOUR, MOVEMENT

6. Jubilate Deo 5-part canon

Michael Praetorius (1571–1621)
Text underlay: A. Gottfried Wolters, B: Fritz Jöde

7. Jubilate 6-part canon

Michael Praetorius (1571–1621)
Text underlay and ostinati: Gottfried Wolters

Ostinati:

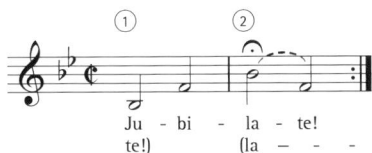 

I. CANONS, HUMOUR, MOVEMENT

8. Laudemus Virginem

From the Llibre Vermell
de Montserrat (pp. XIII–XIV)

9. Splendens Ceptigera

From the Llibre Vermell
de Montserrat (pp. XIII–XIV)

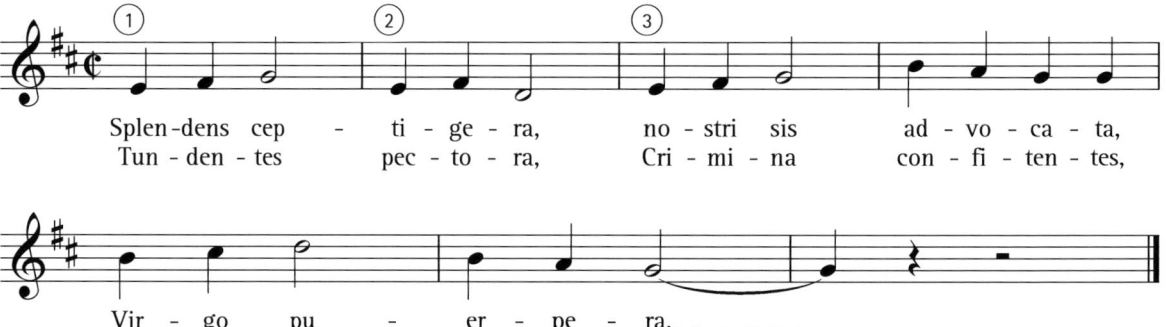

Performance tip

These two canons can be sung separately or at the same time.

Acoustic experiments and improvisation
1. Closer canon entries: The entry intervals can also be each half bar. It is possible to have more than three entries.

2. Acoustic experiments: These two canons lend themselves particularly well to acoustic experimentation and improvisation as explained on page 236-237.

I. CANONS, HUMOUR, MOVEMENT

10. Dona nobis pacem 3-part canon

Traditional

Descant part

Michael Gohl

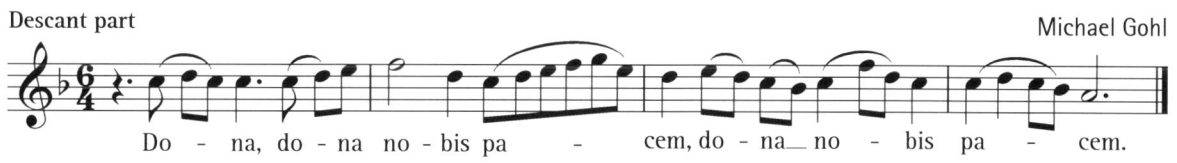

© 2014 by C. F. Peters

11. Jahreszeiten-Kanon / Seasons Canon 4-part canon

Music: Peter Dubs (1977)
English words: Richard George Elliott

© Theres Gysi-Dubs, Barbara Dubs, Susann Dubs

Fades away at the end

I. CANONS, HUMOUR, MOVEMENT

12. Apollo 4-part lied-canon

Music: Michael Gohl
German words: Heinrich Heine
English words: Richard George Elliott

1. Ich bin der Gott der Mu-si-ka, ver-ehrt in al-len Lan-den;
1. I am the god of har-mo-ny, Re-vered in ev'-ry land;

Mein Tem-pel hat in Grä-zi-a auf Mont-Par-nass ge-stan-den.
My tem-ple did in an-cient Greece on Mount Par-nas-sus stand.

*) At the end, hold the note until all the voices have reached it.

2. Ich sang – und wie von selbst beinah
   die Leier klang, berauschend.
   Mir war, als ob ich Daphne sah,
   aus Lorbeerbüschen lauschend.

2. I sang – and of its own accord,
   The lyre rang out enchanting.
   I thought that I did Daphne see,
   In laurel thicket hearkening.

3. Ich sang - und wie Ambrosia
   Wohlrüche sich ergossen,
   es war von einer Gloria
   die ganze Welt umflossen.

3. I sang – and like Ambrosia,
   Sweet fragrances spilled forth,
   And bathèd in a Gloria
   Was this our earthly orb.

(From *Der Apollogott*)

Performance suggestions

- Initial polyphony: can also be sung with just two or three parts.
- Can be sung with more than four parts if desired.
- Cluster version: an oscillating cluster effect is created when a new voice starts on each crochet, with as many voices deployed as desired. Or when each part comes in on a different note in a different key. (See "Acoustic Experiments and Improvisation" p. 236.)

© 2014 by C. F. Peters

I. CANONS, HUMOUR, MOVEMENT

13. Give It Up! 5-part canon

Michael Gohl

Suggested movements

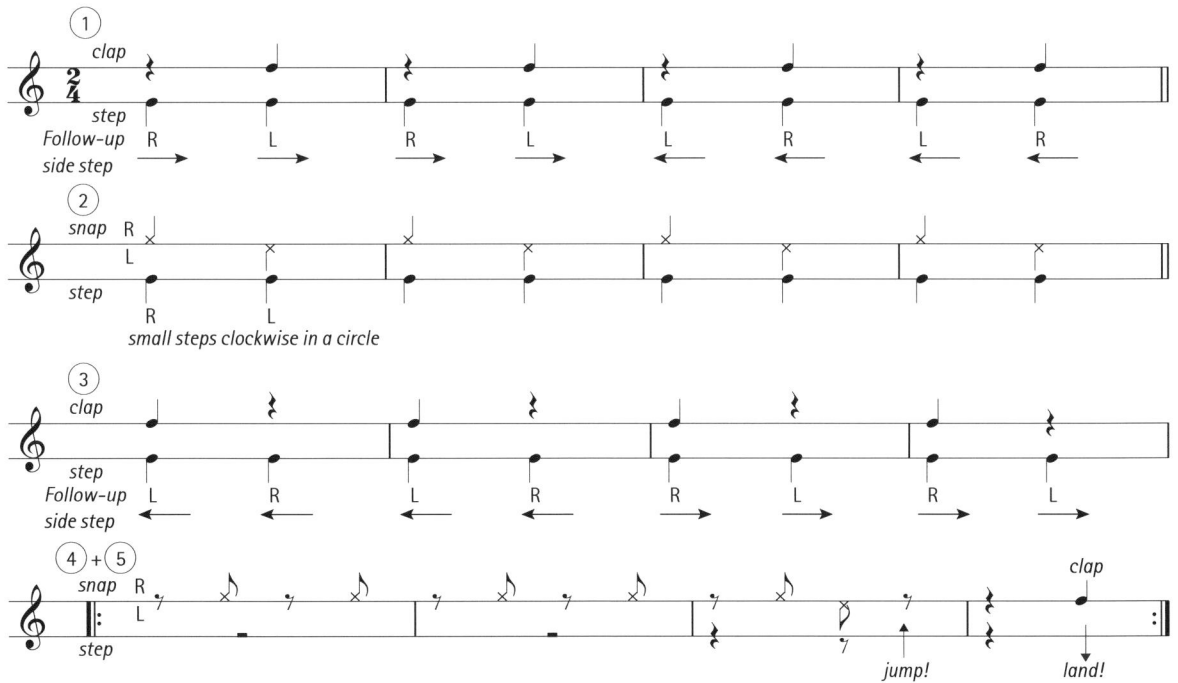

© Verlag Schweizer Singbuch

I. CANONS, HUMOUR, MOVEMENT

14. Hello 3-part canon

Fredi Fluri (1991)

Possible order of events:

The voices arrive on stage one after the other:

- Bass greets the public with the ostinato, accompanied by an off-beat snap
- First canon voice greets the public with the salutation (across a third) of the first bar ("Hel-lo_")
- Second canon voice greets the public with the salutation (across a third) of the first bar ("Hel-lo_")
- Third canon voice greets the public with the salutation (across a third) of the first bar ("Hel-lo_")

Simplified version: no glissando at the end of the first fermata

Suggested movements

With each "hello", wave briefly with upstreched hand to someone in the audience. Alternate hands.

⬇ A video of the song can be found at www.editionpeters.com/singalong

© Fredi Fluri

I. CANONS, HUMOUR, MOVEMENT

15. Goodbye 4-part canon

Fredi Fluri

Score (excerpt)

© Fredi Fluri

I. CANONS, HUMOUR, MOVEMENT

16. Good Morning (Evening) 5-part canon

Robert Sund (b 1942)

© Robert Sund, Sweden

I. CANONS, HUMOUR, MOVEMENT

17. Lai-la

Czech folk tune
Arr.: Michael Gohl

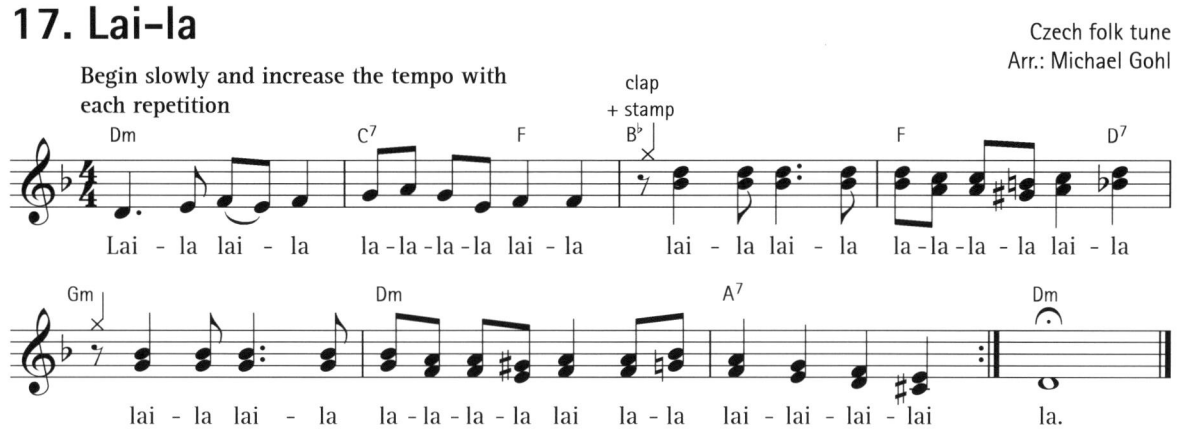

© Verlag Schweizer Singbuch

Suggested movements and performance tips

Variant 1:

While singing the song, stamp feet and clap hands in each of the two rests. Speed up with each repetition. Traditionally the song would be accompanied by an accordion rather than piano, and percussion in the form of a tambourine on the off-beat, in time with the right hand of the piano.

Variant 2:

In bar 2, step to the side, alternately to the left and to the right, and clap hands on beats 2 and 4. Speed up with each repetition. Move straight into this variant from variant 1 without a break, beginning slowly again.

Variant 3:

In bar 2, step to the side, alternately to the left and to the right. At the same time, clap hands on every other quaver (as per right hand of the piano accompaniment). Speed up with each repetition. Move straight into this variant from variant 2 without a break, beginning slowly again.

I. CANONS, HUMOUR, MOVEMENT

18. Ding dong 4-part canon

Oral tradition
German words: Michael Gohl

Ding dong, when I was walk-ing on a May__ morn-ing, I heard the birds sing. *)
Ding dong, *im* *Mai* in *Ba*-*sel**) rings-um singt's__ und klingt's, und al-les singt mit!

*) Adapt the words to the relevant situation or find new words!

© 2014 by C. F. Peters

Suggested movements

Form rows or stand in a circle, facing inwards.
Right hand (palm upwards) supports left hand of person on the right and vice versa.

Bar 1:
clap

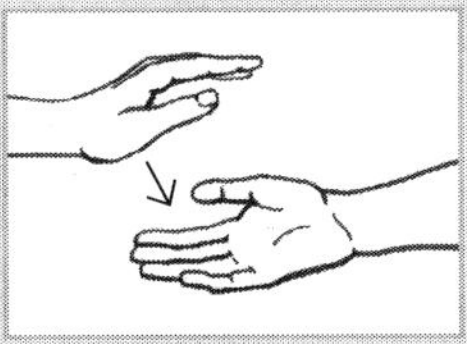

| l. h. on r. h. | 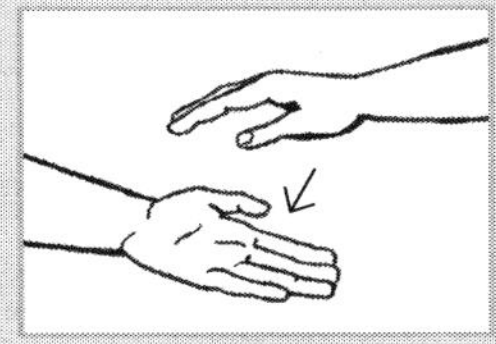 r. h. on l. h. | 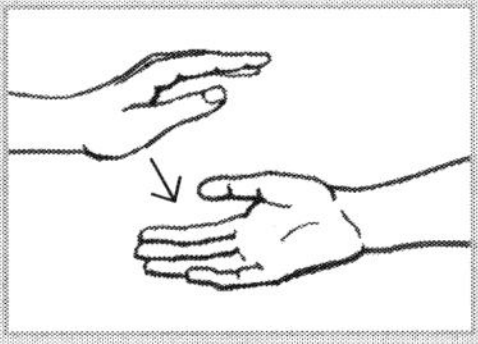 l. h. on r. h. |

Bar 2:
pat

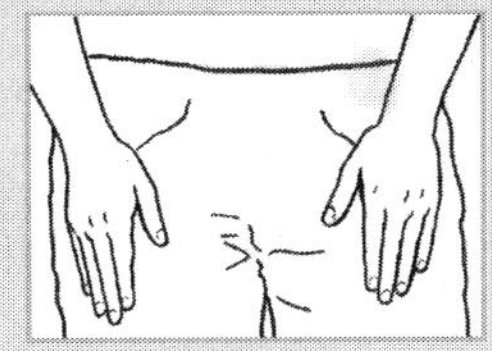

| parallel | 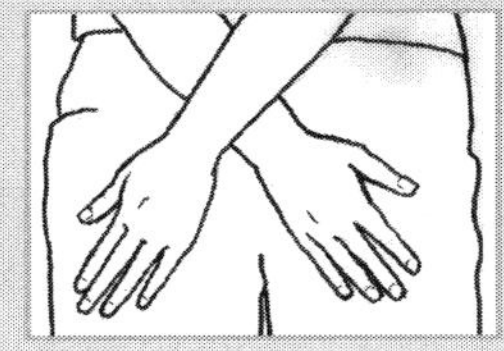 crossed | 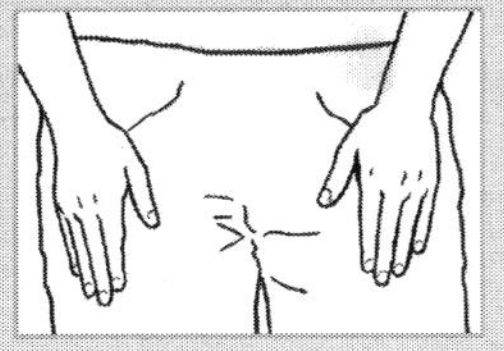 parallel |

Bar 3:
clap

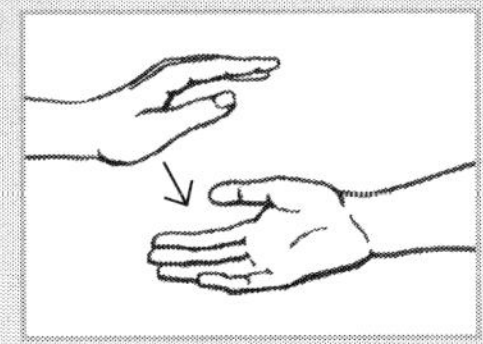

| l. h. on r. h. | 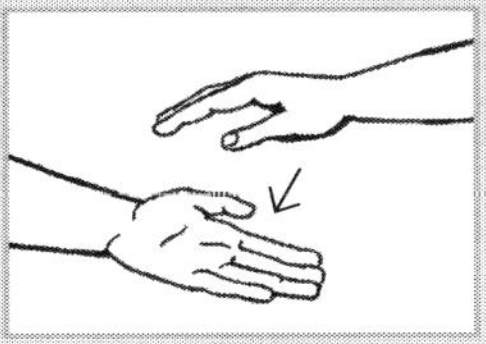 r. h. on l. h. | 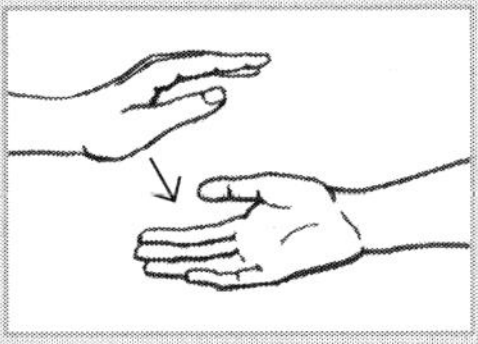 l. h. on r. h. |

Bar 4:
2 x "candle",
1 x finger snap

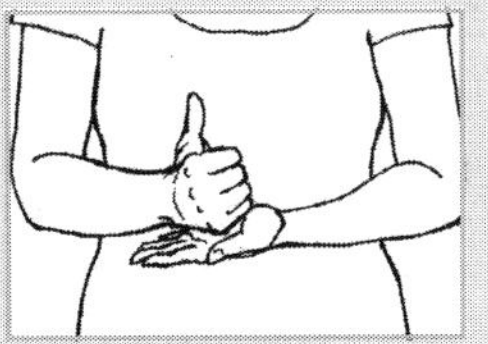

| r. h. on l. h. | 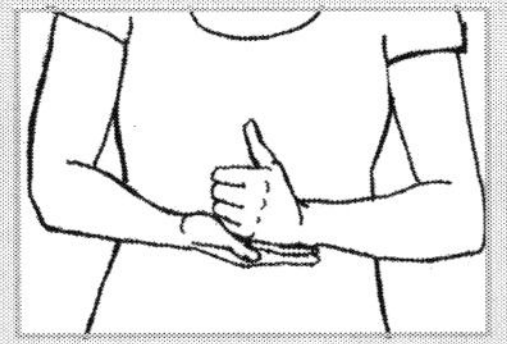 l. h. on r. h. | 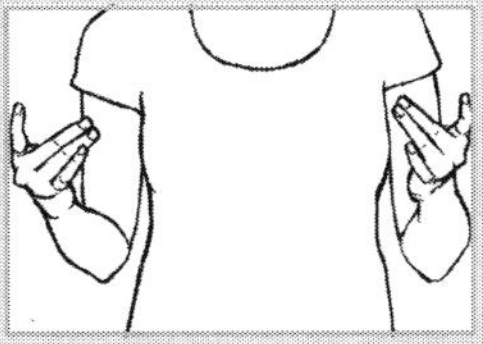 snap fingers (both hands) |

Variant 1 (in canon):
Each canon group performs the actions independently.

Variant 2 (challenging):
All the singers make the same movements as the first canon group, while nevertheless singing in canon.

I. CANONS, HUMOUR, MOVEMENT

19. Ayelevi

Trad. Ghana

Translation:

Ayelevi, may your soul dance happily on!
Yes, may it dance, son of Ayele.

Suggested movements

Form rows or stand in a circle, facing inwards. Right hand (palm upwards) supports left hand of person on the right and vice versa.

In the transition from bars 4 to 5 and 8 to 1, the group side-steps to the left: step to the left with left leg (bar 4/8 on first beat), follow-up side step with right leg to the left (bar 5/1 on first beat).

Bars 1/5

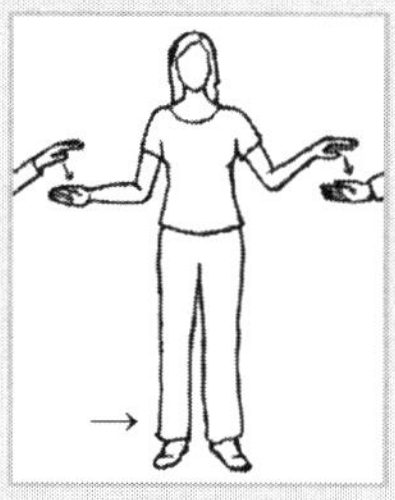

l. h. on r. h.
(l. leg follow-up side step)

change hands

Bars 2/6

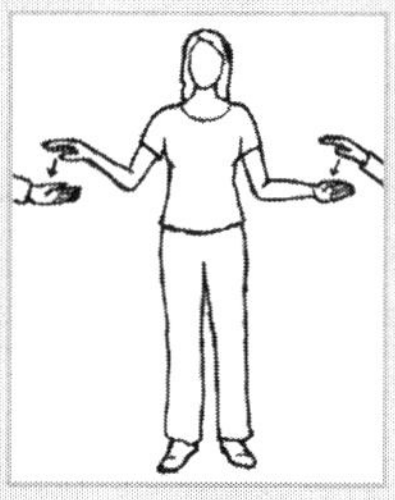

r. h. on l. h.

Bars 3/7

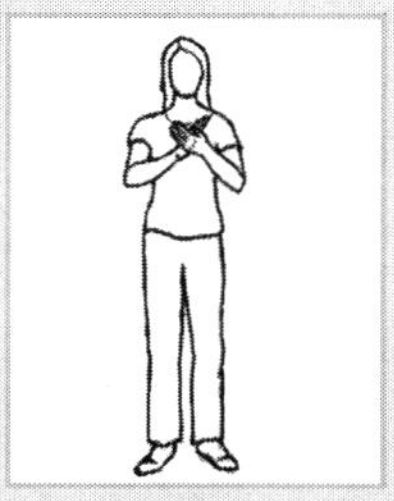

clap

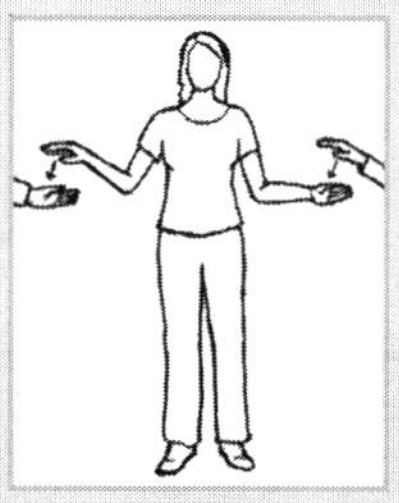

r. h. on l. h.

Bars 4/8

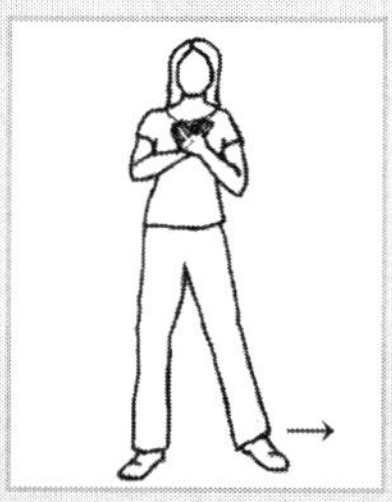

clap + side-step to the left

© 2015 by C. F. Peters

Edition Peters 11401

I. CANONS, HUMOUR, MOVEMENT

20. Branle du Quercy

Music: French instrumental dance *)
Words: Suzanne Forel

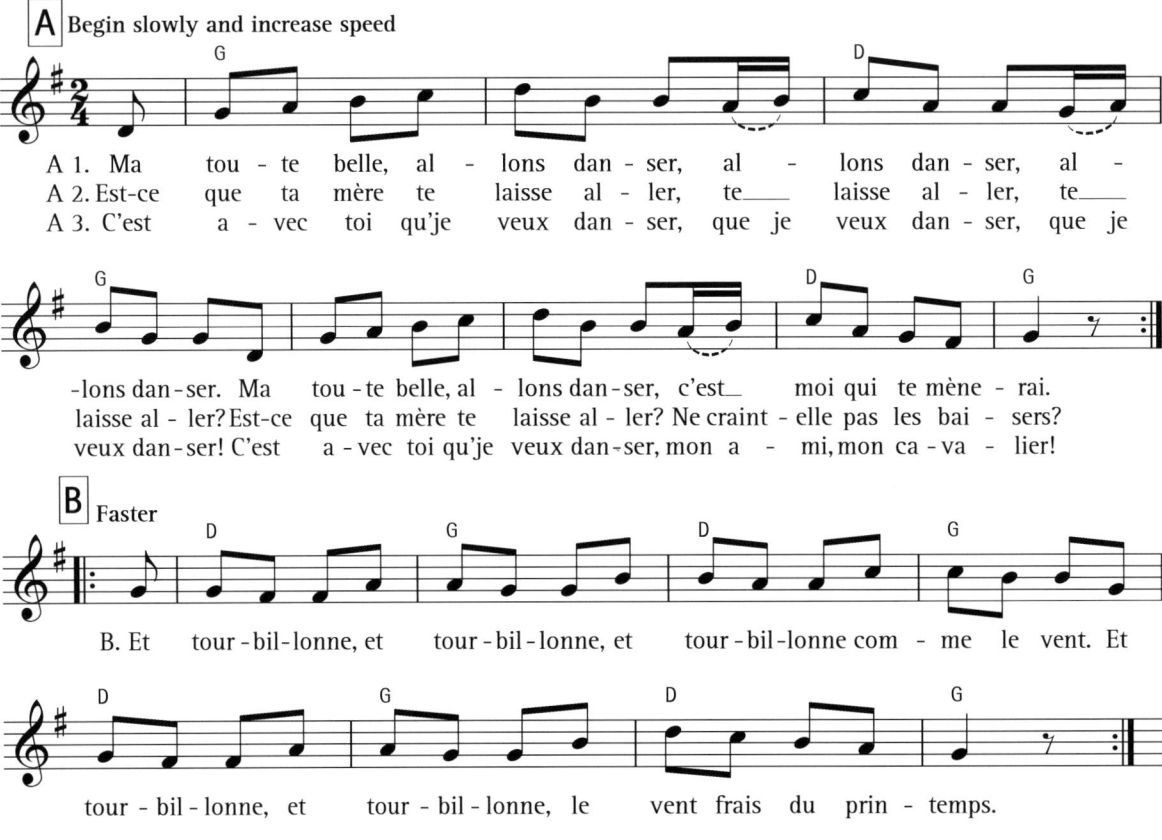

© Copyright Michael Gohl

*) This dance music was originally performed by instruments only. However, it also makes a delightful, cheerful dance-song that can be sung either to "la-la-la" or to the texts presented below!

Gist translation:

A.
1. Hey, do you want to go dancing with me,
   Dancing with me, dancing with me?
   Hey, do you want to go dancing with me,
   Do you want to go and dance?

2. But are you allowed to go dancing with me,
   Dancing with me, dancing with me?
   But are you allowed to go dancing with me,
   Are you allowed to go and dance?

3. Of course I'm allowed to go dancing with you,
   Dancing with you, dancing with you!
   Of course I'm allowed to go dancing with you
   I'm allowed to go and dance!

B.
We're dancing like a whirlwind, a whirlwind, a whirlwind!
We're dancing like a whirlwind, we're dancing like the wind!

Movement suggestions

A1: Rotate in a circle to the left, holding hands and swinging forearms to the front.

A2: Move towards the centre, taking two steps and a hop, while continuing to swing arms up and to the front. Then move back to original position. Perform this routine twice in total.

A3: Male partner positioned behind female partner, left arms stretched out and holding hands. Right hand on the hip of female partner, sideways gallop to the left.

B: Rotate to the right, arm in arm with free arm raised and inclined over head, repeat towards the left.

I. CANONS, HUMOUR, MOVEMENT

21. Robinson

Trad. German children's song
English words: Richard George Elliott
Setting: Max Frey

Also in D or E!

Dance suggestion

	Bars	
The group is distributed evenly about the space	1-2	right, left tap, left, right tap
	3-4	rotate to the right on own axis with arms in the air (to represent the balloon)
	5-6	as in bars 1-2, starting with left
	7-8	as in bars 3-4, rotate to the left on own axis, with arms held as if in an embrace
	9-12	take 4 steps in search of a partner (r snap, l, snap r snap, l snap)
	13-16	with partner – link right arms and turn, take leave!

© Gustav Bosse Verlag, Kassel

I. CANONS, HUMOUR, MOVEMENT

22. Heigh-Ho! Anybody home? 3-part canon
Trad. England

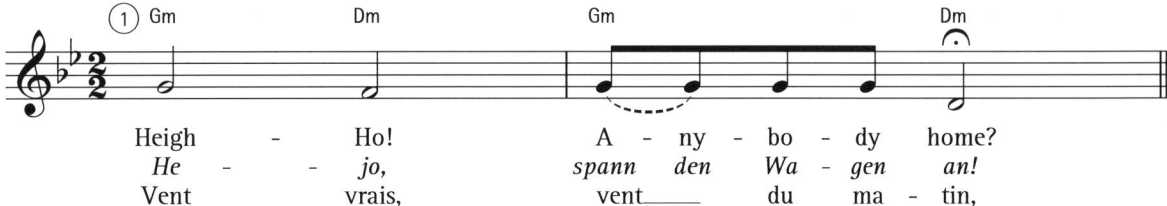
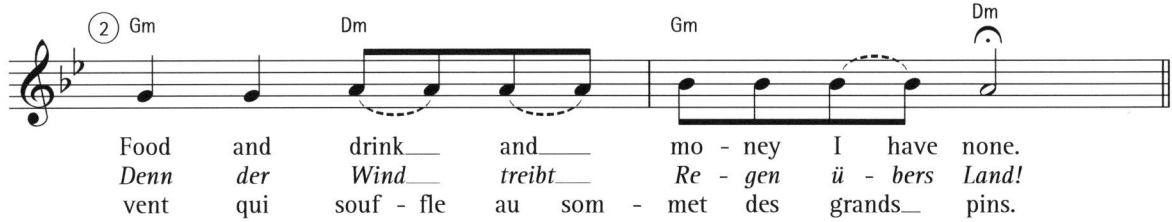
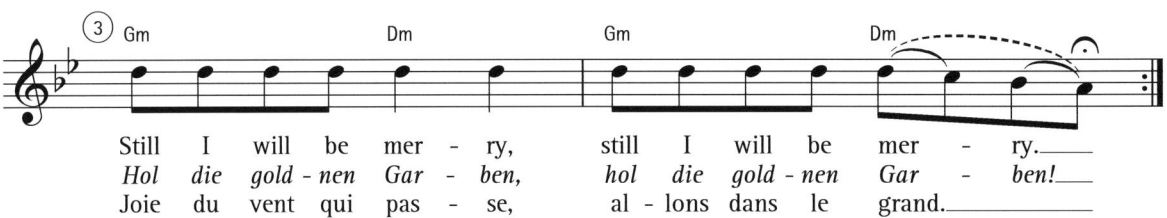

© 2015 by C. F. Peters

23. Hine ma tov u'manayim 2-part canon
Trad. Israel

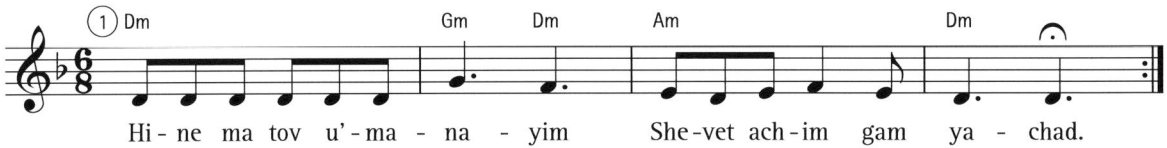

Look how wonderful and how pleasant it is
when brothers live together in unity.

Psalm 133,1

© 2015 by C. F. Peters

I. CANONS, HUMOUR, MOVEMENT

24. Frère Jacques 4-part canon

Trad. France

Danish:
Mester Jakob, Mester Jakob,
sover du, sover du?
Hører du ej klokken,
hører du ej klokken?
Bim, bam bum. Bim, bam, bum.

Finnish:
Jaakoo kulta, Jaakoo kulta,
herää jo, herää jo?
Kellojasi soita, kellojasi soita.
Piu, pau, pou. Piu, pau, pou.

Italian:
Frà Martino, campanaro,
dormi tu, dormi tu?
Suona il campane,
suona il campane.
Din, dan, don. Din, dan, don.

Latin:
Quare dormis, o Iacobe,
etiam nunc, etiam nunc?
Resonant campanae,
resonant campanae.
Din, din, dan. Din, din, dan.

Dutch:
Vader Jacob, Vader Jacob,
Slaapt gij nog, slaapt gij nog?
Alle klokken luiden,
alle klokken luiden.
Bim, bam, bom. Bim, bam, bom.

Romanian:
Frate Ioane, Frate Ioane,
Oare dormi tu, oare dormi tu?
Suna clopotelul, suna clopotelul.
Ding, dang, dong. Ding, dang, dong.

Spanish:
Martinillo, Martinillo,
¿Donde esta, donde esta?
Toca la campana, toca la campana.
Din, don, dan. Din, don, dan.

Turkish:
Yakop usta, Yakop usta,
uyuyormussun, uyuyormussun?
Çani duymadimi, çani duymadimi
Ding, dang, dong. Ding, dang, dong.

© (for the Latin text) by Philip Reclam jun., Stuttgart

© 2015 by C. F. Peters

I. CANONS, HUMOUR, MOVEMENT

25. Ja dan duia 8-part canon

Soili Perkiö (b 1958)

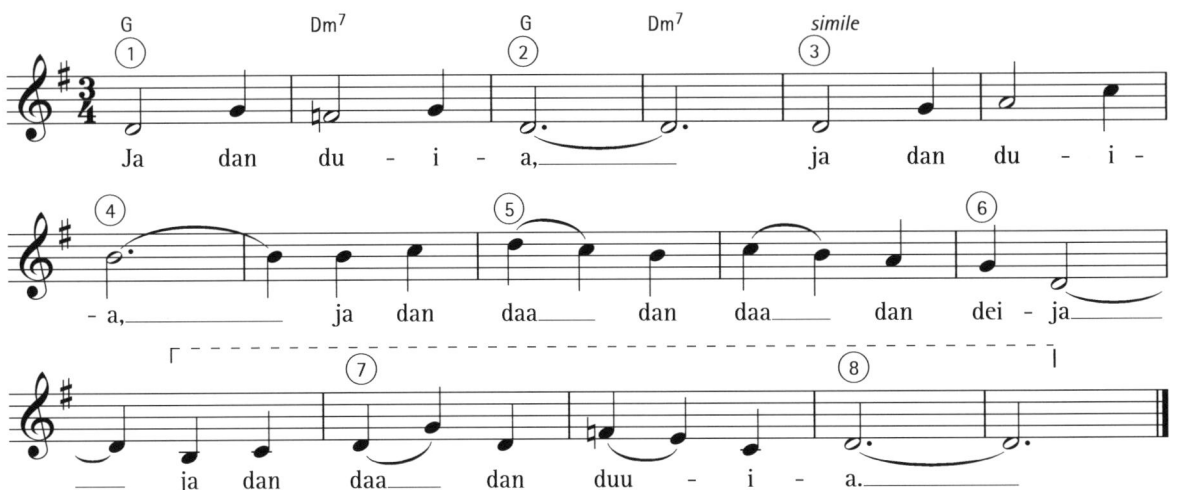

© Soili Perkiö

Ending: Repeat the last 4 bars (with upbeat) until all groups have reached the end, or alternatively end in canon on beat 1 of the G major chord

Tip

This canon forms part of a composition written in summer 2003 by the Finnish composer and music teacher Soili Perkiö for a night-time, open-air performance on the Pühä tunturi (Holy Mountain), a mighty stone wilderness in the vast, open landscape of Lapland. When singing in two parts, a special effect can be achieved if the echo (the second canon entry) is sung either by a soloist or by a small group of singers spatially separated from the rest.

I. CANONS, HUMOUR, MOVEMENT

26. I Like The Flowers 3-part canon

Oral tradition

Note:
Both canons have the same harmonical structure: I-VI-II-V. If sung in the same key (e.g. D or E) they can be combined. Even more "1-6-2-5"-songs can be added!

27. Zwei Schritt nach links 4-part canon

Oral tradition
English words: Richard George Elliott

Suggested movements and performance tips

1. Bars 1–2: two Follow-up side-steps to the left, two Follow-up side-steps to the right.
2. Bars 3–4: cross arms in front of your body and shake your neighbour's hand.
3. Bar 5: jump up on "Sprung" / "jump", bar 6: clap hands on "Klatsch" / "clap".
4. Bars 7–8: with arms raised, rotate clockwise on own axis.

© 2015 by C. F. Peters

I. CANONS, HUMOUR, MOVEMENT

28. Move On! (6-part canon, to be done in pairs or in rows)
Maya Barkani, Roni Natzchan

© Michael Gohl

1) on partner's hand
2) on laps
3) vertically on partner's hand

rb = right foot backwards
rf = right foot forwards to original position
lb = left foot backwards
lf = left foot forwards to original position

Performance suggestions

Form rows or stand in a circle, facing inwards.

1. This movement based canon takes on a particularly "groovy" feel when accompanied by one or more improvising instrumentalists (piano and/or drums, percussion etc.). The instrumentalists can choose either a funk or a rock groove, but should also, as far as possible, play the indicated rhythms.

2. This canon with movements can be performed either in pairs or in a normal choir configuration or else using the hall seating.

3. When it is performed in pairs, two people stand opposite one another and perform the same rhythm/line of music at the same time. For claps marked 1), clap hands with the partner standing opposite.

4. In a choral configuration or when using the hall seating, the participants are arranged in rows. For claps marked 1), clap your own hands together. For claps marked 3), clap hands with your neighbours to the left and the right, as in the songs *Ding Dong* and *Ayelevi*.

5. The participants can be divided into canon groups either longitudinally or diagonally across the room or else according to one of the other variants (see the section "Variants in canon division" on p. 243).

⬇ A video of the song can be found at **www.editionpeters.com/singalong**

I. CANONS, HUMOUR, MOVEMENT

29. Dito 3-part canon

Jürg Siegrist

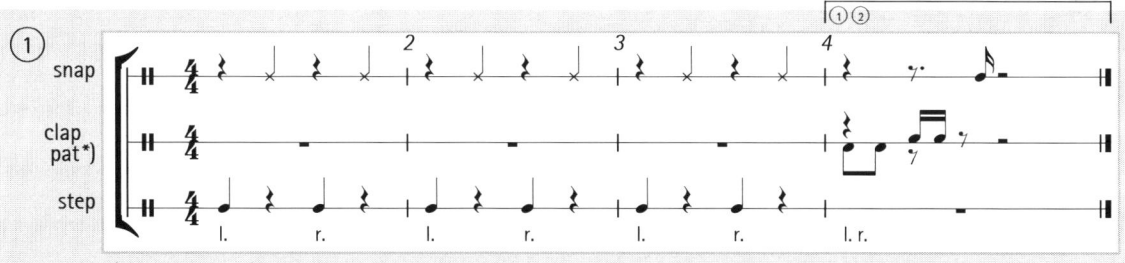

Suggested movements

*) Pat thighs, l. / r. in turn

② Bar 1: Diagonal stretch to left and right in turn: stretch left arm upwards and to the left, extending whole body in a diagonal and splay fingers in a sudden explosion.
Bar 2: On the long **"dai"**, stretch both arms upwards and flutter hands. Then roll forearms rapidly in an upward movement as if in a crescendo.
Bar 3: As per bar 1.
Bar 4: Pat, clap, snap in the rhythm of bar 4 of ①.

③ Bar 1-3: Make horizontal wave movements using both arms and hands, in turn (3x).
Bar 4: Pat, clap, snap as in bar 4 of ①, but with a different rhythm:

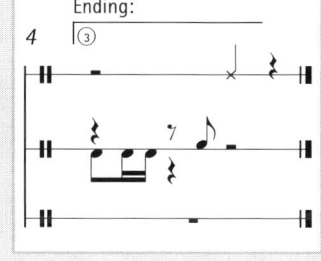

© Verlag Schweizer Singbuch

I. CANONS, HUMOUR, MOVEMENT

30. Makumaná 4-part canon

Jesús Debón

© Jesús Debón

Suggested movements

Form rows or stand in a circle, facing inwards.

① Nod head to left on "**Nim**-ba", "ka-**lim**-ba", "**Lim**-ba", "ka-**lim**-ba **kim**-ba-**lé**" (in each case righting it again on "ba").

② Side-step to the right. On "yem-**be**", bend arm over the head to the right. On "ku-**lé**", extend right arm and index finger towards the ceiling. The second time, wave instead of pointing.

③ "Zulu step" (see *Sangena*, p. 75): r. foot forward, l. foot following, r. foot back, l. foot following. Move right shoulder and bend arm forward and back in tandem with leg.

④ Side-step to the left while simultaneously waving arms and hands in parallel right to left ("windscreen wiper").

On the final note, stretch arms and hands up towards the ceiling and wave.

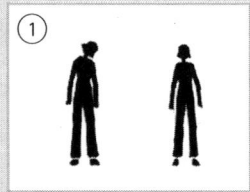

⬇ A video of the song performed with dance actions can be found at **www.editionpeters.com/singalong**

I. CANONS, HUMOUR, MOVEMENT

31. Hotaru Koi 3-part (or more) canon

Trad. Japan

Translation:

Come, firefly, come!
The water over there is bitter.
Here the water is sweet.

© Verlag Schweizer Singbuch

32. The Big Band 3 to 6-part canon

Words: Ute Kühlmann
Music: Joachim Fischer

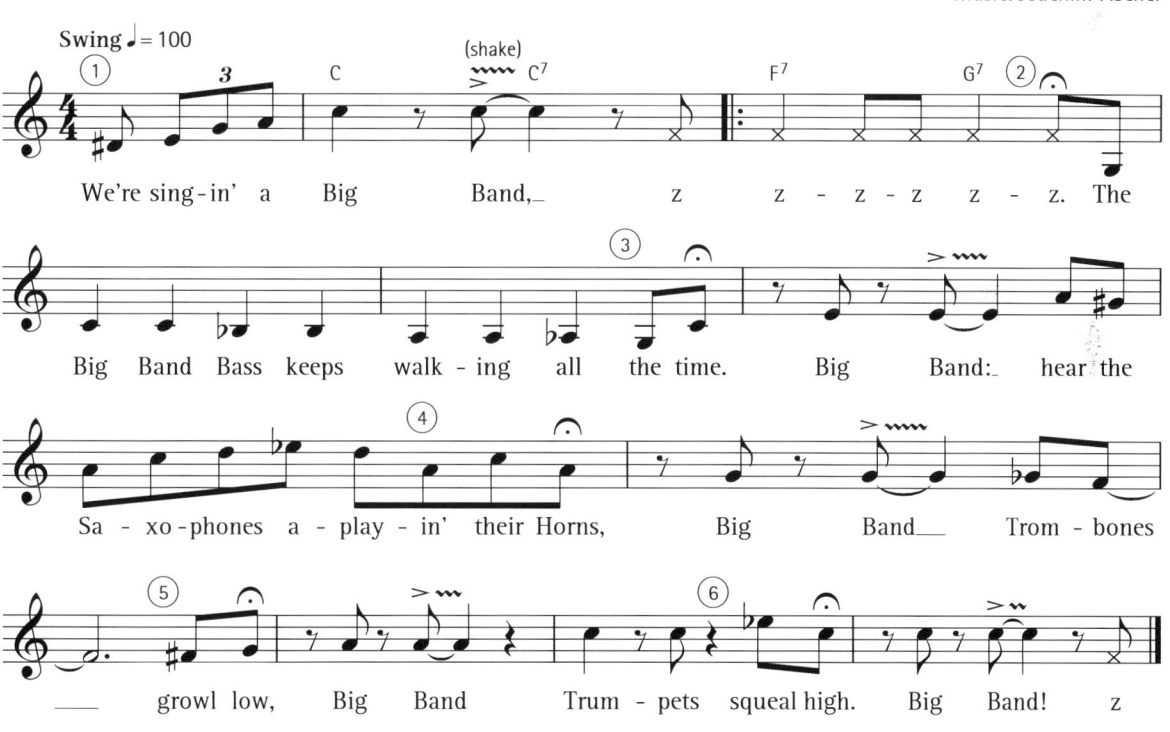

© Fidula-Verlag, Boppard/Rhein www.fidula.de

I. CANONS, HUMOUR, MOVEMENT

33. Fruit canon 3-part canon

Oral tradition

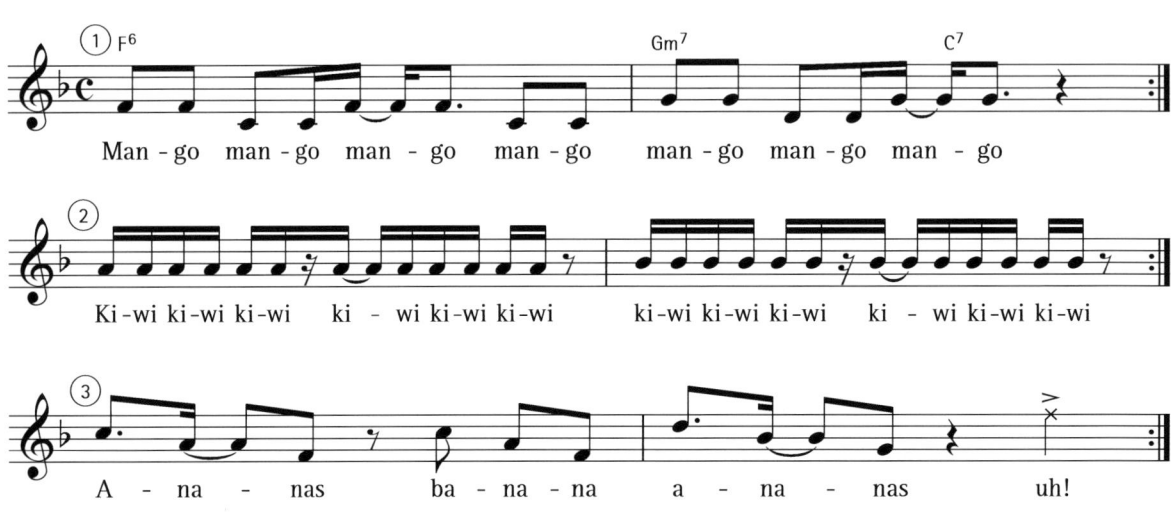

Piano accompaniment

Michael Gohl

Suggested movements

Form rows or stand in a circle.

1. Dance on the spot, alternating right leg and left leg in time to the music.

2. Turn to the left, then walk towards the left and mark the quavers by pointing with the left index finger in the direction of movement. On the repeat, rotate 180° and run and point to the right.

3. On "Ananas" (pineapple), reach into the air with the right arm and wave.
   On "banana", poke the left cheek with the left index finger while bending forward slightly with the upper body.
   On "uh!", throw both arms up into the air.
   Option: the women perform the "Ananas" action and the men perform the "banana" action.

© 2015 by C. F. Peters

A video of the song can be found at www.editionpeters.com/singalong

I. CANONS, HUMOUR, MOVEMENT

34. Calypso 3-part canon

Music and words: Jan Holdstock

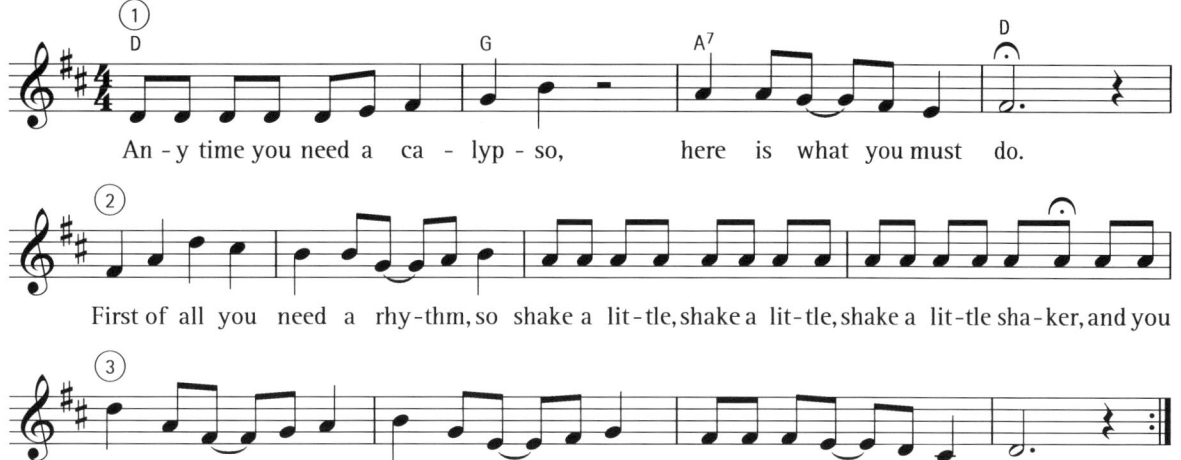

A-ny time you need a ca-lyp-so, here is what you must do.

First of all you need a rhy-thm, so shake a lit-tle, shake a lit-tle, shake a lit-tle sha-ker, and you bang a drum and you sing and strum and then there's a ca-lyp-so for you.

© Jan Holdstock

Suggested movements

Michael Gohl

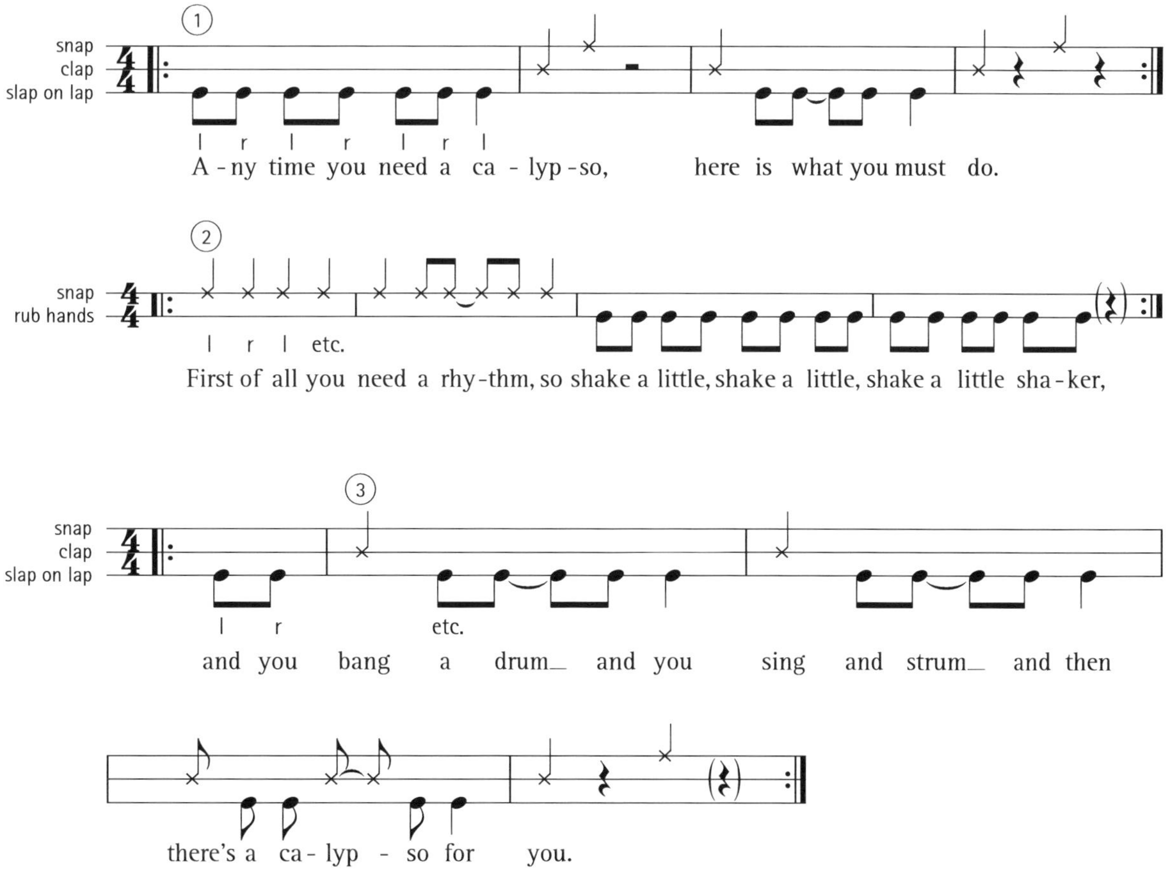

snap / clap / slap on lap

A-ny time you need a ca-lyp-so, here is what you must do.

snap / rub hands

First of all you need a rhy-thm, so shake a little, shake a little, shake a little sha-ker,

snap / clap / slap on lap

and you bang a drum and you sing and strum and then there's a ca-lyp-so for you.

I. CANONS, HUMOUR, MOVEMENT

35. Funky Goodbye

Text and music:
Markus Detterbeck (2013)

I. CANONS, HUMOUR, MOVEMENT

© Helbling, Innsbruck-Esslingen-Bern/Belp

Performance tip

The lead can either be sung solo with instruments or accompanied by choral voices, which can come in one after another, imitating the sound of the instruments as indicated!

In funk, the most important thing is a feel for the main beat of the bar. "But where is the ONE?", asked James Brown when his guitarist played him a guitar riff. It is therefore important to really stress the beginning of the bar, to sing this note "late" (laid back) and with real weight.

The bass groove begins and builds a foundation and the tenors add to the groove with their funk guitar patterns. As soon as these two parts have interlocked rhythmically, the female voices come in with the keyboard part.

Finally a soloist or small group sings the lead over the accompaniment. This vocal style lends itself well to performance with the open singing concert audience as a farewell song, with the audience singing the lead, accompanied by the choir.

I. CANONS, HUMOUR, MOVEMENT

36. Me and Jack

Jonathan Rathbone (b 1957)

I. CANONS, HUMOUR, MOVEMENT

37. Vanitas Vanitatum 4-part canon

Music: Jan Pieterszoon Sweelinck
(1562–1621)
Words: Old Testament
(Prayer 1, 2)

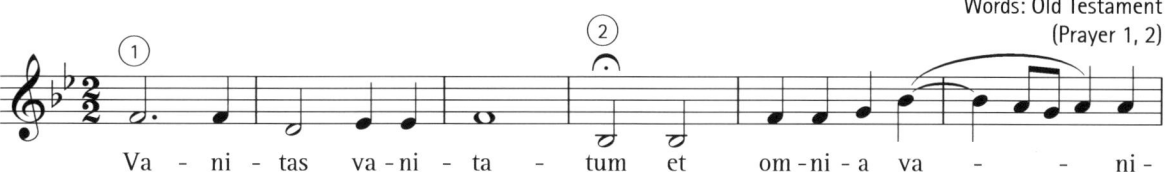

38. Spring

Words and music: Thord Gummesson (b 1930)

© Notfabriken Music Publishing AB. Printed by permission

39. Flying 3-part canon

Alan Simmons

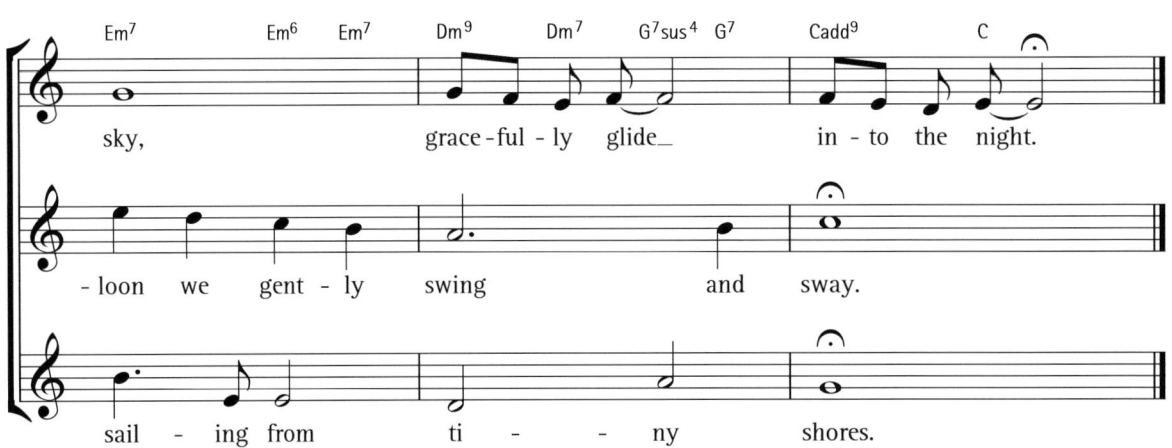

© Copyright Alan Simmons Music
All Rights Reserved. Used by Permission.

I. CANONS, HUMOUR, MOVEMENT

40. Sambabrasil 3-part canon

Thord Gummesson (b 1930)

Piano accompaniment

Michael Gohl

Performance tip

With the appropriate adjustment to key, this canon can be combined with the canon Alpen-Rumba (p. 46) and/or sung with the vocal percussion accompaniment to Alpen-Rumba.

© Notfabriken Music Publishing AB. Printed by permission.
Klavierbegleitung: © 2014 by C. F. Peters

I. CANONS, HUMOUR, MOVEMENT

41. Alpen-Rumba 3-part canon

Uli Führe (b 1957)

A quick glossary by Uli Führe:

„*Chlungi*": two guys having a chat

„*Halunki*": nickname (Halunke in High German = rascal)

„*däne dobe*": the quarrel can be heard "over there", even the "reg di nit so uf" (don't get so worked up)

„*Schlumbä*": a chicken feed, the reason for the dispute

„*rigedigag*": pecking hens

„*bing*": the sound of the evening bells

(Comment: don't take it so seriously...!)

This canon can be combined with the canon Sambabrasil (see p. 45). A suitable piano accompaniment (in C major) is also provided on that page.

© Fidula-Verlag, Boppard/Rhein www.fidula.de

Suggested movements

1. On "**Chlun-gi**" and "**Halun-ki**", twitch the right shoulder upwards and move the upper body slightly to the right (diagonally).
On "**ribeli rabeli räbeli robeli böll**", make rolling motion with hands and forearms while leaning forward with upper body.
On "**So chumm!**" (so come!), make a gesture of invitation towards the audience.

2. On "**Dä-ne-do-be**", point up to the sky with the right arm and index finger.
On "**dätsch**", make as if to slap right cheek with right hand while turning head away to the left. On "**reg di nit so uf!**", stretch arms out to the front in a relaxed manner.

3. On "**ri**-gedi, **ga**-gedi **bing**", point right, left, right with the (right, left, right) thumbs. On "**reg di nit so uf!**", stretch arms out to the front in a relaxed manner.

I. CANONS, HUMOUR, MOVEMENT

42. Samba-style percussive accompaniment to Alpen-Rumba

(Vocal percussion)

Michael Gohl

I. CANONS, HUMOUR, MOVEMENT

43. Goli goggoli!!!

Wolfram Buchenberg (b 1962)

© Wolfram Buchenberg

I. CANONS, HUMOUR, MOVEMENT

Performance tip

Parts A to E can be combined in any number of ways. We would advise an incremental build-up from A to E, with all the parts ringing out together at the end. (In order to find the note, it may be necessary to make the whirly tubes sound for a short while in advance.) Entries can also be staggered, for example with B starting on the second bar of A. In A, the canon entries may also follow at half-bar intervals.

I. CANONS, HUMOUR, MOVEMENT

44. Taga del i öst och väst
(Join Along in East and West)

Words and music: Gunnar Eriksson (b 1936)
English words: Wouter Tukker

© Gunnar Eriksson and Bo Ejeby Förlag

Performance suggestions

Try: unison all themes A–F with accompaniment. B, C and F in canon. Suggestion for form: all sing theme A in unison, the alto part gradually switching over to C, tenor to D, soprano to B respectively. E and F can be inserted ad lib.

Experiment in different directions: chaos > order, order > chaos. Accompaniment can be salsa type, for example with theme D as a starting point, plus bass notes. Start on first beat of last bar of preceding song.

I. CANONS, HUMOUR, MOVEMENT

45. A Summer's Over 3-part canon

Githe Christensen

Michael Gohl

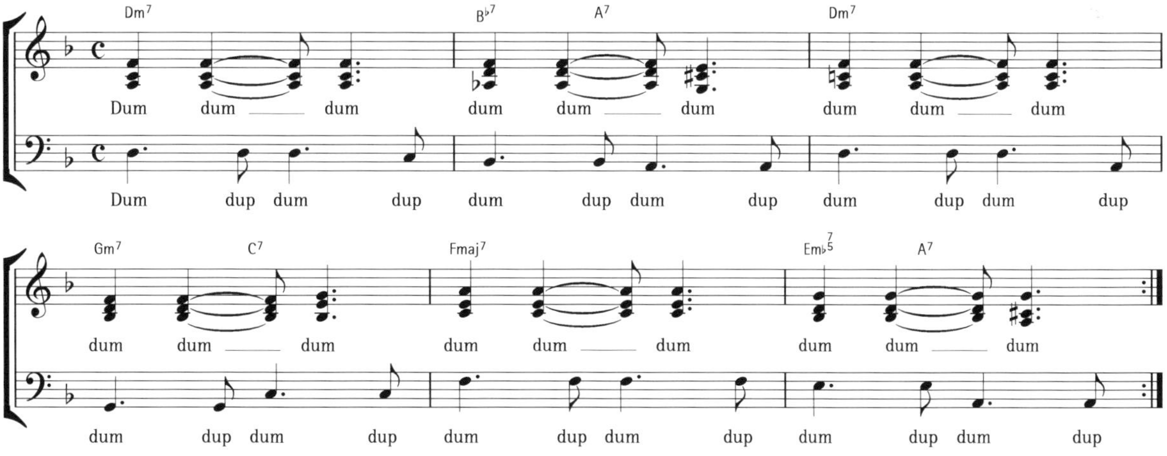

Bossa nova rhythm (clave)

Canon © Githe Christensen
Accompanying rhythm © 2014 by C. F. Peters

I. CANONS, HUMOUR, MOVEMENT

46. Polska efter Jon-Sebastian or Bach goes to Delsbo*

Music: Göran M Hägg

Copyright © 2007 Wessmans Musikförlag AB, Visby.
Printed with permission.

* Imagine that Johann Sebastian Bach actually visited the bandsman meeting in Delsbo in 1732. Imagine further that he was so touched by what he heard that he wrote a Polish Fugue. To conclude, imagine that this document was found in a barn outside Delsbo in modern times.

I. CANONS, HUMOUR, MOVEMENT

I. CANONS, HUMOUR, MOVEMENT

47. The First Commandment of Art / Das erste Gebot der Kunst

from: Die zehn Gebote der Kunst
Joseph Haydn (1732–1809)

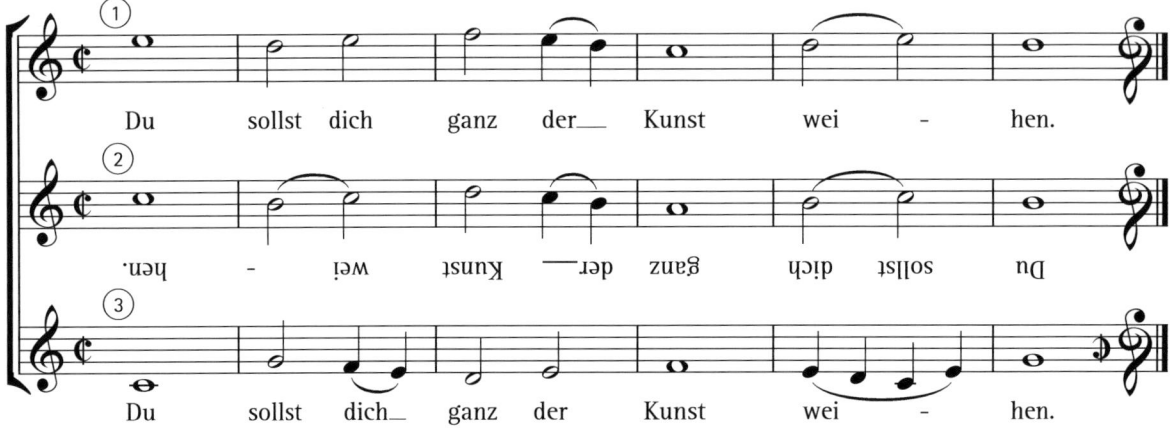

Note

This canon can be sung forwards, backwards, and then rotated 180° and sung forwards and backwards again. It is the first of ten canons composed by Haydn under the title The Ten Commandments of Art.

© 2015 by C. F. Peters

48. Von guten Mächten   4-part canon

Music: Michael Gohl (2000)
Words: Dietrich Bonhoeffer (1906–1945)
English words: Arne Muus

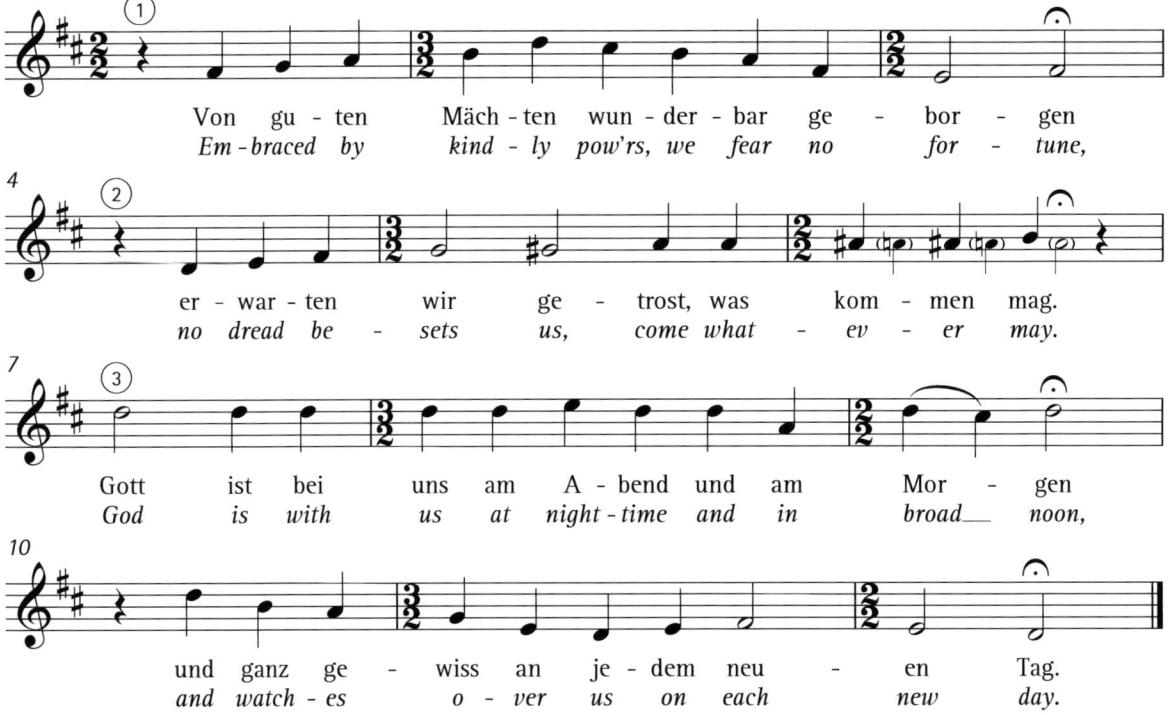

Music © 2015 by C. F. Peters
German text © Gütersloher Verlagshaus, Gütersloh, in der Verlagsgruppe Random House GmbH

II. Around the world

*Schläft ein Lied in allen Dingen,
die da träumen fort und fort.
Und die Welt hebt an zu singen,
triffst du nur das Zauberwort.*

Joseph von Eichendorff

*Un poquito cantas,
Un poquito bailas,
Un poquito lelola,
Com un canario.*

South American folk song

II. AROUND THE WORLD

49. Un poquito cantas

Trad. South America

Translation:
1. Sing a little, dance a little,
2. A little vine, a little air,
3. Play a little, love a little,
4. A little winds, a little shadows
   Lelola (!) a little, Like a Canario
   (= resident of the Canary Islands)

As a choral accompaniment can also be used the song *Salsa Beach Band* (no. 153, p. 195).

Accompanying pattern for the refrain:

Michael Gohl

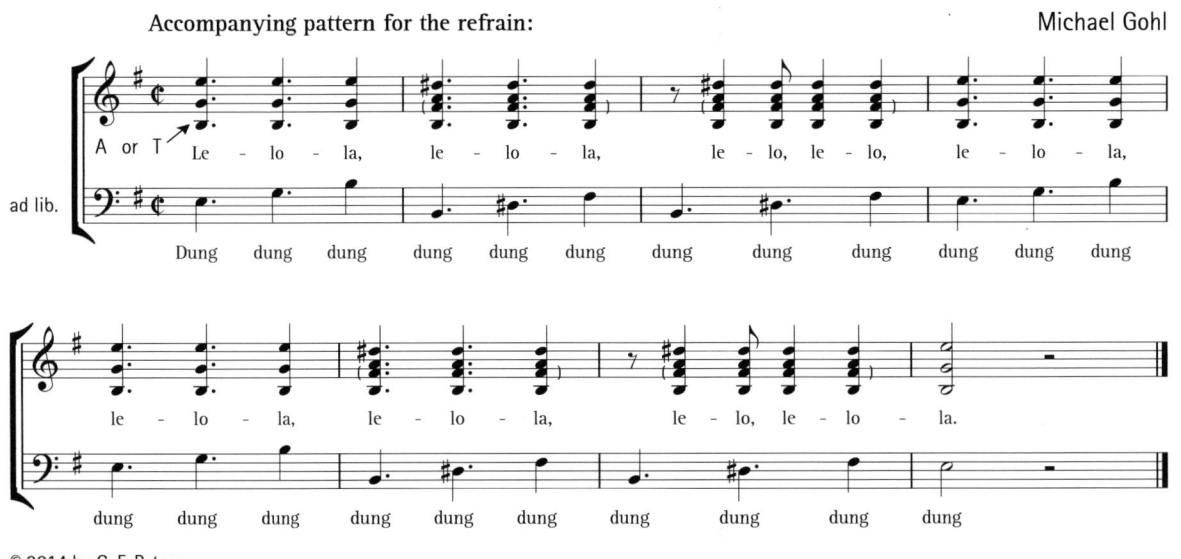

© 2014 by C. F. Peters

II. AROUND THE WORLD

50. Sakura

Trad. Japan
Choral setting: Hansruedi Willisegger

*) Can also be sung SSA

© Arr. Verlag Schweizer Singbuch

Translation:

Cherry blossom, cherry blossom, as far as the eye can see. Over field and mountain and village, a haze of cherry blossom, a cloud of cherry blossom resplendent in the morning sun. Cherry blossom, cherry blossom at its most beautiful!

II. AROUND THE WORLD

51. Evening Rise

Indian folk song

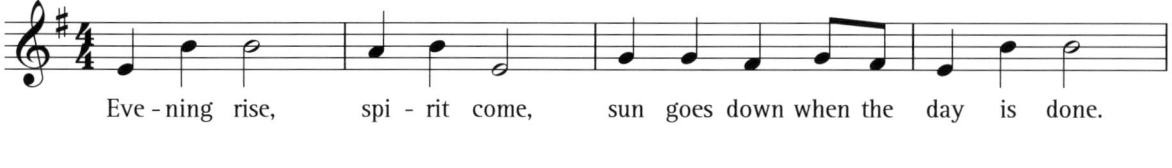

Eve-ning rise, spi-rit come, sun goes down when the day is done.
Mo-ther Earth a-wa-kens me with the heart-beat of the sea.

52. Evening Rise (4-part setting)

Arr.: Meinhard Ansohn

Performance suggestion

Begin softly and gradually raise the volume by increasing the number of voices,
climaxing in the tutti (order: Mel. – A2 – A1 – B – T – Descant).
Then repeat the tutti softly and let it fade away.
Variation: a flute or violin improvises to the hummed song.

© Setting: Meinhard Ansohn

II. AROUND THE WORLD

II. AROUND THE WORLD

53. Let me fish off cape St. Mary's

Words and music: Otto P. Kelland
Choral setting: Diane Loomer

© by Star Quality Music / Musik Edition Discoton GmbH (Universal Music Publishing Group)

Performance suggestion

First verse in unison / as solo
Second and third verses in two parts (tune sings text, canon voice sings "Oo")
Fourth verse in three parts

II. AROUND THE WORLD

54. Shenandoah

Trad. USA

1. O Shenando', I long to see you, away, you rolling river, o Shenando', I long to see you, away we're bound away, across the wide Missouri.
2. O Shenando', I love your daughter, away, you rolling river, o Shenando', I love your daughter, a-
3. O Shenando', I long to see you, away, you rolling river, o Shenando', I'll not deceive you,

Accompanying parts

Michael Gohl

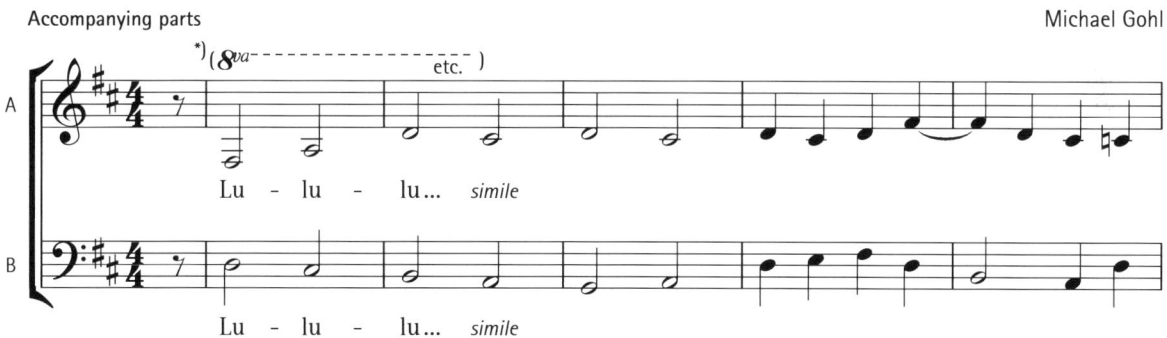

Lu - lu - lu... *simile*
Lu - lu - lu... *simile*

© Arr. Verlag Schweizer Singbuch

*) Can also be sung as descant

II. AROUND THE WORLD

55. La Bamba
Trad. Mexico

Pa-ra bai-lar la Bam - ba, pa-ra bai-lar la Bam - ba, se ne-ce si-ta u-na po-ca de gra - cia, u-na po-ca de gra - cia y o-tra co - si-ta, y a-rri-ba, y a-rri-ba. Ay arr-i-ba, y a-rri-ba, por ti se-ré, por ti se-ré, por ti se-ré. Yo no soy ma-ri-ne-ro, yo no soy ma-ri-ne-ro, soy ca-pi-tan, soy ca-pi-tan, soy ca-pi-tán. Bam-ba, bam - ba. Bam-ba, bam-ba. Bam-ba, bam - ba. Bam-ba, bam.

Bass ostinati
Anja Merusch

① dum du dum du dum du dum dum
② dum dum dum du dum dum ba du ba
③ dum p tz dum dum tz du dum p tz du dum ba du ba

© 2014 by C. F. Peters

II. AROUND THE WORLD

56. Janie Mama 4-part canon

Trad. from the Caribbean
Arr.: Klex Wolf

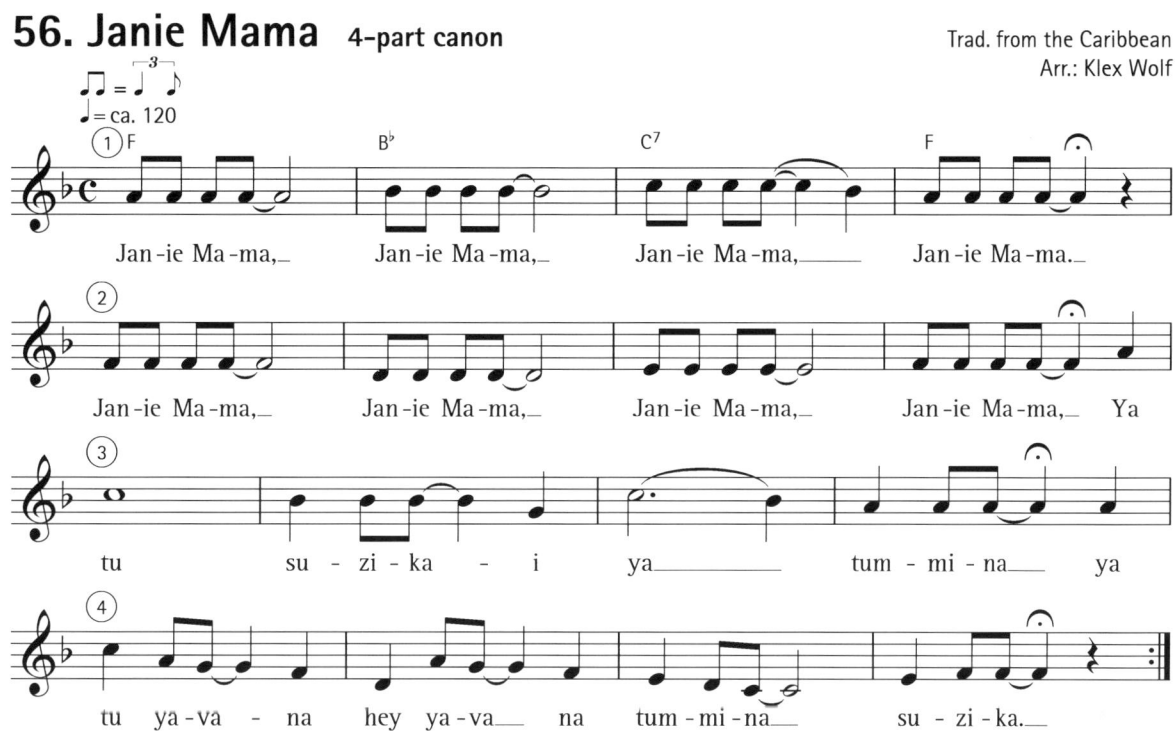

© Helbling, Innsbruck-Esslingen-Bern/Belp

Meaning of text unknown.

57. Hue Gim Go (Glow-worm)

Trad. Taiwan

II. AROUND THE WORLD

58. Mo Li Hua / 茉莉花 (Jasmin Flower)

Chinese folk song
18th century
Arr.: Anja Merusch

Literal Translation:

What a beautiful jasmine flower
What a beautiful jasmine flower
Sweet-smelling, beautiful, stems full of buds
Fragrant and white, everyone praises
Let me pluck you down
Give to someone else
Jasmine flower, oh jasmine flower

© 2015 by C. F. Peters

59. Arirang

Korean folk song

Note

Arirang is the most popular Korean folk song and was inscribed on the UNESCO Intangible Cultural Heritage list in 2012. Young Jo Lee has interwoven a popular Korean rhythm into his version.

II. AROUND THE WORLD

60. Arirang / 아리랑 (SATB)

Korean folk song
Arr. Young Jo Lee
(2014)

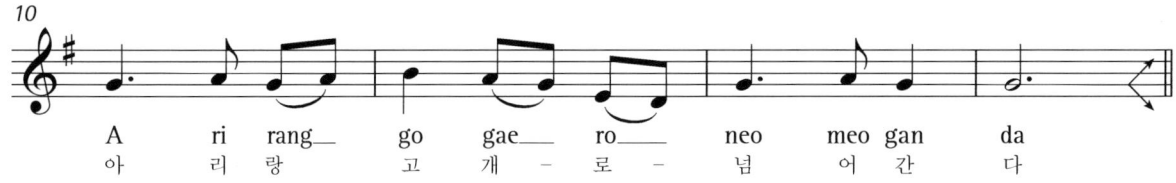

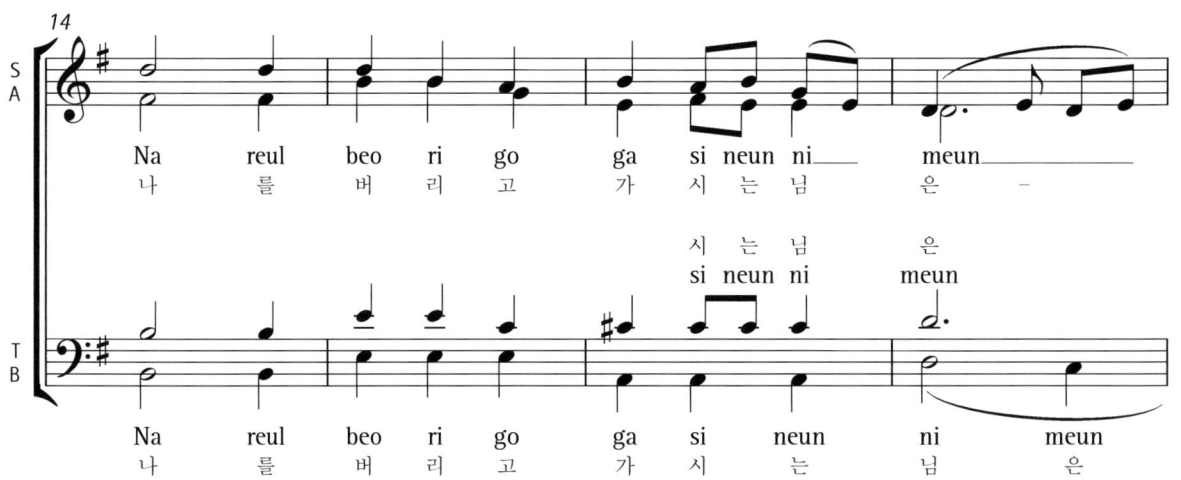

© Young Jo Lee. Reproduced by permission.

II. AROUND THE WORLD

II. AROUND THE WORLD

II. AROUND THE WORLD

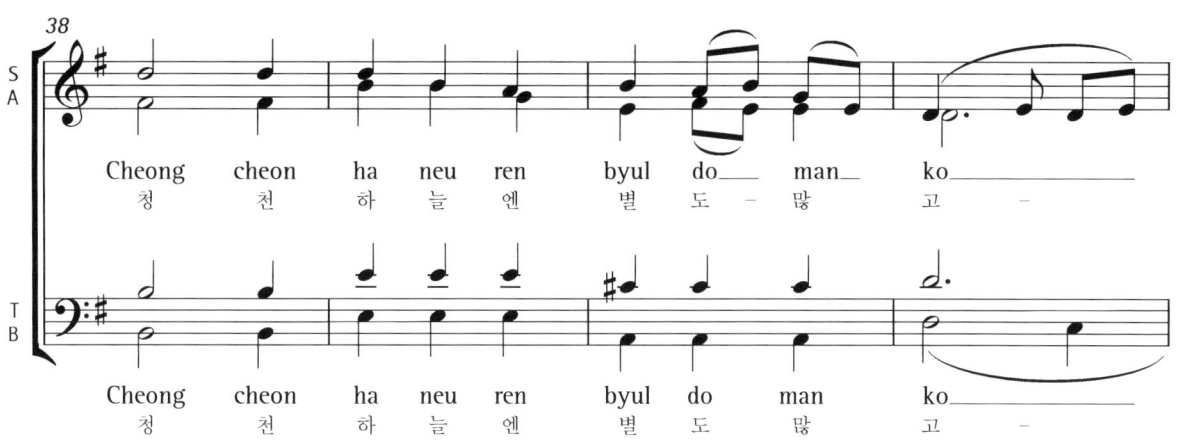

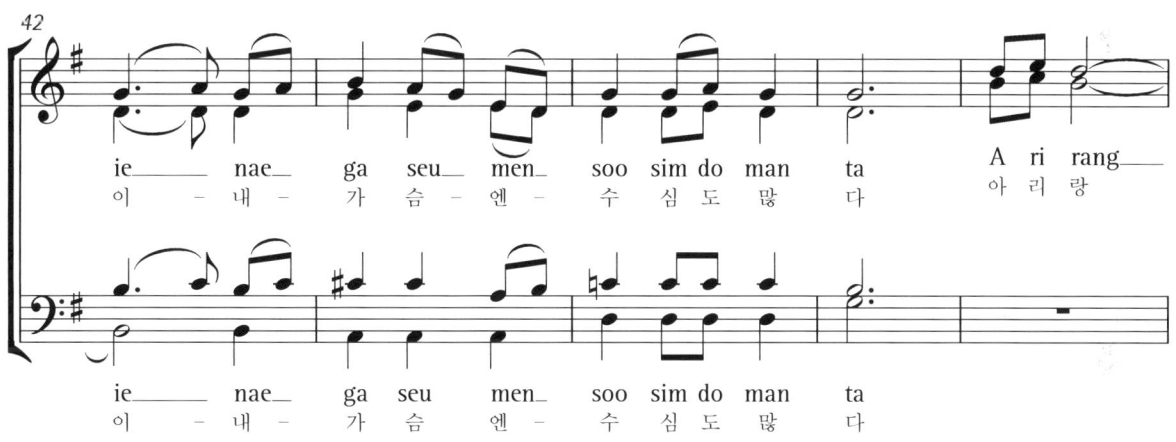

II. AROUND THE WORLD

61. Minoi, Minoi

Samoan dancing song
Arr.: Christopher Marshall

© C. J. Marshall, 1994. Vaia'ata Print. Reproduced by permission.

Piano accompaniment available for download at www.editionpeters.com/singalong

II. AROUND THE WORLD

Translation:

Move, move like an ant *(loi)* when you dance,
Swaying from side to side,
Dipping into rich coconut cream, *(pe'epe'e)*
As sweet as baked fruit. *(poi)*

Ah, my pigeon, *(lupe)*
Crying out to me,
I wish you could keep dancing like that,
So move, move, move my darling. *(la'u pele)*

Note

Minoi Minoi is a dancing song, the words describing the movements of the dance. It is foreign to the Samoan spirit to allow the pursuit of a completely authentic performance to stand in the way of the shared enjoyment of singing.

Pronunciation guide:
The letter "g" should be promounced as "ng" like in "singing". The apostrophe is a gentle glottal stop as in the English "oh-oh". When a diphtong is sustained, sustain the second vowel, for example in "Minoi" sustein the "i", not the "o". The dotted rhythm should be performed like a triplet (swung: ♩♪).

II. AROUND THE WORLD

62. O-re-mi Nigerian high day song

Words: Trad. Nigeria
Music: Robert Bucknor
Choral setting: Mike Brewer

© 1999 by Faber Music Ltd, London WC1B 3DA
This arrangement © 2014 by Faber Music Ltd, London WC1B 3DA
Reproduced from Hamba Lulu: Five African Songs by permission of the publishers
All Rights Reserved

II. AROUND THE WORLD

Performance suggestions

Translation:

Let us dance.
Father and mother dance.

Variant 1:
Sing the song in unison or as a 2-part canon (entries at 1 and 3).

Variant 2:
Sing the song in unison the first time, then as a 2-part canon (entries at 1 and 3) and then as a 4-part canon.

Variant 3:
Sing the song in unison the first time, then as a 4-part canon and then add the coda (arr. M. Brower).

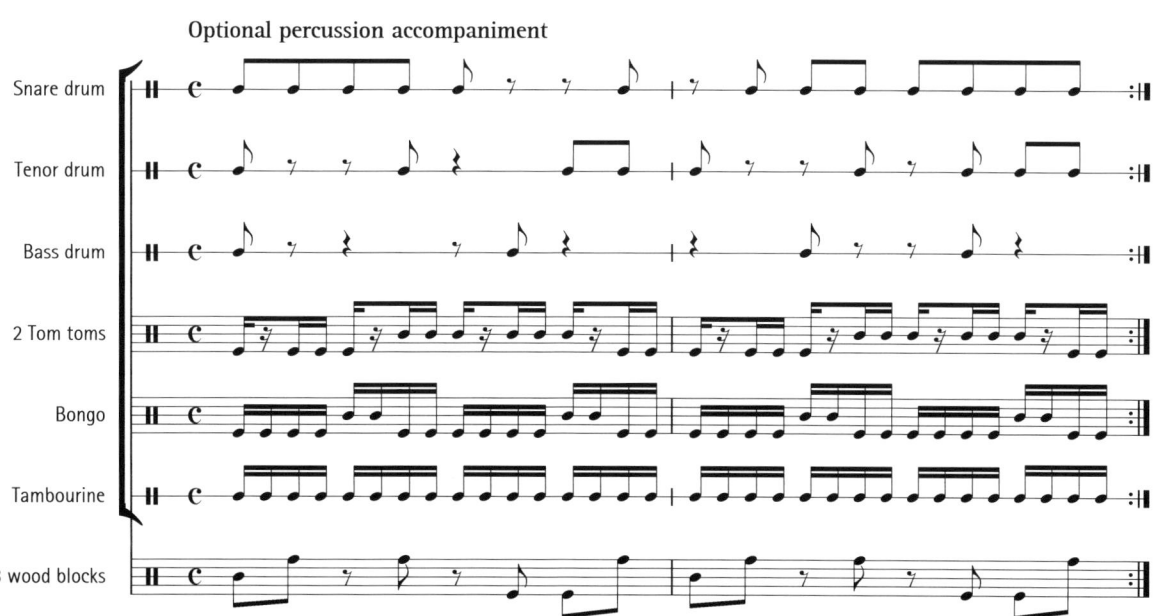

63. Si ya hamba

Trad. South Africa

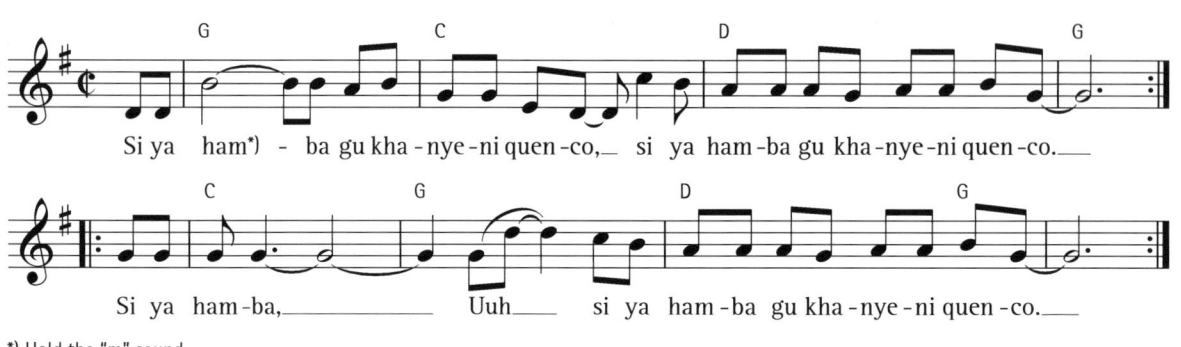

*) Hold the "m" sound

English lyrics:
We are marching in the light of God.

Arr.: Franziska Gohl

4-part setting:

© Arr. Verlag Schweizer Singbuch

*) Can also be sung SSA, without male voice

II. AROUND THE WORLD

64. Sangena (Wedding song)

Traditional Zulu, South Africa
Arr.: Prof. M. Khumalo

*) Bass part can can also be sung 8va in an SSA version

Initially alto part in unison, then all three voices.

Sangena – Greetings!
Sangena thina – We greet you!
Wema – Mother, mummy

Suggested movements

A From bar one and from bar 22: Zulu step

The **Zulu step** is a common basic dance step in the Zulu tradition:
1. Right foot forward (turned slightly inwards) while at the same time utwisting right shoulder and elbow forward ("attack")
2. Left foot on-the-spot step.
3. Right foot back, straighten upper body while twisting right shoulder and elbow backward.
4. Left foot on-the-spot step.

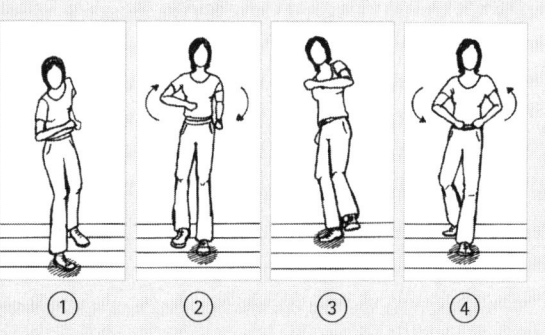

B From bar 14:

Stand with legs together.
Stretch arms in parallel (including hands and fingers) diagonally to the right in a downard direction (twice) and then diagonally to the left in a downard direction (twice). Alternate direction.

This score has been supplied by the SAMRO (Southern African Music Rights Organisation), on behalf of the Composer/Arranger, who is a member of SAMRO. The work may be performed only under licence from SAMRO, or an affiliated performing right society. All public performances must be notified to SAMRO. This score may not be photocopied or reproduced in any manner or form, without prior written permission from SAMRO. Permission to make a recording of this work or any part thereof, must be obtained beforehand, in writing, from SAMRO or from one of its international affiliates
© SAMRO

II. AROUND THE WORLD

II. AROUND THE WORLD

II. AROUND THE WORLD

65. Nginesi Ponono

Trad. South Africa
Arr.: Michael Gohl

© 2014 by C. F. Peters

*) SSAA version: T can be sung by A1; B can be sung by A2, an octave higher as necessary.

Gist translation:
My lover lives in Durban. I have a lover in Durban.

II. AROUND THE WORLD

66. Noyana

Trad. South Africa
Arr.: Franziska Gohl

Translation:

Noyana – are you going?
Nigini – what are you saying?
Noyana Pezulu – are you going to paradise? (will you enter heaven?)

© Franziska Gohl

Note

In the South African tradition, polyphony is generally improvised. The vocal setting presented here is intended as a suggestion. It can also be expanded, transposed to equal voices or accompanied by percussion. The rhythmic staggering of the voices and interspersing of E♭ flats are features of this song tradition.

67. African Alleluja

Words and music:
Markus Detterbeck

Performance tip

Possible performance variants:

A) To start with, everyone sings the melody (lower line) in unison. After several repetitions, it is sung as a canon.
B) Everyone sings the lower line in unison while a small group of soloists sings the upper staff.
C) In the case of a mixed (SATB) choir, the basses sing the lower line. Tenors and female voices then come in with the upper line, singing the text variants ad lib.

Pronunciation of the Zulu text Uyingcwele baba ("You are holy, my Lord"): the "c" in the group of letters "gcwe" is sounded as a click consonant with the tongue. Alternatively it can be pronounced as "que".

© Markus Detterbeck

II. AROUND THE WORLD

68. Ah ya zein

Trad. Arabic
Choral setting: Hansruedi Willisegger

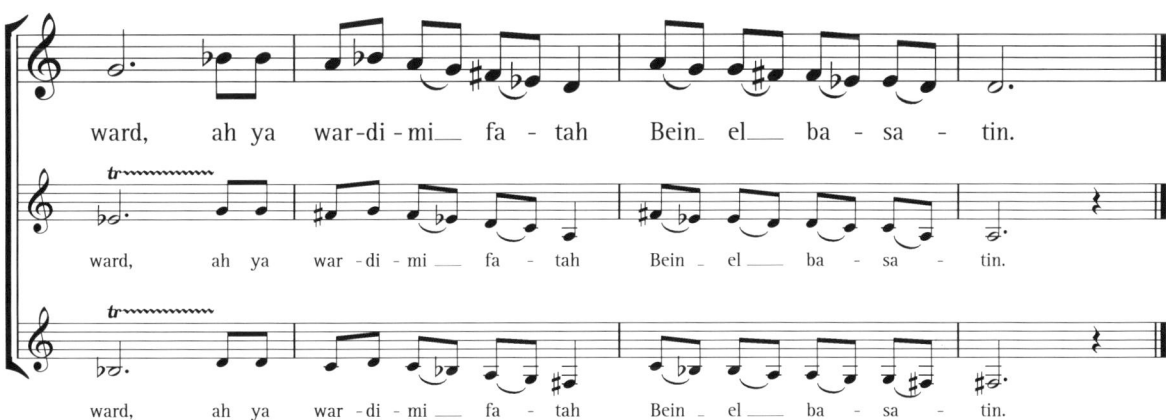

© Arr. Verlag Schweizer Singbuch

Translation:

Ah, thou divine Zein el Abedin, seeing thee is like seeing the fairest of roses.

Note

Ah ya Zein is a well-known love song throughout the Arab world. With modern jazz, music from outside Europe often came in to focus, and more than ever before a song like this can today be a bridge over to other cultures. It can also rub itself off onto our own music.

II. AROUND THE WORLD

69. Keshet l'vana / A White Rainbow

Music: Josef Hadar
Words: Bruria Schweitzer

© All rights reserved to Joseph Hadar, Bruria Schweitzer and ACUM. Used by permission.

*) The lowest part can also be sung by male voices an octave lower

70. Samiotissa

From Greece (Isle of Samos)

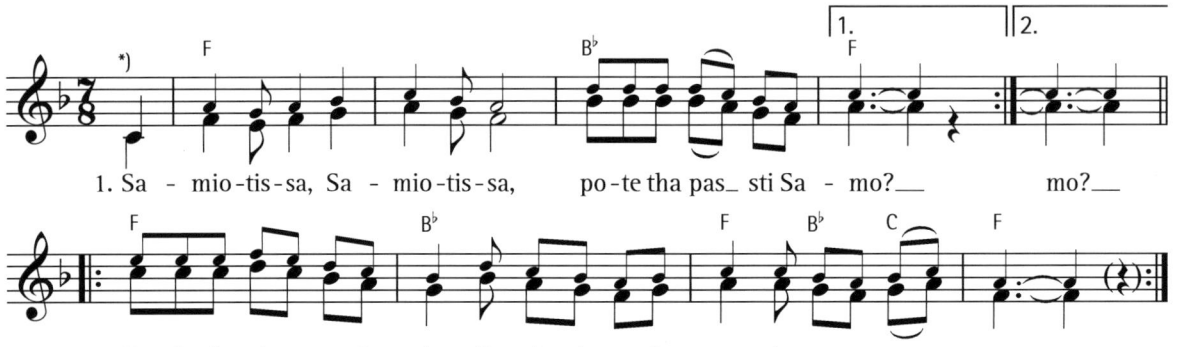

*) High voice comes in on repeat

2. Me ti varka pu tha pas chrisa pania tha valo,
   malamatenia ta kupia, Samiotissa, ja nartho na se paro
3. Samiotissa me tis elies ke me ta mavra matia
   mu'kanes tin kardhula mu, Samiotissa, saranta dhio kommatia.

Translation:

1. Samiotissa*, Samiotissa when do you leave for Samos? I will scatter roses on the shore, Samiotissa, when I come to fetch you.
2. And the ship that carries you will I bedeck with golden sails and gilded oars, Samiotissa, when I come to fetch you.
3. Samiotissa with your beauty marks and black eyes. You shatter my heart, Samiotissa, into forty-two fragments.

*Samiotissa = a woman or girl from the isle of Samos

71. El haderech

Trad. Israel
Music: Nurit Hirsch
Words: Schimrit Or
Arr.: Michael Gohl

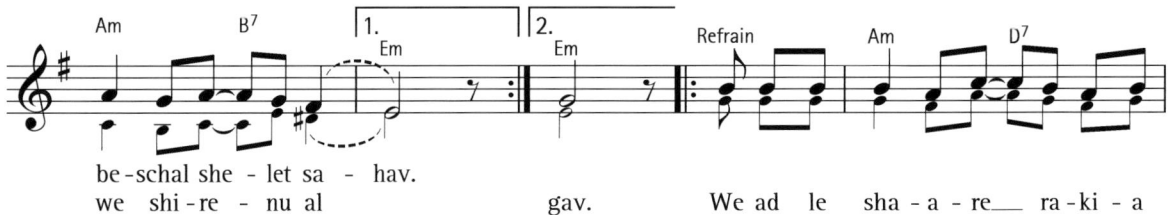

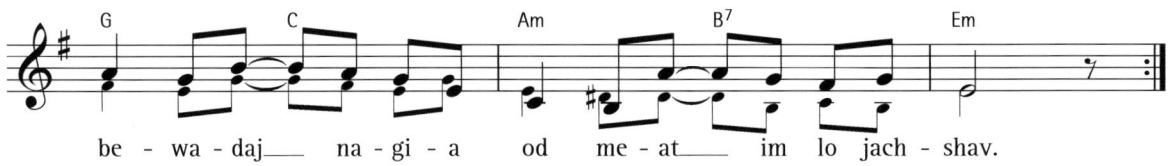

© M/T: with the authors
© Arr.: Schweizer Singbuch Verlag

II. AROUND THE WORLD

71. Što mi e milo

Trad. Macedonia

Gist translation:

How lovely it would be to have a shop in Struga; to be able to sit there and watch the young women carrying water in their colourful pitchers.

Note

*) *Što mi e milo* would originally have been sung by men. It can therefore also be sung with mixed or exclusively male voices with the key adjusted accordingly.

II. AROUND THE WORLD

73. Istanbul Kasap Havası

Turkish-Greek traditional
Dancing tune from Istanbul

Optional part

*) Start slowly and accelerate slowly, repeat the song as much as you like. Add part C between A and B as you wish.

74. Çayeli'nden öteye

Turkish folk song
Arr.: Murat Başman

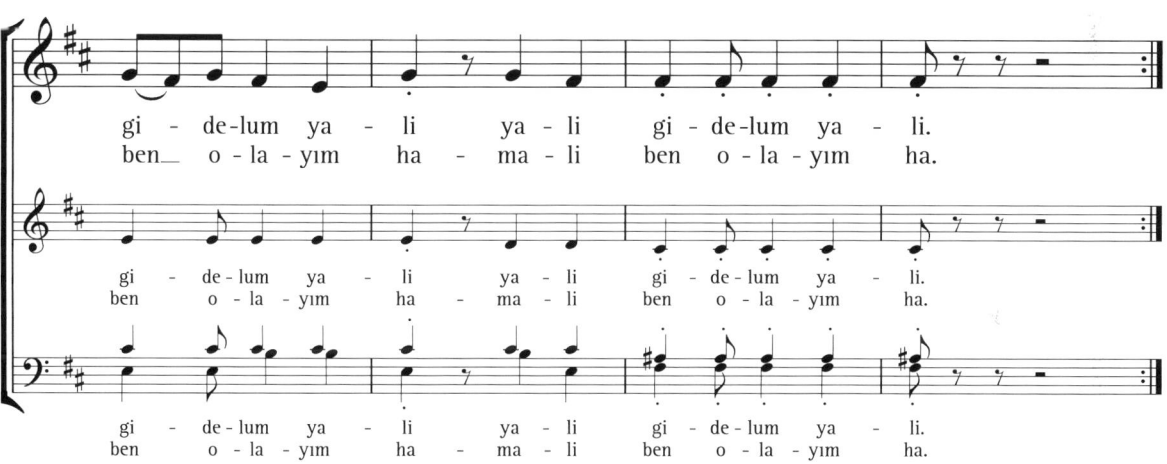

© Murat Başman. Reproduced by permission.

Performance suggestion

1. Play the melody twice with instruments.
2. Sing the song three times: First line of text once, second line of the text twice.

Different variations including dialogues between man and woman are traditional.

II. AROUND THE WORLD

75. Tiliseb From Estonia

Music and 4-part setting: Leonard Virkhaus (1910–1984)
Words: J. Oro (1901–1941)
English words: Richard George Elliott

Ti - li - seb, ti - li - seb ai - sa - kell, lu - mi hell, lu - mi hell,
Ti - li - seb, ti - li - seb, sleigh bells sound, snow lies soft - ly on the ground,

ti - li - seb, ti - li - seb ai - sa - kell, kiir - gab mets ja hiil - gab maa.
ti - li - seb, ti - li - seb, sleigh bells ring, the froz - en earth is glis - ten - ing.

1. Möö - du - vad saa - nid, reed pi - ki teed, tal - vist teed,
1. Be - neath the star - ry can - o - py, through the snow - y land glide we,
2. Hel - gi - vad tu - led eel, tal - ve - teel, kü - la - teel,
2. Hark, the church bells' mer - ry peal, song of an - gels filled with zeal

ü - le soo ja kar - ja - maa, ü - le hei - na - maa.
Win - ter for - est ra - diant white, young and old de - light.
rõõm - sad pü - had i - gal pool, ü - le ko - gu - maa.
See you bright and cheer - ful glow, thith - er now we go.

Suggested movements for children (for the English version)

Bars 1–8: Run on the spot, possibly with bells either held in the hand or attached to the ankles.

First verse:
Bars 9–12 "canopy" (vault of heaven): describe a big arc above the head, moving the right hand from left to right.
Bars 13 and 14 "Winter forest": stand like fir trees.
Bars 15 and 16 "delight": spread arms.

Second verse:
Bars 9–12 "Hark": sing quietly with the right hand behind the ear as if listening.
Bars 13 and 14 "See": shield eyes with hand.
Bars 15 and 16 "thither": with outstretched arm and index finger, point to a spot in the distance.

Melody © Fennica Gehrman Oy, Helsinki.
Printed with permission

II. AROUND THE WORLD

76. Nocturne

Words and music: Evert Taube
Choral setting: Anders Öhrwall

Translation:
Sleep in my arms. The night shelters your glowing cheeks under its wings.
Happy and warm, you're soon dreaming, escaping from me as waves flee the wind.
You're caught again. You pant. You struggle. You don't want to. You do want to. And are kissed again.
Slumber my darling! The night advances. And love watches over you, tender and still.

© Gehrmans Musikförlag AB.
Printed with permission.

II. AROUND THE WORLD

77. Dobrú noć

Trad. Czech Republic
Choral setting: Jos Van den Borre

Do - brú noć má mi - lá, do - brú noć má mi - lá,

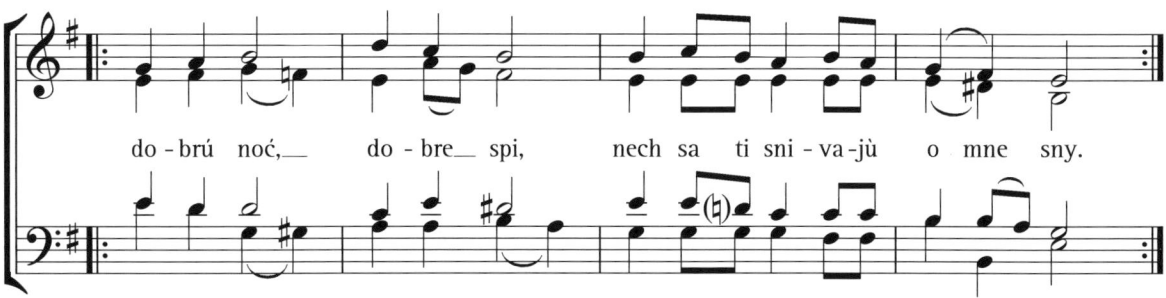

do - brú noć, do - bre spi, nech sa ti sni - va - jù o mne sny.

Gist translation:
Good night my sweetheart, sleep well.

Copyright © by Möseler Verlag, Wolfenbüttel

Open singing, Europa Cantat Turin 2012, Piazza San Carlo: concluding evening with Michael Gohl (© Festival Europa Cantat Torino 2012)

78. Mu Süda, Ärka Üles
Wach' auf, mein Herz, und singe

Cyrillus Kreek (1889 - 1962)
from Estonia

1. Mu sü-da, är-ka ü-les ja kii-da Loo-jat laul-des, kes
2. Mu Ju-mal, nii kui öö-se, mind hoi-dis si-nu kä-si, nii
3. Ka töös mind ik-ka ai-ta, mis õi-ge, mul-le näi-ta! Su
4. Su hel-dus jää-gu mul-le, mu sü-da temp-liks sul-le: su

kõik hääd mei-le an-nab ja mu-ret ik-ka kan-nab.
päe-va ka mind kan-na, mull' ing-lid var-juks an-na.
hool-de kõik ma jä-tan, mis ii-al et-te võ-tan.
sõ-na mind siin toit-ku, teed tae-va poo-le näit-ku.

Original German lyrics by Paul Gerhardt (1648):

1. Wach auf, mein Herz, und singe
dem Schöpfer aller Dinge,
dem Geber aller Güter,
dem frommen Menschenhüter.

2. Heut' als die dunkeln Schatten
mich ganz umgeben hatten,
bedecktest du mich Armen
mit göttlichem Erbarmen.

3. Sprich „Ja" zu meinen Taten,
Hilf selbst das Beste raten;
den Anfang, Mittel, Ende,
ach Herr, zum Besten wende.

4. Mit Segen mich beschütte,
mein Herz sei deine Hütte;
dein Wort sei meine Speise,
bis ich gen Himmel reise.

1. Mu sü-da, är-ka ü-les ja kii-da Loo-jat laul-des, kes

kõik hääd mei-le an-nab ja mu-ret ik-ka kan-nab.

© www.edition49.de

II. AROUND THE WORLD

79. Leijoo

Trad. Lapland
Arr.: Sanna Valvanne (b 1971)

Performance suggestion

First time: everyone sings the S2 part in unison.
Second time: two voices (S1 part added).
Third time: three voices (S1, S2, A).

Lei-joo loi lae loi la pronunciation guide:
"joo", "ei" and "ae" should be pronounced as in the English words "y<u>o</u>del", "s<u>ay</u>" and "<u>ah eh</u>" respectively.

© Sanna Valvanne

II. AROUND THE WORLD

80. Flikkain polska

Trad. Finland
Choral setting: Kari Ala Pöllanen

1. Mi - tä net toul - laa - sek - ki laat - ti - al - le me - nöö; kyl - lä sin - ne pa - rem - mak - ki tuk - kii,
Mi - tä me - nöö, pa - rem - mak - ki tuk - kii,

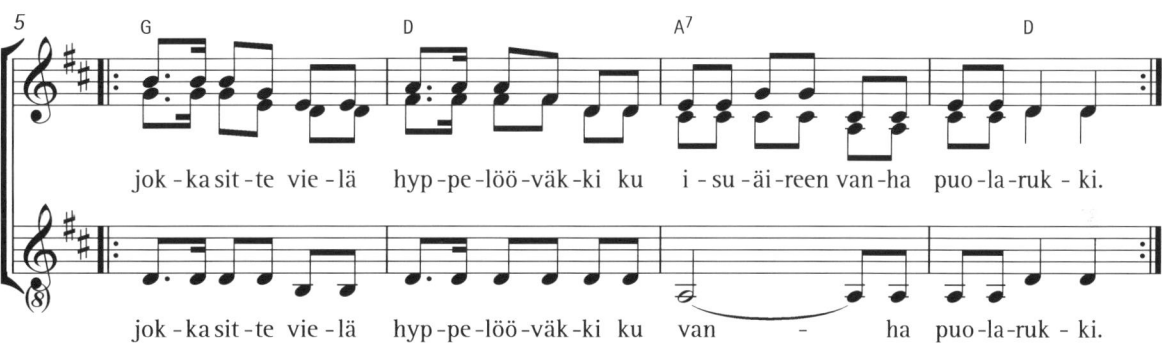

jok - ka sit - te vie - lä hyp - pe - löö - väk - ki ku i - su - äi - reen van - ha puo - la - ruk - ki.
jok - ka sit - te vie - lä hyp - pe - löö - väk - ki ku van - ha puo - la - ruk - ki.

Arr. © Fennica Gehrman Oy, Helsinki. Printed with permission.

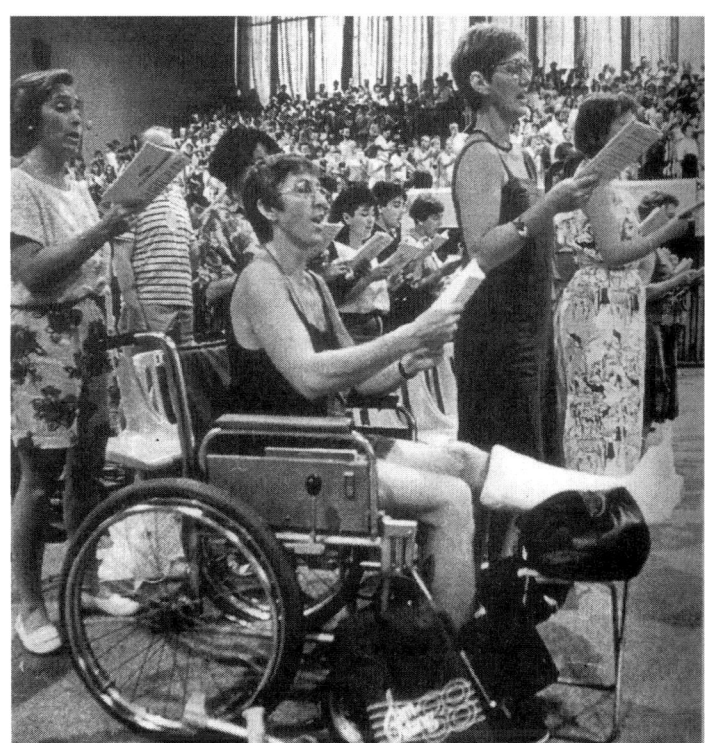

Open singing: Pécs, 1988

2. ‖: Soot tullu **muhun** ja moon tullu **suhun**
   ja pappani pani mun **sua** meinaamahan. :‖
   ‖: Jonsen mä sua **saa**, niin voi-voi herran tähären,
   kyllä se olis **mammallekki** paha. :‖

3. ‖: Kyllä muaki **sitte** hyppelemään **vietääs**,
   jos ne **tietääs**, jotta mul on **lehemä**. :‖
   ‖: Mutta kun ei **tierä**, niin ei liioon vierä;
   pahakos sen **lehemällisen** kerjää! :‖

4. ‖: Menin luttihin **maata** ja jätin oven **haata**,
   orottelin **poikia perähäni**. :‖
   ‖: Aamulla heräsin ja yksin makasin,
   voi pirnales, kun **pisti nenähäni**. :‖

In the second to fourth verses the third voice sings only the words printed in bold.

81. Gamla Moder Jord

Trad. Sweden
German and English words: Markus Detterbeck
Choral setting: Markus Detterbeck

© Helbling, Innsbruck-Esslingen-Bern/Belp

II. AROUND THE WORLD

82. Vem kan segla förutan vind

Swedish folk song
Arr.: Gunnar Eriksson

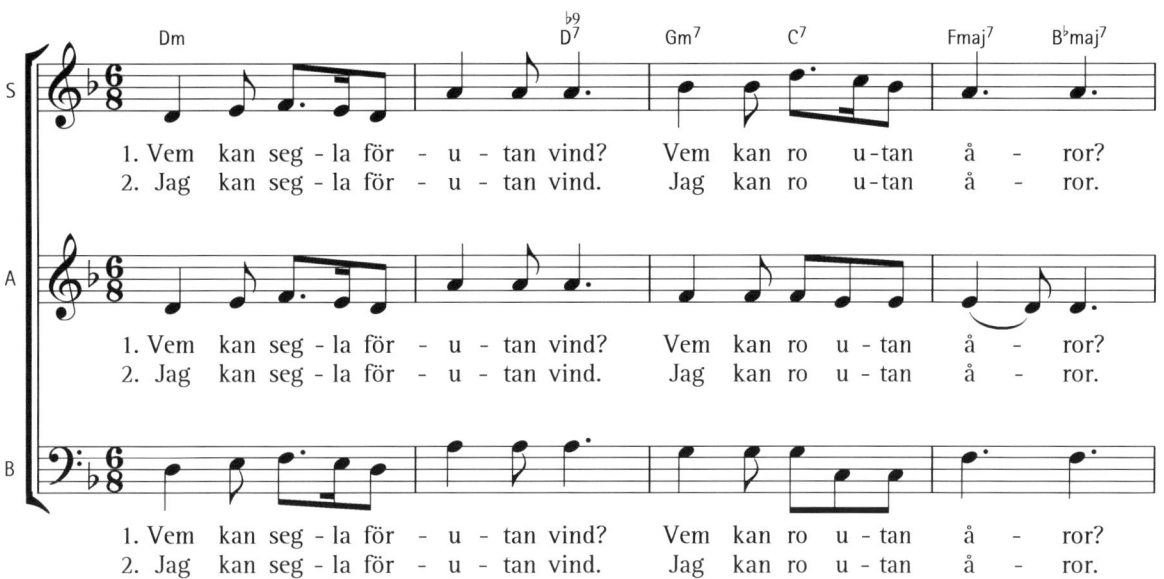

Translation:

1. Who can sail without wind?
   Who can row without oars?
   Who can be parted from his sweetheart
   without shedding tears?

2. I can sail without wind,
   I can row without oars,
   But I can't be parted from my sweetheart
   without shedding tears.

Copyright © 2014 Bo Ejeby Förlag and Gunnar Eriksson.

II. AROUND THE WORLD

83. Kom!

Monica Åslund (b 1952)

Afro-inspired marching tune, with great spirit

© Gehrmans Musikförlag AB, Stockholm. Printed with permission.

II. AROUND THE WORLD

II. AROUND THE WORLD

84. All through the Night

Trad. Wales
Choral setting: Malcolm Goldring (b 1949)

© With the kind permission of SCHOTT MUSIC, Mainz

II. AROUND THE WORLD

85. Autumn Comes

Trad. England
Choral setting: Anja Merusch
Descant part: Michael Gohl

© 2014 by C. F. Peters

Performance tip

The voices accompanying the tune are optional. The descant part, to be performed by a female soloist, a small group or a single instrument, should only join in later on.

II. AROUND THE WORLD

86. Greensleeves

Trad. England/Scotland (16th century)

1. A-las, my love, you do me wrong to cast me off dis-cour-tous-ly; and
2. If you in-tend thus to dis-dain it does so more en-rap-ture me, and
3. A-las, my love, that you should own a heart of wan-ton va-ni-ty, so
4. Ah, Greens-leeves, now fare-well, a-dieu, to god I pray to pro-sper thee, for

I have lov-ed you so long, de-light-ing in your com-pa-ny.
e-ven so, I still re-main, a lov-er in cap-ti-vi-ty.
must I me-di-tate a-lone u-pon your in-sin-ce-ri-ty.
I am still thy lov-er true, come once a-gain and love me.

Refrain

Green-sleeves was all my joy, Green-sleeves was my de-light.

Green-sleeves was my heart of gold, and who but my la-dy Green-sleeves.

Accompaniment

Hansruedi Willisegger

Instrumental or vocal

© setting: Verlag Schweizer Singbuch

II. AROUND THE WORLD

87. Porompom pón (El Porompompero)

Trad. Spain
Arr.: Guido Helbling

© Setting: Verlag Schweizer Singbuch

Percussion accompaniment

Performance suggestion

Part A
Intro: 1x guitar and then add percussion instruments
with each successive repeat.
+ piano
+ 1st voice
+ 2nd voice
+ 3rd voice
- repeat 2x with all voices

Part B
Free rhythmic improvisations with any imaginable forces
Form: A – B – A – B' – A + Coda

This is a simplified version of the chorus of the popular Spanish song "El Porompompero" by Ochaita-Valerio-Solano (recorded by the group EL CHATO).

II. AROUND THE WORLD

88. Lili eder bat

Trad. Basque Country (Spain)
Arr.: Javier Busto (b 1949)

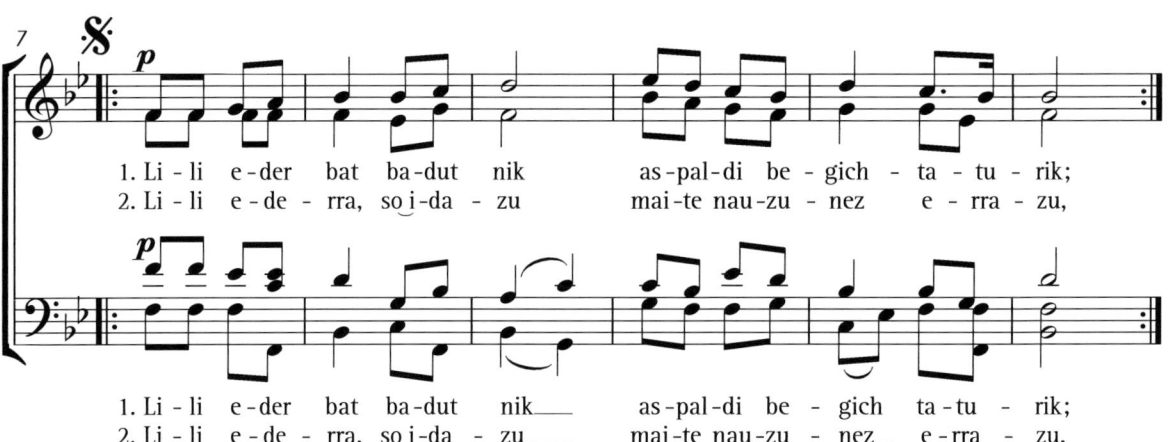

© Bustovega. Printed with permission.

Translation:

I have had my eye on this lovely flower for a long time, but I haven't dared touch her.

Had I the courage, I would approach her. Beautiful flower, look at me and tell me whether you love me.

The look in your eyes has broken my heart and I feel I'm dying.

II. AROUND THE WORLD

II. AROUND THE WORLD

89. Santa Lucia

Trad. Italy

© Arr. Verlag Schweizer Singbuch

Note on the Swedish text (Sankta Lucia)

Santa Lucia is a Neapolitan song from the nineteenth century in which a seafarer praises the beauty of the port of Borgo Santa Lucia.

The high point of the Swedish Christmas celebrations is the festival of St. Lucy on 13 December. In this Swedish version of the text (there are various others), Lucia, the "Bride of the Light", a girl dressed in white wearing a crown of lights, is asked for her blessing.

II. AROUND THE WORLD

90. Sankta Lucia (4-part setting)

Swedish words: Sigrid Elmblad
Arr.: Carl-Bertil Agnestig

© Gehrmans Musikforlag AB. Printed with permission.

II. AROUND THE WORLD

91. Pique la baleine or „Le navire merveilleux"

Words and music: Patrick Denain
Choral setting: Luc Guilloré

© 2011 ÉDITIONS À CŒUR JOIE, »Les Passerelles«, 24 avenue Joannès Masset, F-69009 LYON. *Tous droits réservés.*

2. Sa coque, elle est en bois rouge (Pique...) / Ses mâts d'ivoire brillant. (Pique...)
3. Son doublage en cuivre fin... / Ses avirons en argent...
4. La mâture est tout en marbre... / Et les haubans en rubans...
5. Les voiles sont en dentelles... / Travaillées fort joliment...
6. Les cordages du navire... / Sont de fils d'or et d'argent...
7. Son gréement garni de perles... / Ses ancres sont en argent...
8. Le pavillon du navire... / Allait jusqu'au firmament...

II. AROUND THE WORLD

92. Una mattina

Trad. Italy

2. O partigiano, portami via, o bella ciao...
   O partigiano, portami via che mi sento di morir.

3. Se io muoio da partigiano, o bella ciao...
   Se io muoio da partigiano, tu mi devi seppelir.

4. Mi seppellirai lassú in montagna, o bella ciao...
   Mi seppellirai lassú in montagna sotto l'ombra
   d' un bel fior.

5. E tutti quelli che passeranno, o bella ciao...
   E tutti quelli che passeranno diranno che bel fior.

6. E questo è il fiore del partigiano, o bella ciao...
   E questo è il fiore del partigiano morto per la libertà.

Gist translation:

Early one morning we encountered the enemy.
O partisans, take me with you, even if it means I will die.
If I perish as a partisan, bury me up in the mountains.
Plant a flower on my grave. And passers-by
will see the beautiful flower and say: this is the flower of the
partisan who died for the sake of everyone's freedom.

Note

"Bella ciao" means "Here's to a happy reunion". This is an Italian partisans' song from the Second World War and is probably the best-known song of the resistance movement. The Italian partisans were an underground organisation who fought to liberate their country from occupation by the troops of Nazi Germany. The tune derives from an old Lombard cotton pickers' melody.

© 2015 by C. F. Peters

II. AROUND THE WORLD

93. Ritsch, ratsch fidirullala

Swiss folk dance
English version: Michael Gohl

© 2014 by C. F. Peters

Suggested movements

Simple form (can be executed in the smallest space, even with seating)

- **A** Bar 1: On "ritsch" and "ratsch", clap hands, raising one hand energetically from below and bringing the other down energetically from above, as if playing the cymbals. In bars 2–4 hold hands with your neighbours. In each bar take one side-step (with follow-up step) to the left or right as applicable.

- **B** Place hands on hips. In each bar, hop twice on one foot and perform a "heel-toe" tap with the other. Change side with each bar. This a classic polka step.

- **C** With both arms raised in the air, turn on the spot anti-clockwise in a small circle. With each step, snap fingers on same side. Repeat: change direction. Increase tempo gradually with each repetition of the song. You could also raise the key in semitone increments if you wish.

Swiss folk dance (any number of pairs in free formation or else arranged in rows or in a circle)

- **A** Bar 1: On "ritsch" and "ratsch", clap hands, raising one hand energetically from below and bringing the other down energetically from above, as if playing the cymbals.
  Bars 2–4: Link right arms with partner and trot around in a circle clockwise. Repetition: change direction.

- **B** Place hands on hips. In each bar, hop twice on one foot and perform a "heel-toe" tap with the other. Change side with each bar. This a classic polka step.

- **C** Take hold of both of partners' hands. Dance in a clockwise direction (taking a sideways "skip and a jump") and stamp foot on last beat to mark the change of direction.

  Repetition: change direction. No stamp on last note. Option: change parter with each repetition of the song. Gradually increase tempo.

94. Der Hasbācher

Trad. Austria

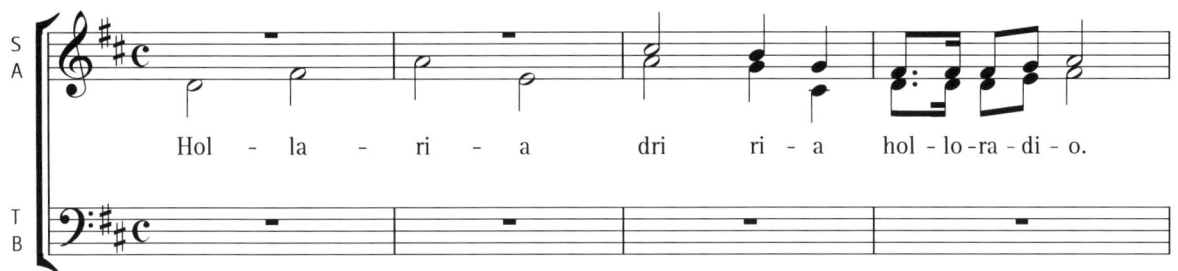

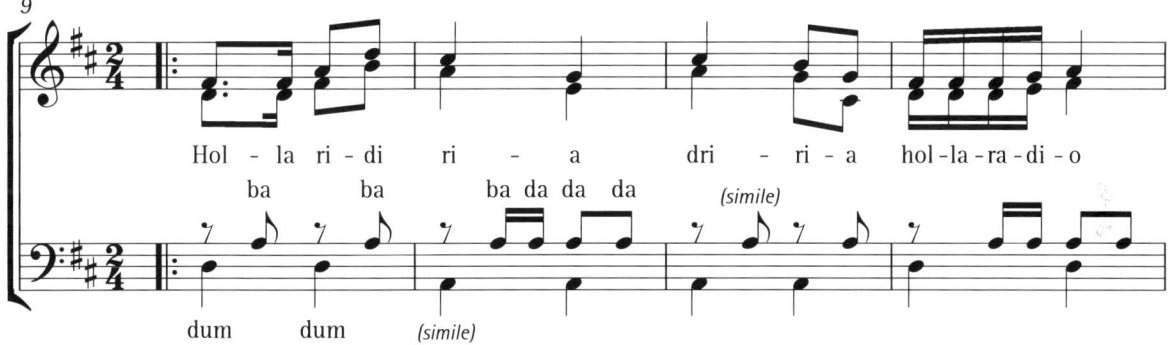

Second time through a whole tone higher

II. AROUND THE WORLD

95. Schläft ein Lied in allen Dingen

Music: Michael Gohl
Words: Joseph von Eichendorff

96. Der Mond ist aufgegangen

Words Matthias Claudius (1740–1815)
Melody: Johann Abraham Peter Schulz (1747–1800)

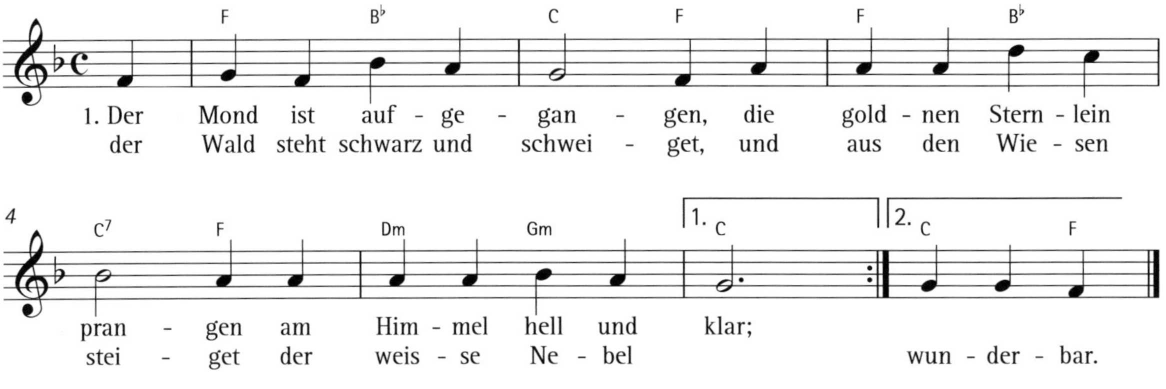

© 2014 by C. F. Peters

II. AROUND THE WORLD

2. Wie ist die Welt so stille
und in der Dämm'rung Hülle
so traulich und so hold,
als eine stille Kammer,
wo ihr des Tages Jammer
verschlafen und vergessen sollt!

3. Seht ihr den Mond dort stehen?
Er ist nur halb zu sehen
und ist doch rund und schön.
So sind wohl manche Sachen,
die wir getrost belachen,
weil unsre Augen sie nicht sehn.

4. Wir stolzen Menschenkinder
sind eitel arme Sünder
und wissen gar nicht viel;
wir spinnen Luftgespinste
und suchen viele Künste
und kommen weiter von dem Ziel.

5. Gott, lass dein Heil uns schauen,
auf nichts Vergänglichs trauen,
nicht Eitelkeit uns freun;
lass uns einfältig werden
und vor dir hier auf Erden
wie Kinder fromm und fröhlich sein!

6. Wollst endlich sonder Grämen
aus dieser Welt uns nehmen
durch einen sanften Tod!
Und, wenn du uns genommen,
lass uns in Himmel kommen,
du, unser Herr und unser Gott!

7. So legt euch denn, ihr Brüder,
in Gottes Namen nieder,
kalt weht der Abendhauch.
Verschon uns, Gott, mit Strafen
und lass uns ruhig schlafen
und unsern kranken Nachbar auch!

97. Der Mond ist aufgegangen
(4-part setting)

Words: Matthias Claudius (1740–1815)
Melody: Johann Abraham Peter Schulz (1747–1800)
Choral setting: Adolf Seifert (1902–1945)

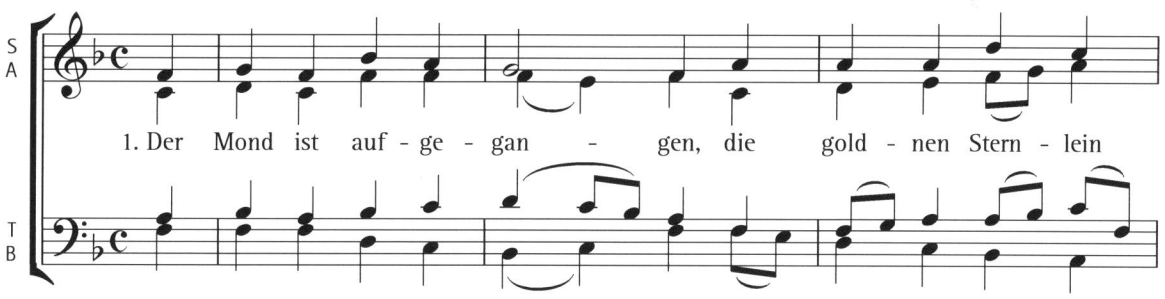

II. AROUND THE WORLD

98. Du fragsch mi, wär i bi

Bernese Oberland, Switzerland
Words: Hans Zulliger
Music: Heidi Stucki
Choral setting: Willi Gohl (1925–2010)

*) Can also be sung SAB

Gist translation:

You ask me who I am,
You ask me what I can do,
You want to know, don't you, why
I won't let you out of my sight.

I don't know who I am,
I don't know what I can do,
All I know is I'm drawn to you,
I cannot let you go.

© Arr. Verlag Schweizer Singbuch

II. AROUND THE WORLD

99. All mein Gedanken, die ich hab

From Lochamer Liederbuch, c. 1450/60
Arr.: Michael Gohl
English words: Richard George Elliott

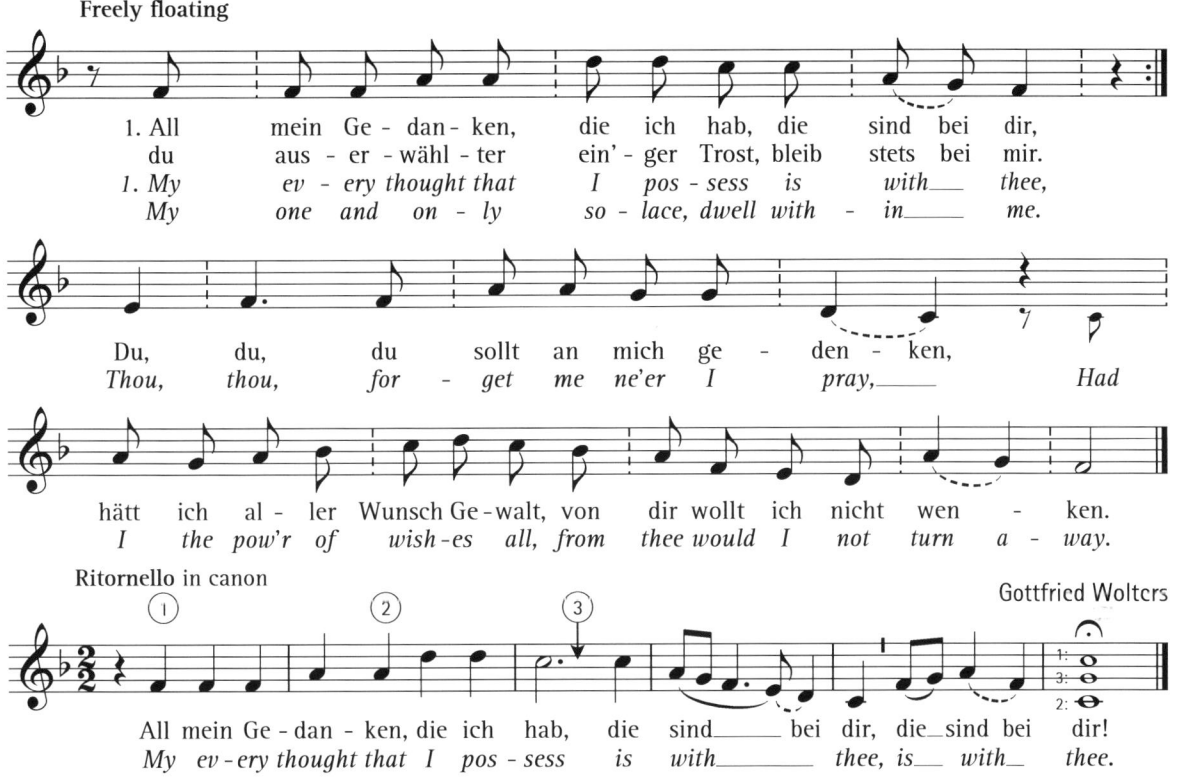

Gottfried Wolters

Copyright © by Möseler Verlag, Wolfenbüttel

2. Du auserwählter ein'ger Trost, gedenk daran:
Leib und Gut das sollst du ganz zu eigen han.
Dein, dein, dein will ich ewig bleiben,
du gibst mir Freud und hohen Mut und kannst
mir leicht vertreiben.

2. My one and only solace, this be known:
My life, my goods belong to thee alone.
Thine, thine, thine will I ever stay,
Thou giv'st me joy and courage and canst my sorrows
drive away.

Performance suggestions

Variant 1:
At a sign from the conductor, a solo voice begins the song, following which all the other singers then enter, individually and in their own tempo. All singers allow the final note of the phrase (or line) to slowly die away.

This results in the creation and subsequent fading away of a melodic sound cloud. The conductor indicates the start of each new phase and directs the fade.

Variant 2:
As in variant 1, the conductor indicates which section of singers is to start first, for example from left to right or from the back to the front. This way, the melodic sound cloud will move through space.

Variant 3:
The conductor organizes each phrase as a canon. Various different entries are possible, for example after every two or every four syllables (in other words quavers). The number of entries can also be freely determined.

The ritornello can be sung either between verses or as an ending.

Arrangement by J. Brahms
The choral setting by J. Brahms on the following pages can follow on seamlessly from one of the performance variants described above. In such a case the keys of the two versions will need to be coordinated. The original version of the song can also be performed in unison or by a single soloist, intonation-like, before the setting by Brahms.

II. AROUND THE WORLD

100. All mein Gedanken, die ich hab (4-part setting)

Words and music:
Lochamer Liederbuch, c. 1450/60
Choral setting: Johannes Brahms
(1833–1897)

Moderato, not too slow, to be performed somewhat freely
With expression

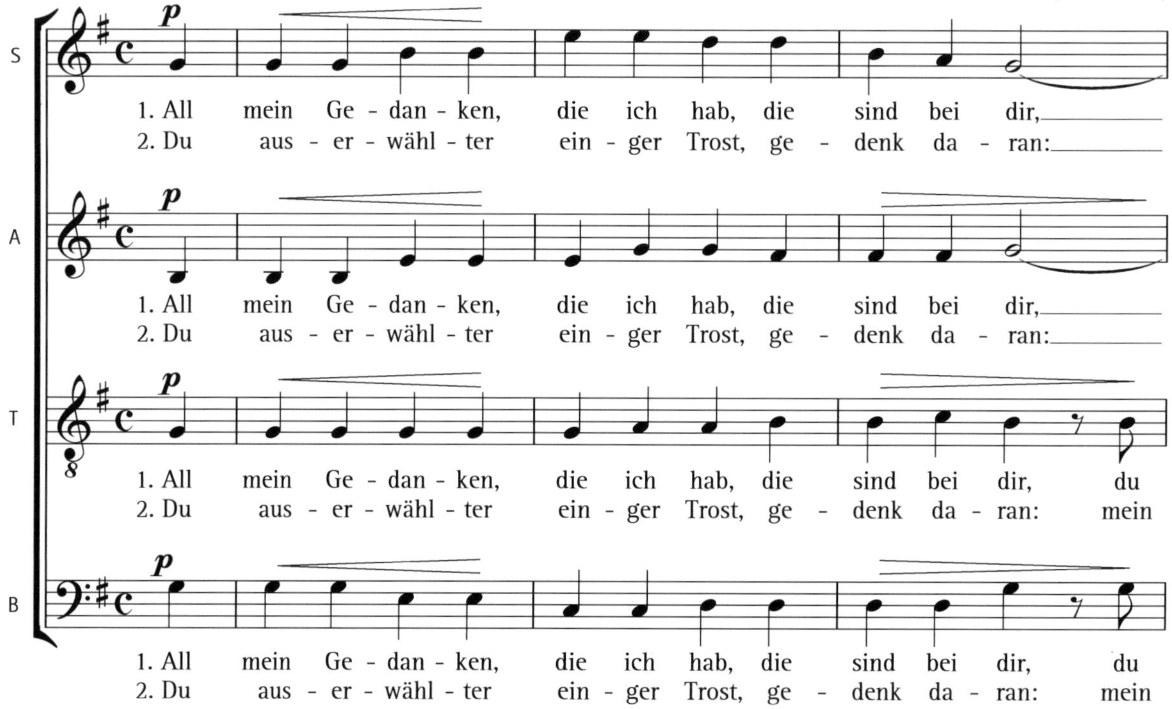

II. AROUND THE WORLD

II. AROUND THE WORLD

101. The River She is Flowing

Indian Song

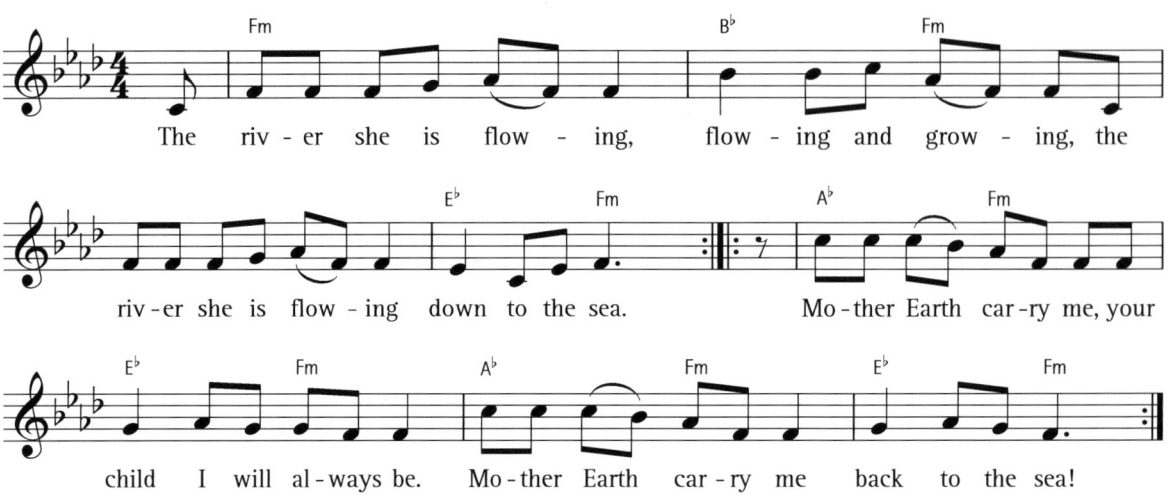

Arr.: Michael Gohl

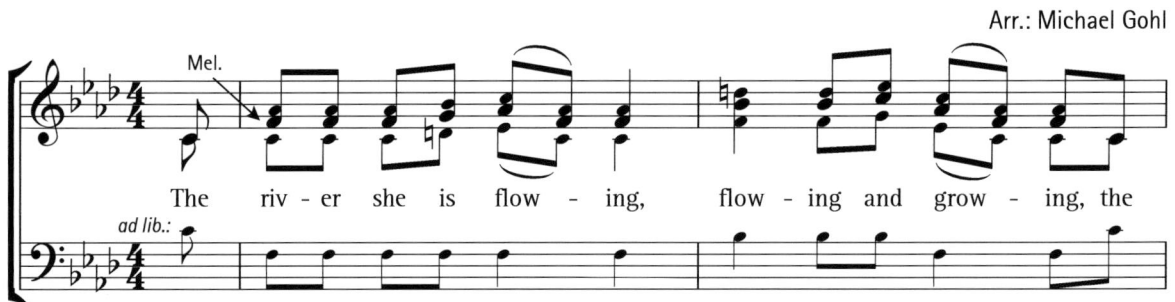

© Arr. Verlag Schweizer Singbuch

III. CLASSICAL AND SACRED

*Toute musique qui s'approche avec révérence
du Divin, du Sacré, de l'Ineffable, est
vraiment une musique religieuse dans toute la
force du terme.*

Olivier Messiaen

*Come, come ye sons of art, come, come away.
Tune all your voices and instruments play
To celebrate, to celebrate this triumphant day.*

Henry Purcell

III. CLASSICAL AND SACRED

102. Da pacem Introitus

Early Christian
Arr.: Burkhard Kinzler

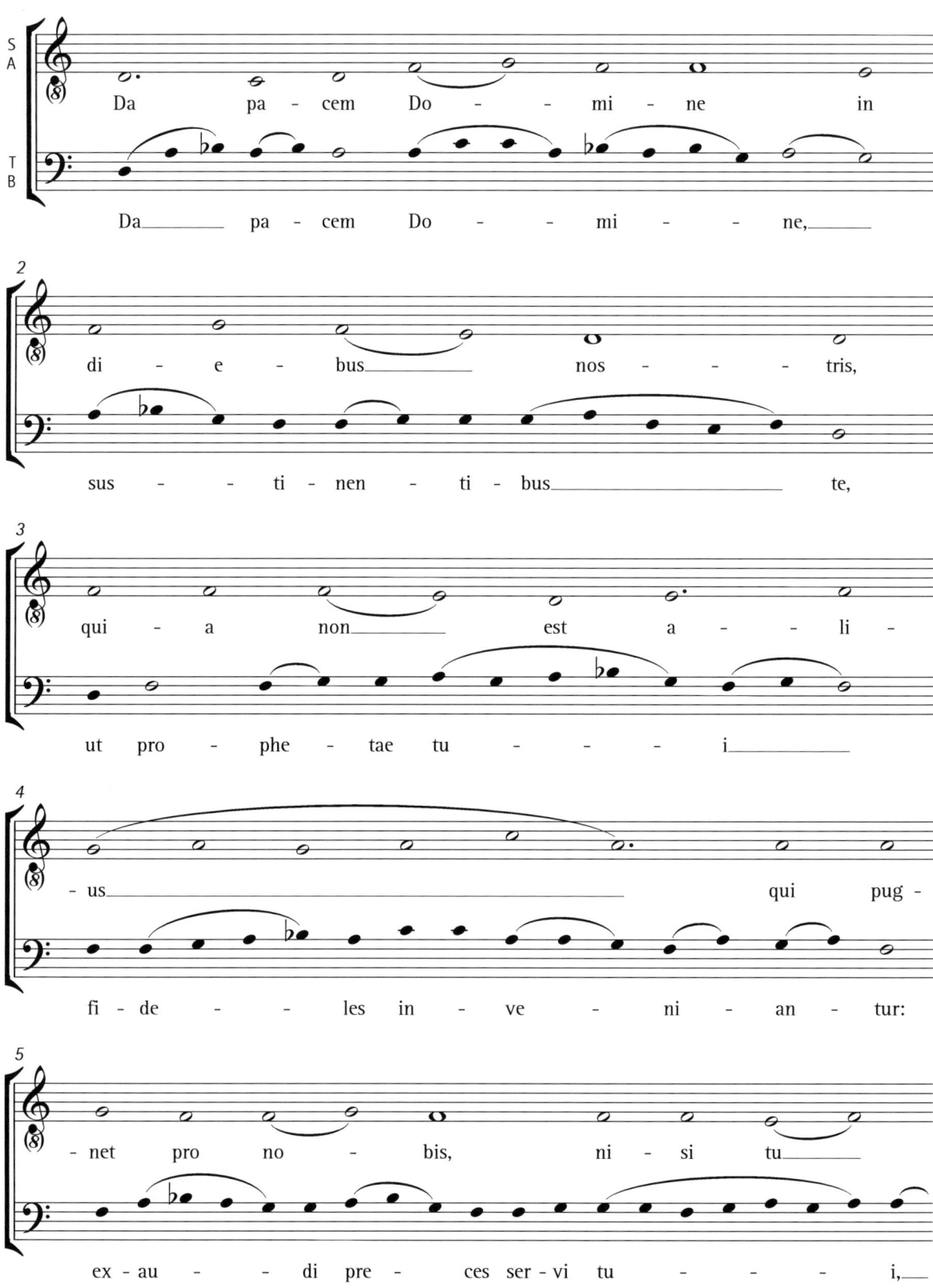

III. CLASSICAL AND SACRED

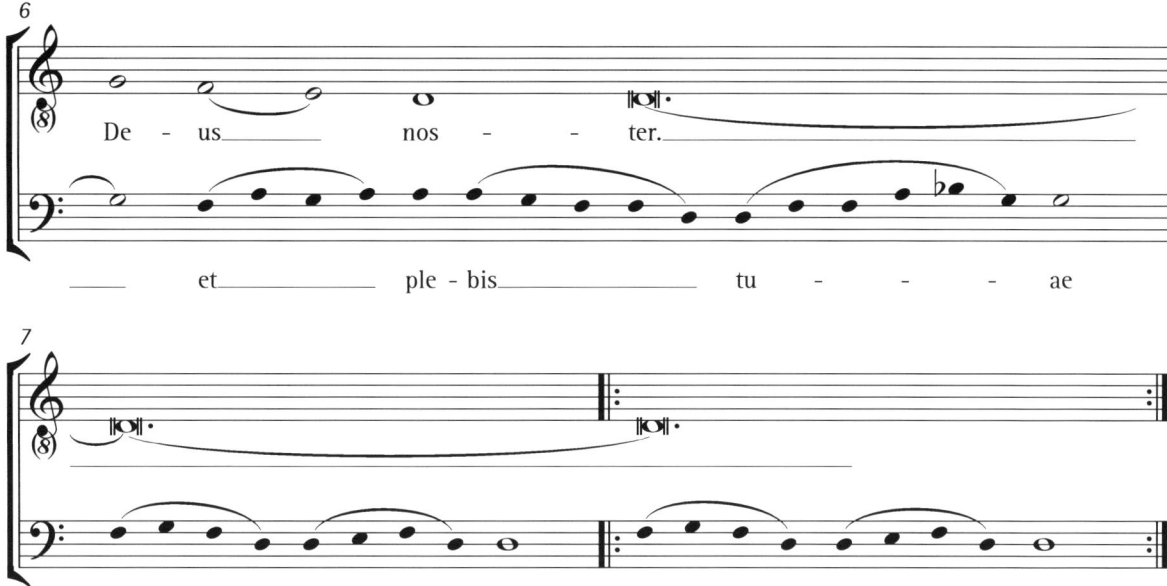

© Burkhard Kinzler. Reproduced by permission.

Performance suggestions

As far as possible, the female and male voices should be organized into separate groups. While singing, they can move around and intermingle. The rhythmic notation is meant as a guide only ("in the Gregorian style"). The female and male voices do not need to be precisely coordinated metrically.

Variant 1: two voices + ad lib. drone:
Men and women sing their respective Gregorian melody in unison, with or without drone.

Variant 2: 3-part canon:
The female voices sing their melody as a 3-part canon (each entry as per "Da pacem").
The men sing their Gregorian line independently of the above, repeating the phrase "Israel" at the end until all the female voices have reached the final d.
Drone ad lib.

Variant 3: polyphonic proportional canon:
Everyone begins on the same note. The female voices sing the proportional canon.

"Proportional canon" means that the first woman (or the first group of women) sings the fastest tempo and those following each sing a little more slowly. Basic rule: the second note may only be sung once it has been sung by the previous voice. This generates a dense sound texture.

The men sing the melody in unison.

Ending as per variant 1, although the men also repeat the last phrase, "Israel", in free canon form or as a proportional canon.

Drone ad. lib.

III. CLASSICAL AND SACRED

103. Miserere mei Domine 2 x 2-part canon

Jan Pieterszon Sweelinck
(1562–1621)
Arr.: Michael Gohl (2013)

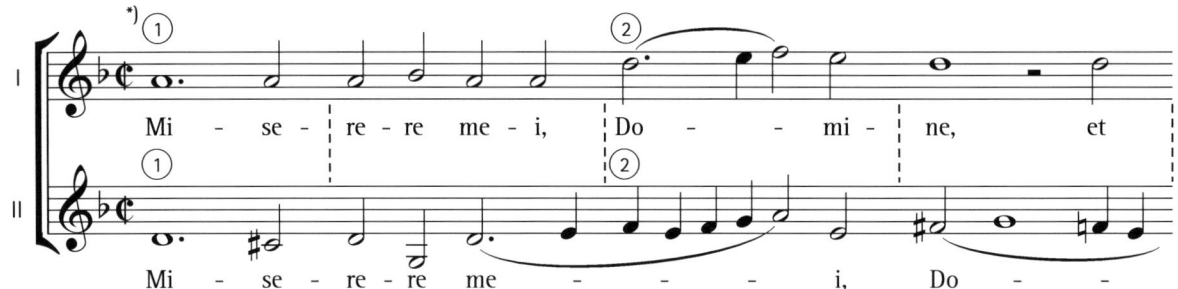

*) Can also be sung in different keys or with mixed voices.

The original key is G Dorian.

Performance suggestions

Variant 1:

Initially, sing the work in just two parts (possibly even two soloists) and then sing through twice as a canon, very softly the second time.

Variant 2:

With mixed voices: start with tenor and bass and then add soprano and alto. This is the form in which the motet was originally composed (source: complete edition of the Royal Society for Music History of the Netherlands).

Variant 3:

With equal voices: physically separate the two groups, in the manner of a double choir, and proceed as per Variant 1.

© 2014 by C. F. Peters

III. CLASSICAL AND SACRED

104. Canon angelicus – Sanctus 18-part canon

Romano Micheli
(ca. 1575–1659)

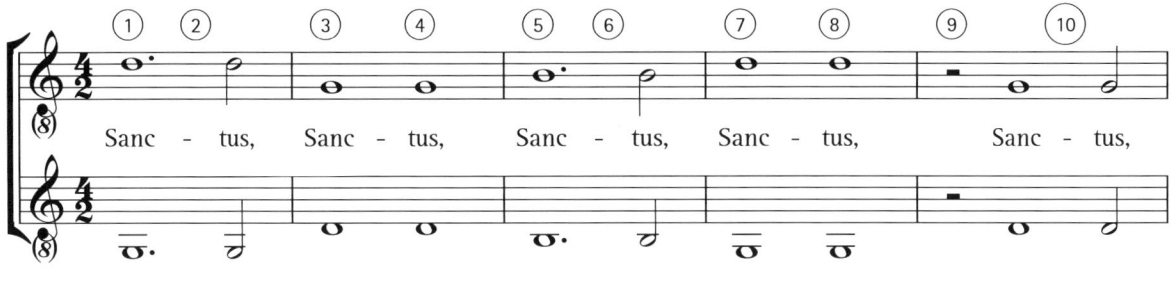

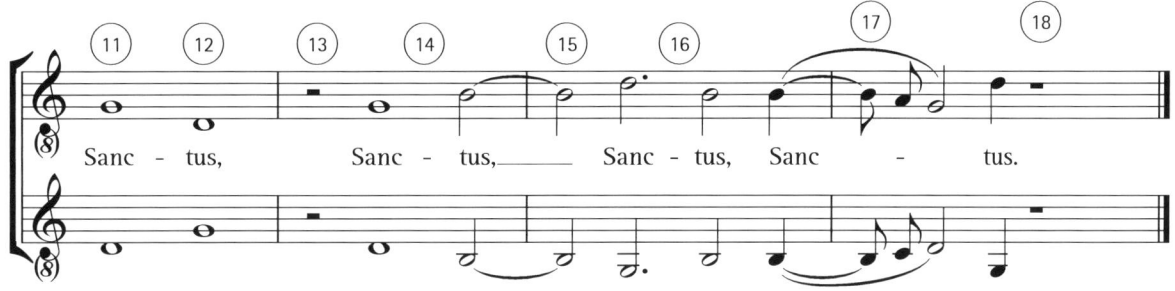

Sanctus
5-part canon

Clemens non Papa (ca. 1510–1555)

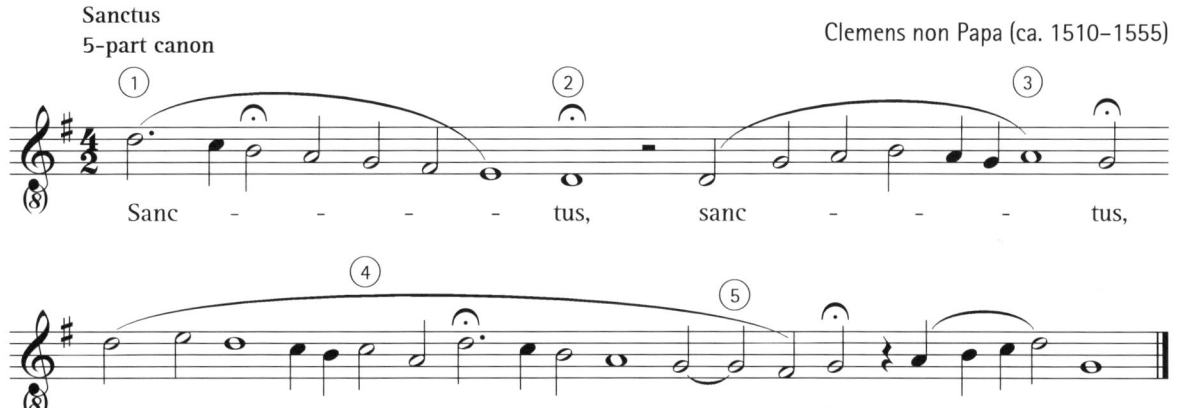

Copyright © 2014 Bo Ejeby Förlag and Gunnar Eriksson.

Acoustic experiment with Gunnar Eriksson

This music lends itself to a wonderful sound experiment in space. The – if you will – 36-part "canon of angels" produces a D major sonority that can be used as a framework for the moving 5-part Sanctus. (Don't forget to try out the Sanctus in a different key, for example A major or, with high sopranos, B flat, at the same time. The more stable the G major foundation, the more freely the high register can be coloured.)

Also think stereophonically, in terms of two or more choral units that either complement each other or vie for attention. The singers can also move around, orbiting the audience like satellites.

In short: these works, either individually or combined, call for anything but a conventional choral configuration with a conductor hanging up washing in the space between the choir and the audience. The imagination knows no bounds!

Gunnar Eriksson

III. CLASSICAL AND SACRED

105. Magnificat — My soul doth magnify the Lord

Jacques Berthier (1923–1994)

First canon

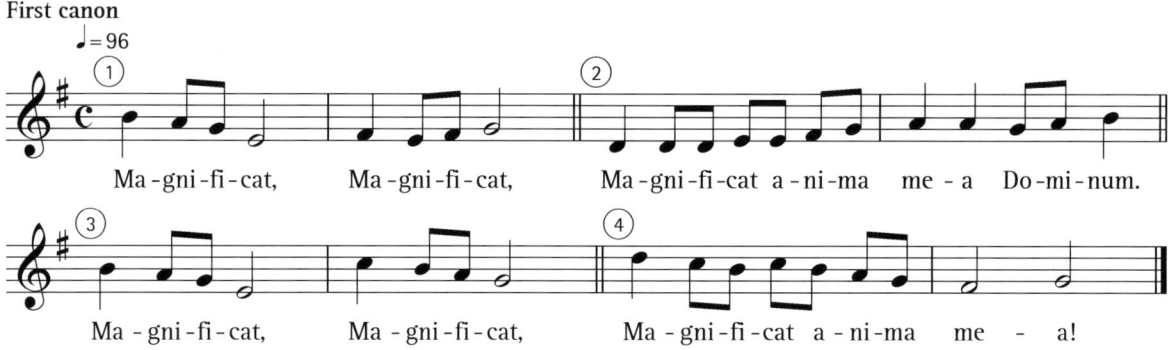

Second canon (or unison choir with trumpet)

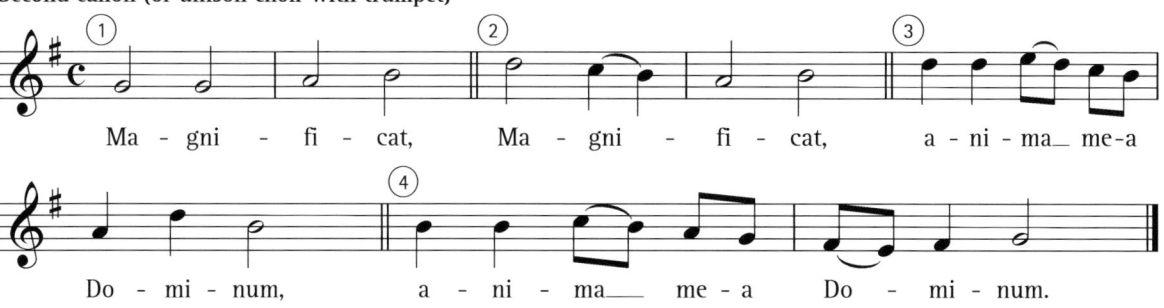

Optional 4-part canons

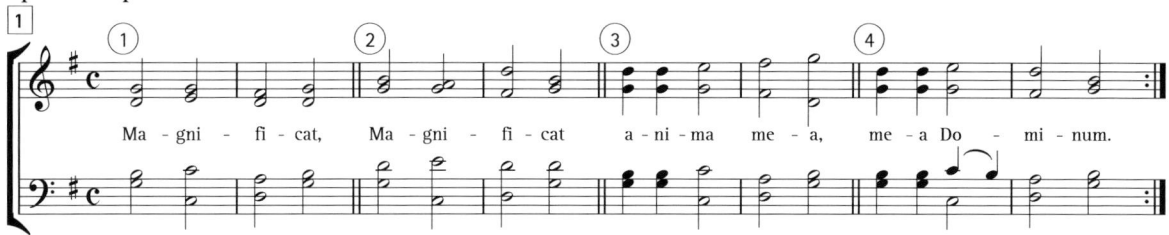

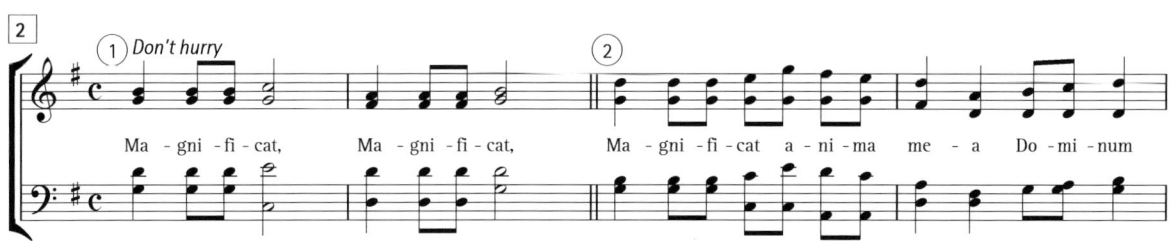

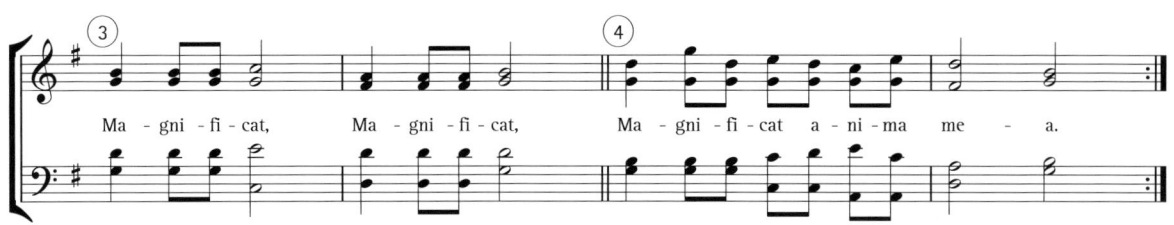

© Ateliers et Presses de Taizé, 71250 Taizé, France.

III. CLASSICAL AND SACRED

106. Nada te turbe

Jacques Berthier (1923–1994)
Words: St. Teresa of Avila

Let nothing disturb you, let nothing daunt you: whoever has God lacks nothing. God alone suffices. (St. Teresa of Avila)

*) choice

In Christ I place my trust, to him alone have I bound myself. From his exhaustion I draw courage, in his emulation I find peace. In him lies my steadfastness, my security, the touchstone of my truth, the example of my fortitude.

© Ateliers et Presses de Taizé, 71250 Taizé, France.

III. CLASSICAL AND SACRED

107. Tebe pojem (We Praise You)

From the Serbian Orthodox liturgy
Music: Stevan Stojanovic Mokranjak (1856–1914)

III. CLASSICAL AND SACRED

Translation:

We sing to you,
we praise you,
we thank you, O Lord,
and we pray to you, our God.

108. Nun ruhen alle Wälder

Melody: Heinrich Isaac (um 1450–1517)
Words: Paul Gerhardt (1607–1676)
Choral setting: Johann Sebastian Bach (1685–1750) *)

2. Der Tag ist nun vergangen,
die güldnen Sternlein prangen
am blauen Himmelssaal;
also werd ich auch stehen,
wann mich wird heißen gehen
mein Gott aus diesem Jammertal.

3. Auch euch, ihr meine Lieben,
soll heute nicht betrüben
kein Unfall noch Gefahr.
Gott lass euch selig schlafen,
stell euch die güldnen Waffen
ums Bett und seiner Engel Schar.

*) from the St. Matthew Passion BWV 244, no. 10
(original text: "Ich bin's, ich sollte büßen")

III. CLASSICAL AND SACRED

109. Alta Trinità Beata

Italian *lauda* (15th century)
Arr.: anonymous (19th century?)

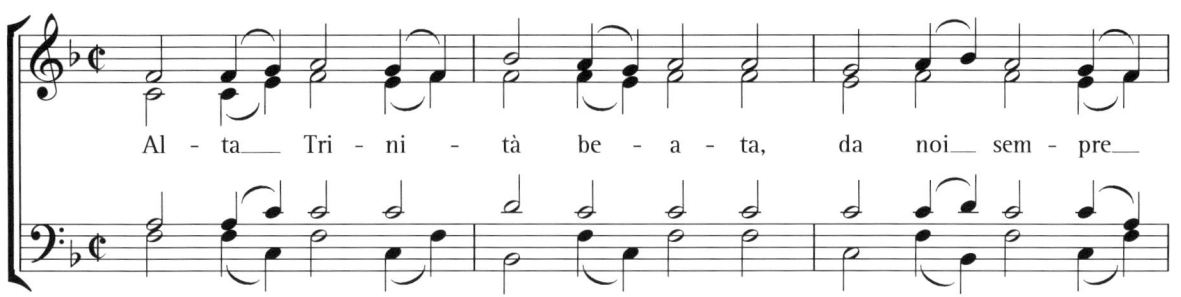

III. CLASSICAL AND SACRED

110. Veni Creator Spiritus

Pál Esterházy (1635–1713)

Performance tip

Each section of this piece is sung initially by a solo soprano. The section is then repeated with all four voices.

III. CLASSICAL AND SACRED

111. Come Ye Sons of Art

Henry Purcell (1658–1695)

Repeat twice:
1st time from B
2nd time from C

112. Alleluja

Traditional
Arr.: Willi Gohl

© Michael Gohl

III. CLASSICAL AND SACRED

113. Stabat Mater

Zoltán Kodály (1882–1967)
Arr. SATB: Imre Sulyok (1912–2008)

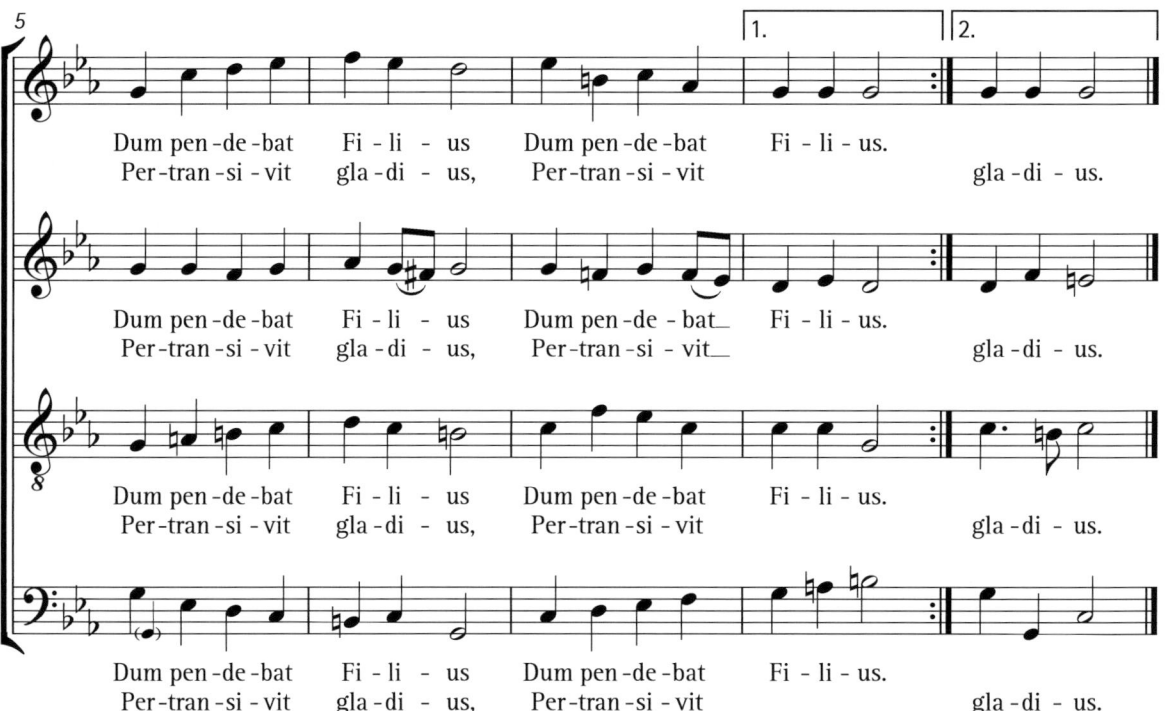

© 1997 by Editio Musica Budapest

III. CLASSICAL AND SACRED

114. Immortal Bach

Johann Sebastian Bach (1685–1750)
Arr.: Knut Nystedt (1915–2014)

Viens, douce mort, viens, repos éternel, emporte-moi en paix!
Come, sweet death, come, eternal rest, carry me away in peace!

Performance suggestion by Knut Nystedt:

1. Sing the choral once as written (Use German text).
2. Then: All begin on "Komm" and sustain the chord for 4 seconds and – without a break sing the first 2 measures according to the following scheme: some holds each quarter-note 4 seconds, others: 6 – 8 – 10 – 12 seconds. (Divide SATB in 5 in each group).
3. When you get to "Tod", sustain your note until all are singing their note on "Tod".
4. Sopranos begin 2nd phrase, holding the Eb for 4 seconds before the ATB enter simultaneously, and everyone sings the 2nd phrase according to the scheme, sustaining your note on "Ruh" until all are singing their note on "Ruh".
5. All begin measure 5 together and sing according to the scheme, holding the final note until al are singing their note on "-de". The chord will be sustained with the fermata.
6. Scale *pp* and increase to forte by measure 5. Then begin a gradual decrescendo, ending the piece pianissimo.

This piece will take appr. 5 minutes.

Proposal for the choirs standing arrangement:

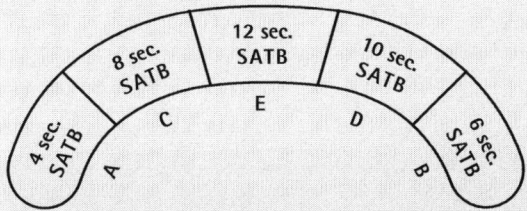

The singers are placed one by one in a long row around the hall.

Copyright © 1988 by Norsk Musikforlag A/S, Oslo. Printed with permission

III. CLASSICAL AND SACRED

115. Olson III (1967)

Terry Riley (b 1935)

© Associated Music Publishers Inc./G- Schirmer Inc. Edition Wilhelm Hansen GmbH.
Mit freundlicher Genehmigung der Bosworth Music GmbH, Berlin.
All Rights Reserved. International Copyright Secured.

Performance suggestions

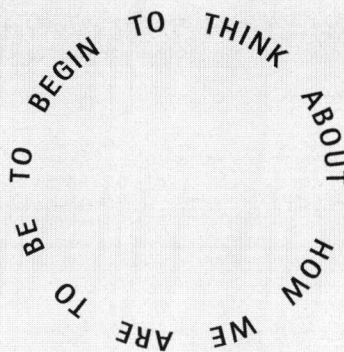

"Olson III" is built on the same principle as Terry Riley's better known instrumental piece "In C". All start with the first cell, repeat it an optional number of times, then go on to the next, and so on, until all cells have been passed. Studies: work first only with cells 1 and 2.

1. SATB each with a principal, starting at the same time but moving on to cell 2 at different times. Try different types of articulation (staccato/legato, etc.). Take great care with intonation, as this will give the right effect to the different intervals arising out of the collisions between parts. Sing softly throughout, unless the contrary should be motivated. Record and listen to the result, if possible.

2. Expand the possibilities by having two or three parts sing with double note values (augmentation), and with dotted note values, causing 2:3 proportions, respectively.

3. Do the same thing again, this time with equal parts (female voices / male voices). This way we can slowly and organically learn to better understand this kind of music, and the possibilities it carries of creating external and internal tranquillity, of letting us focus on all things small, of teaching us patience. What it really is is a sort of criticism of civilization, an appeal to the non-rational, non-efficient, non-splendid.

4. Try now using a larger number of cells: 1. 1–10, which have a uniform tone material. Note how all low A's become important and require extra attention as regards singing technique and intonation. 2. Make your own choice of cells, presenting the whole text (see above). 3. Do a quick version, including only the modulating cells: e.g. 1, 11, 21, 25, 30.

After these time-consuming exercises it will be easier to sense how to arrange the parts, also if it is to be the conductor, the principal or just intuition that decides when each singer should change cell.

Common problem: throat fatigue after a while. Cure:

1. Take care testing for a non-tiring singing technique, individually.

2. "Emergency duty" in each part. 3. Proper breaks for each part – this is also in order to listen to the different stages of the music.

Sadly to say, performing this piece instrumentally is probably simpler! A mixture of voices and instruments is probably the very best. It is important to find a choir formation where sound will benefit maximally (although not necessarily with an audience in mind; reaching outside the choir with this experience is not a self-evident aim).

Do not hesitate to use only smaller parts of the material for a concert. This has actually been suggested by the composer.

This sort of material is specially suited as a bridge between two other concert pieces.

Gunnar Eriksson
(Translated from the Swedish by Rupert Jacobson)

Reprinted from Gunnar Eriksson: *Kör ad lib. Blå*
Copyright © by Bo Ejeby Förlag. Printed with permission.

III. CLASSICAL AND SACRED

116. Breath Soft, Ye Winds

Music: William Paxton (1735–1787)
Words: Anon.

*) This arrangement may be sung in D flat if preferred.

III. CLASSICAL AND SACRED

III. CLASSICAL AND SACRED

117. La Nuit

Melody: Jean Philippe Rameau (1683–1764)
Words: Edouard Sciortino (1893–1979)
Choral setting: Joseph Noyon (1888–1962)

© Éditions Musicales de la Schola Cantorum, Fleurier, Switzerland.

III. CLASSICAL AND SACRED

III. CLASSICAL AND SACRED

III. CLASSICAL AND SACRED

III. CLASSICAL AND SACRED

118. Sweet and low (Lullaby)

Music: Joseph Barnby (1838–1896)
Words: Lord Alfred Tennyson (1809–1892)

III. CLASSICAL AND SACRED

III. CLASSICAL AND SACRED

119. Guten Abend, gut' Nacht

Music: Johannes Brahms
Words: traditional
2nd verse: Georg Scherer (1849)

III. CLASSICAL AND SACRED

English:
1. Lullaby and good night,
with roses bedight,
with lilies bested,
is baby's wee bed.
Lay thee down now and rest,
may thy slumber be blest,
lay thee down now and rest,
may thy slumber be blest.

2. Lullaby and good night,
thy mother's delight,
bright angels around
my darling shall stand.
They will guard thee from harms,
thou shalt wake in my arms,
they will guard thee from harms,
thou shalt wake in my arms.

Text: Natalia Macfarren (1826–1916)

Spanish:
1. Buenas noches mi amor,
duerme bajo el rosal
con las manos en cruz
sobre el corazón.
Que mañana con Dios
ya despertarás,
que mañana con Dios
ya despertarás.

2. Buenas noches mi amor,
que tu ángel guardián
te dirá lo que has de ver
sobre el cielo azul.
Duerme dulce mi bien
en la gracia de Dios,
duerme dulce mi bien
en la gracia de Dios.

Italian:
1. Ninna nanna, mio ben,
riposa seren,
un angiol del ciel
ti vegli fedel.
Una santa vision
faccia i cuori estasiar,
una dolce canzon
possa i sogni cullar.

2. Tutto tace quaggiù
brilla un astro lassù,
riposa tranquil,
bambino gentil.
Al tuo amore divin
voglio un canto innalzar.
Sul tuo cuore piccin
voglia un poco posar.

French:
Bonne nuit, cher enfant
dans tes langes blancs
repose, joyeux
en rêvant des cieux.
Quand le jour reviendra
tu te réveilleras,
quand le jour reviendra
tu te réveilleras.

Portuguese:
Dorme, dorme *(Daniel)*,
ao som desta canção
porque a lua risonha
já começa o seu serão.
Se dormires, amanhã
vamos colher cerejas,
escutar rouxinóis
e o sino da igreja.

(add the name of a child in the first line.)

Basque:
1. Gabon maiteño,
egizu lo itsuarrosapean,
eskuak gurutzatuz
bihotza gainian.
Bihar Jaungoikoarekin
esnatuko zara eta,
bihar Jaungoikoarekin
esnatuko zara eta.

2. Gabon maiteño,
zure aingeruak
ikusi beharrekoa azalduko dizu.
Argia zeru gainean.
Egizu lo enetxo,
Jaungoikoaren graziaz,
egizu lo enetxo,
Jaungoikoaren graziaz.

Dutch:
Goedenavond, goede nacht,
met rozen bedacht
ligt het kindeke teer
daar in 't beddeke neer.
Morgenvroeg, als god wil,
wek ik u, slaap nu stil,
morgenvroeg, als god wil,
wek ik u, slaap nu stil.

Hungarian:
1. Csendes álmot, jó éjt,
majd néz rád az ég,
csak hunyd le szemed,
az angyal veled.
Álom szárnyán ha szállsz,
fönn az égben is jársz,
álom szárnyán ha szállsz,
fönn az égben is jársz.

2. Édes álmot, jó éjt,
amit kis szíved kért.
Amit vártál oly rég,
nézd mily szép most az ég.
Csillagfény ragyog rád,
sok kis fák lombján át,
csillagfény ragyog rád,
sok kis fák lombján át.

Finnish:
1. Levon hetki nyt lyö,
jo joutuvi yö,
pien armaani mun
nuku lauleluhun!
Siipi enkelin on
suojas voittamaton,
seripä turvin sä saat
nähdä untesi maat.

2. Kevätumpunen pien,
unten maille sun vien;
siellä nuokkuvan näät
kultakukkien päät.
Perhot leikkiä lyö,
virran välkkyvä vyö
tuutulaulua soi,
kunnes aamun on koi.

Estonian:
1. Uinu vaikselt, mu lind,
ma valvan ju sind!
Su voodilt ei lae,
nüüd magama jää!
Hommikul ingli tiib
une laugelt sul viib,
hommikul ingli tiib
une laugelt sul viib!

2. Uneinglite lend
ju vangistab Sind!
Ju kinni Su silm,
ju uinumas ilm.
Hommikul ingli tiib
une laugelt sul viib,
hommikul ingli tiib
une laugelt sul viib!

Romanian:
1. Peste dealuri, pe-un nor
plutind ca un gând,
luna trece uşor
aripi de vis legănând.
Si cu ea, rătăcind,
din înalt stele vin,
parc-ar spune, veghind:
Noapte bună copii!

2. Noapte bună, somn lin,
copil drăgălaş!
Fie-ţi somnul senin
dragul mamei îngeraş.
Somn uşor, scump odor
lângă tine voi sta.
Toată noaptea, cu dor,
eu te voi legăna.

Bulgarian:
Leka nosht i lek sun,
spi vsichko navun.
Ti ochichki zatvori,
sun sladuk zaspi.
Utre pak v svetlina
shte te sreshtne denya,
utre pak v svetlina
shte te sreshtne denya.

Slovenian:
Lahko noč, otrok moj,
zatisni oči,
že zvezdic neroj
pokriva nebo.
Lahko noč, lahko noč,
tvoja mamica bdi,
lahko noč, lahko noč,
sanjaj, sladko zaspi.

Text: Jože Humer (1936-2012)

Japanese:
おやすみなさい、
ばらに包まれ、
なでしこ香る
眠りの国へ。
きみは神の
御心により、
明日早く
目を覚ますだろう。
おやすみなさい、
天使がきみを
守ってくれる、
眠りの国で。
眠れ、眠れ、
安らかに、さあ
夢の園を
のぞいてごらん。

III. CLASSICAL AND SACRED

120. Dindirindin (Villancico)

From the Spanish Cancionero de Palacio
Anonymous (16th century)

1. Yo me le-ve un bel ma-tín, ma-ti-ne-ta per la pra-ta;
2. Rui-se-ñor, el rui-se-ñor, fác-te me a-ques-ta em-ba-xa-ta;

en-con-tré el rui-se-ñor que can-ta-ba so la ra-ma,
y di-ga-o-lo a mon a-mí, que yo ya so ma-ri-ta-ta,} din di-rin - dín!

121. Tuonane Paradiso

Trad. Tansania
Arr.: Adrian Schmid

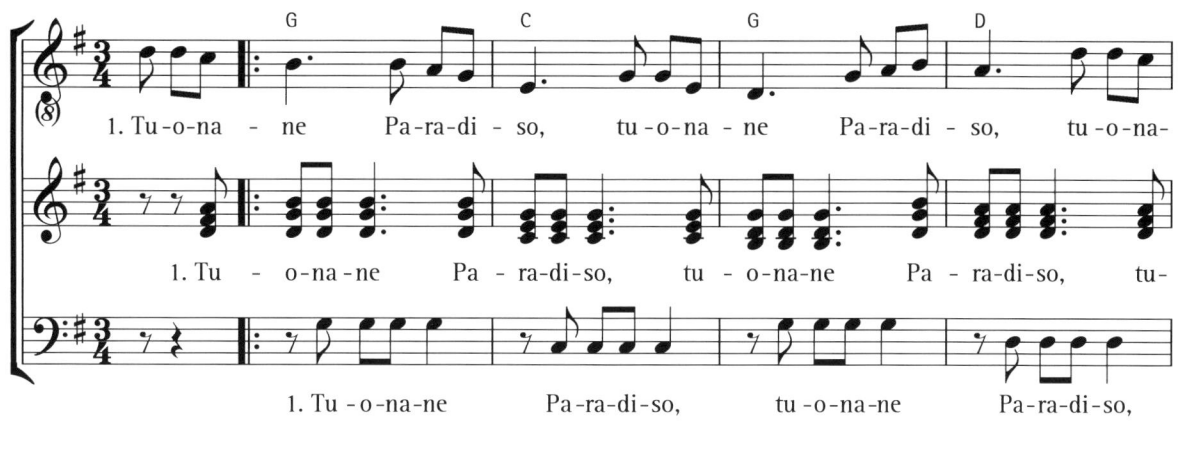

2. Na taji Tutavikwa ... Kwenye mji wa raha.
3. Na Yesu tutamwona ... Kwenye ...
4. Aleluya tutaimba ... Kwenye ...

1. We will meet again in Paradise, in the City of Peace.
2. We will wear the crown in the City of Peace.
3. And we will see Jesus ...
4. Hallelujah will we sing ...

© 1998 Innovative Music, CH-8932 Mettmenstetten

III. CLASSICAL AND SACRED

122. An Irish Blessing

Words: Trad. Ireland
Music: James E. Moore Jr.

May the road rise to meet you, may the wind be al-ways at your

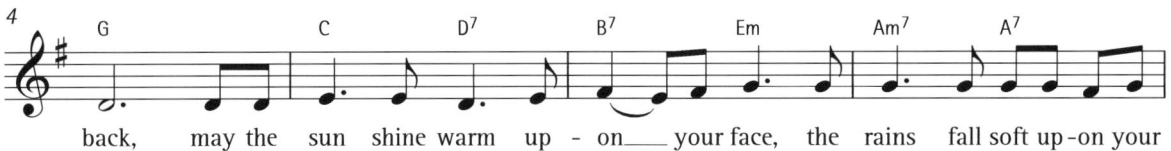
back, may the sun shine warm up-on your face, the rains fall soft up-on your

fields. And un-til we meet a-gain, un-til we meet a-gain may

God hold you in the palm of His hand. hand!

Music © 1987 by GIA Publications, Inc.
7404 S. Mason Ave., Chicago, IL 60638, USA

www.giamusic.com Tel: + 1 800.442.1358
All rights reserved. Used by permission.

Open singing with Robert Sund on the Lorelei (in the rain!), Europa Cantat 2006 in Mainz (Germany)

III. CLASSICAL AND SACRED

123. An Irish Blessing (4-part setting)

Words: Trad. Ireland
Music: James E. Moore Jr.

Music © 1987 by GIA Publications, Inc.
7404 S. Mason Ave., Chicago, IL 60638, USA
www.giamusic.com Tel: + 1 800.442.1358
All rights reserved. Used by permission.

III. CLASSICAL AND SACRED

124. Va, pensiero

From the opera "Nabucco" by
Giuseppe Verdi (1813–1901)

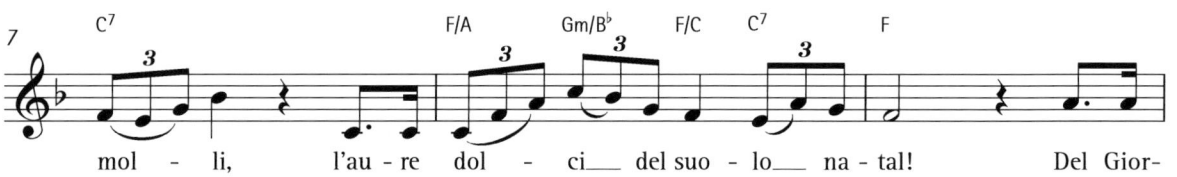

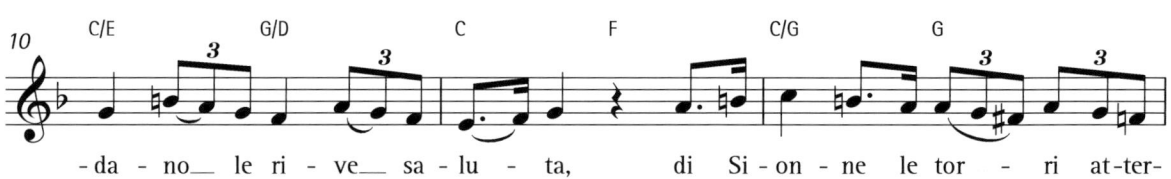

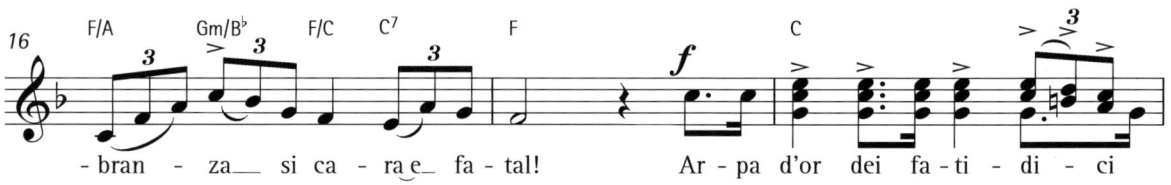

III. CLASSICAL AND SACRED

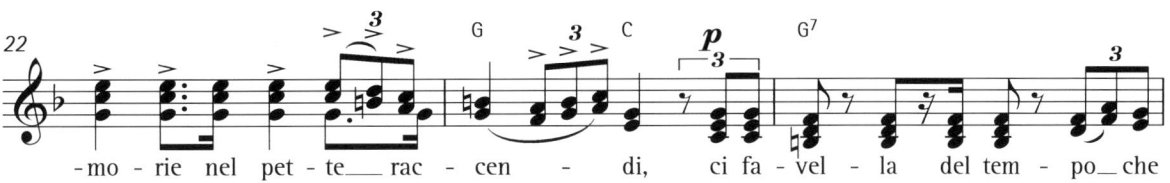
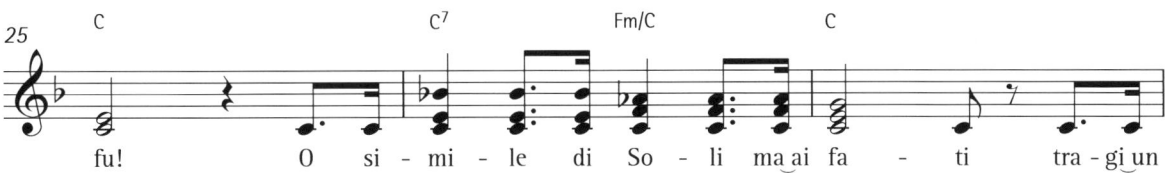
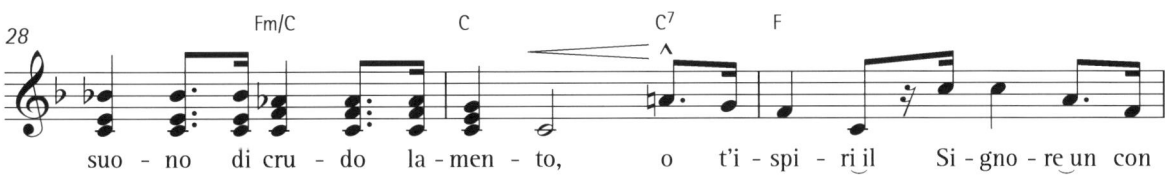
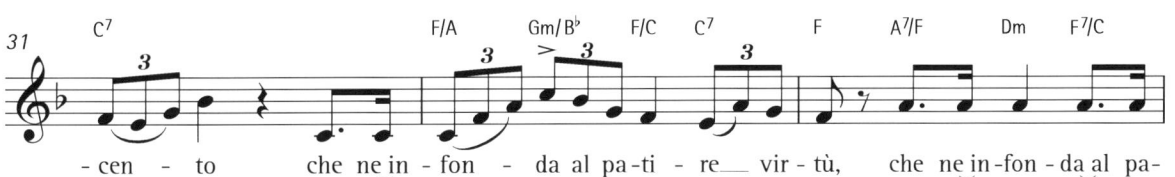

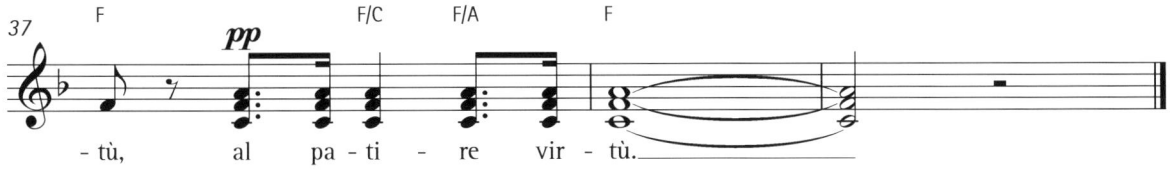

III. CLASSICAL AND SACRED

125. Tábortűznél

Trad. Hungary
Choral setting: Lajos Bárdos (1899–1986)

© 1959 by Editio Musica Budapest.

III. CLASSICAL AND SACRED

III. CLASSICAL AND SACRED

126. Jerusalem

Melody: C. Hubert H. Parry (1848–1918)
Words: William Blake (1757–1827)

Piano accompaniment available for download at www.editionpeters.com/singalong

IV. Advent and Christmas

El Cant dels Ocells
Cançó de Nadal

The Song of the Birds
Catalan carol

Al veure despuntar
el major lluminar,
en la nit més ditxosa,
els aucellets cantant
a festejar-lo van
amb sa veu melindrosa.

As they observe,
On this blissful night,
The brightest of lights ascend,
The little birds,
With graceful voice,
Sing in celebration.

IV. ADVENT AND CHRISTMAS

127. Joy To The World / Freue dich, Welt

On a theme by George Frideric Handel (1685-1759)
Arr.: Beat Fritschi

© Arr. Verlag Schweizer Singbuch

IV. ADVENT AND CHRISTMAS

Open Singing 1964 in the Nevers Cathedral

Spanish Words:

1. ¡Regocijad! Jesús nació, del mundo Salvador;
   y cada corazón tornad
   a recibir al Rey, a recibir al Rey.
   Venid a recibir al Rey.

2. ¡Regocijad! El reinará; cantemos en unión;
   y en la tierra y en el mar
   loor resonará, loor resonará,
   y gran loor resonará.

3. Ya la maldad vencida es; la tierra paz tendrá.
   La bendición del Salvador
   quitó la maldición, quitó la maldición;
   Jesús quitó la maldición.

4. ¡Glorias a Dios cantemos hoy!
   Señor de Israel, la libertad tú le darás
   y tú serás su Dios, y tú serás su Dios,
   Señor, y tú serás su Dios.

128. Halleluja 2-part canon

Melody: Karen Lafferty

*) Bring in the high voice (M. G.) as an addition later on.

© (Maranatha) Universal Music – Brentwood Benson Publishing
Druckr. D, A, CH: Small Stone Media Germany GmbH, Köln

IV. ADVENT AND CHRISTMAS

129. Hark! The Herald Angels Sing

Music: Felix Mendelssohn Bartholdy (1809–1847)
Words: Charles Wesley (1739)
Choral setting: William H. Cummings (1856)

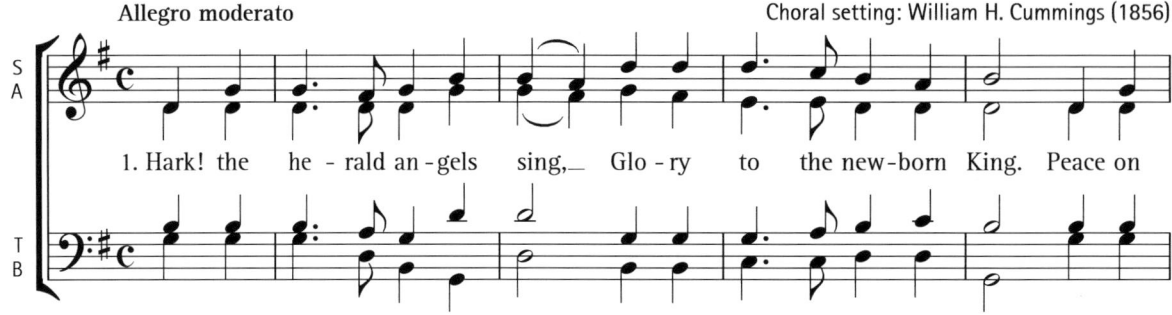

2. Christ, by highest heav'n ador'd,
   Christ, the everlasting Lord.
   Late in time behold Him come,
   offspring of the virgin's womb.
   Veil'd in flesh the Godhead he;
   hail th'incarnate Deity!
   Plea'd as man with man appear,
   Jesus our Immanuel here.

IV. ADVENT AND CHRISTMAS

130. Hail! Blessed Virgin Mary

Italian carol
Words: G. R. Woodward
Choral setting: Charles Wood (1866–1926)

1. Hail! Bless-ed Vir-gin Ma-ry! For so when he did meet thee, Spake might-y Ga-bri-el, And thus we greet thee. Come weal, come woe, Our hymn shall nev-er va-ry, Hail! Bless-ed Vir-gin Ma-ry! Hail! Bless-ed Vir-gin Ma-ry!
2. A-ve, a-ve Ma-ri-a! To glad-den priest and peo-ple, The an-ge-lus shall ring from ev-'ry stee-ple, To sound his Vir-gin-birth, Al-le-lu-i-a! A-ve, a-ve Ma-ri-a! A-ve, a-ve Ma-ri-a!
3. Arch-an-gels chant O-san-na, And Ho-ly, Ho-ly, Ho-ly, Be-fore the In-fant born of thee, thou low-ly, Aye-mai-den child of Jo-a-chim and An-na; Arch-an-gels chant O-san-na. Arch-an-gels chant O-san-na.

Edition Peters 11401

IV. ADVENT AND CHRISTMAS

131. O Little Town of Bethlehem

Melody and choral setting: 17th century
Words: Phillips Brooks (1868)

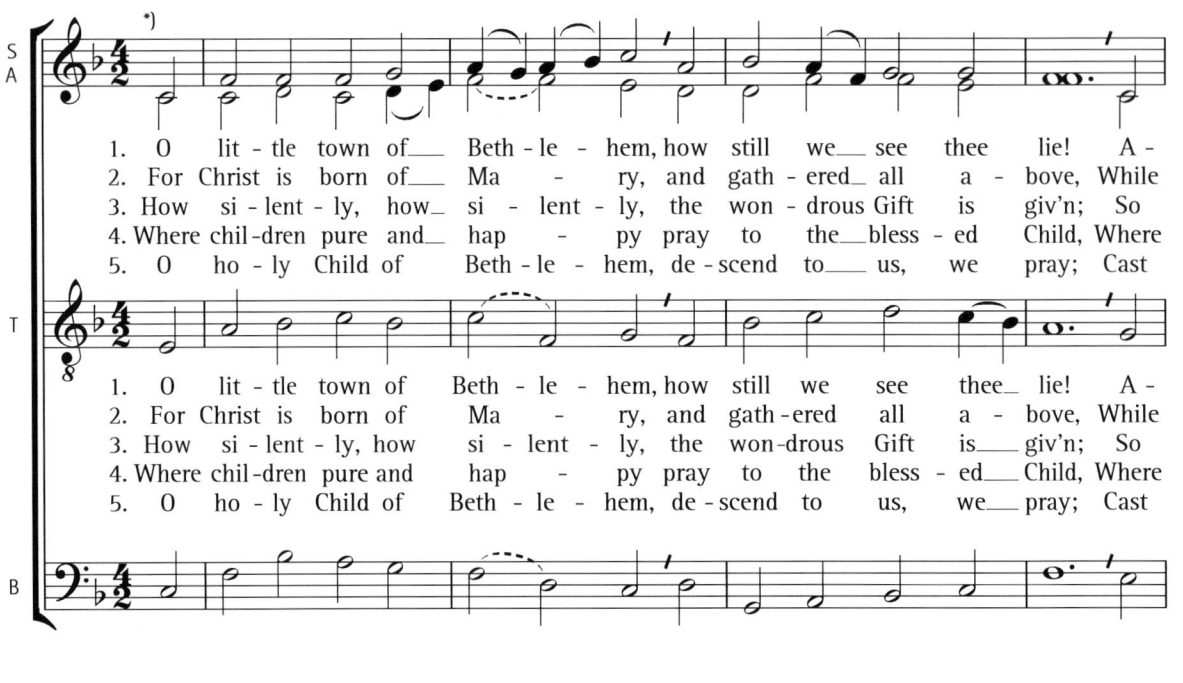

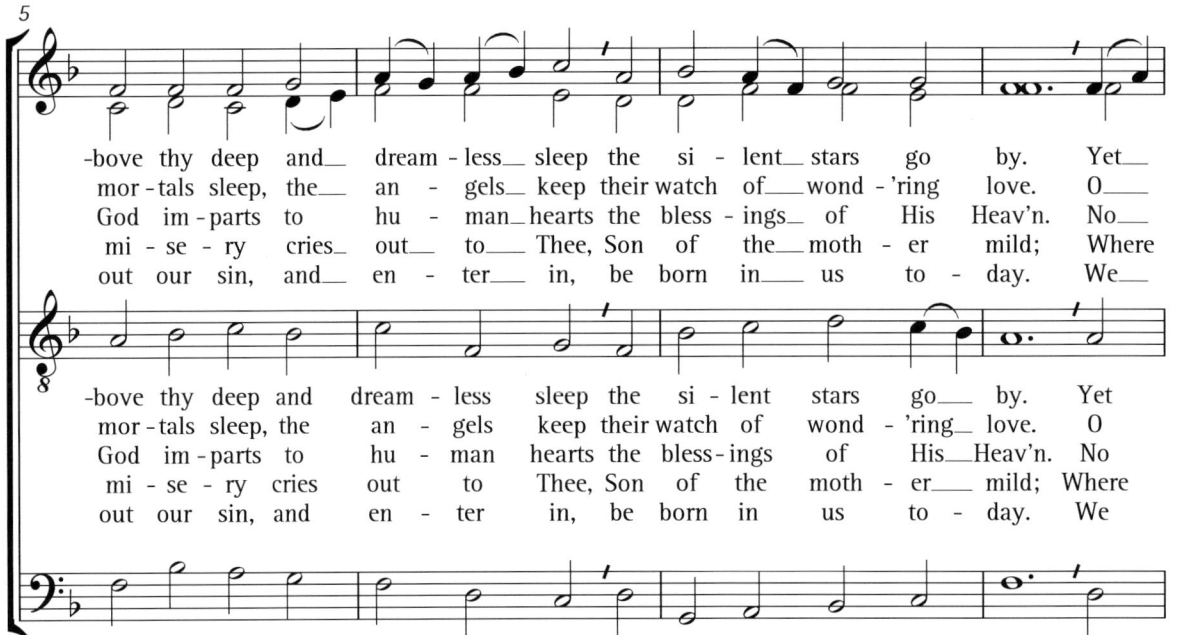

*) Original version in G major

IV. ADVENT AND CHRISTMAS

IV. ADVENT AND CHRISTMAS

132. El cant dels ocells

Trad. Catalonia
Arr.: Pau Casals
Choral setting: Oriol Martorell

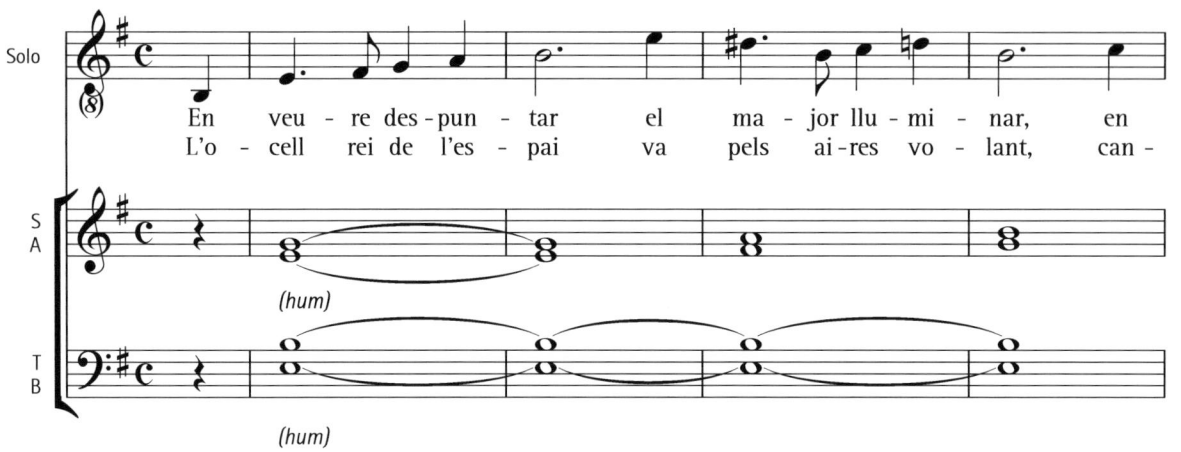
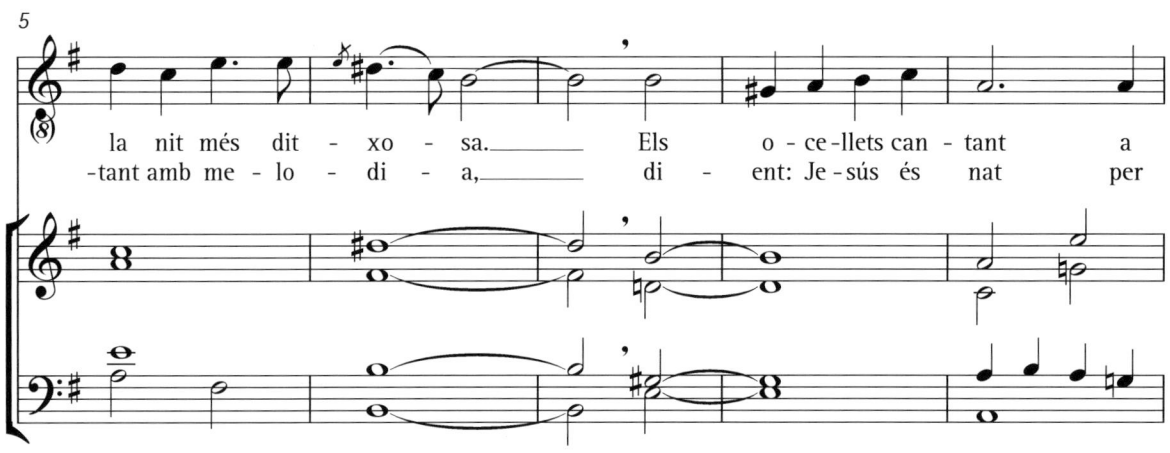
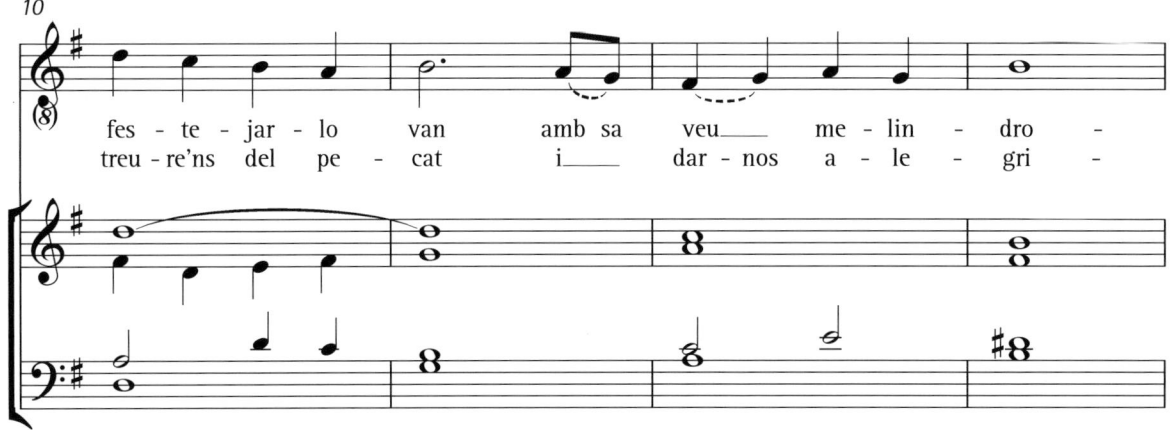

© 2010 by Editorial de Música Boileau, S. L. – www.boileau-music.com

IV. ADVENT AND CHRISTMAS

Translation:

1. As they observe,
   On this blissful night,
   The brightest of lights ascend,
   The little birds,
   With graceful voice,
   Sing in celebration.

2. The king of the air
   Soars high into the sky
   And, singing a melody, announces: Jesus is born
   To bring us great joy
   By freeing us from our sins.

Note

This song was turned into a song of liberation by the world-famous cellist Pablo Casals, who said of it: "When I was living in exile after the Spanish Civil War, I made it my custom to end all my concerts and music festivals with an old Catalan folk song, which is actually a Christmas carol. It is called *El Cant des Ocells* (The Song of the Birds). Since then, this song has become the hymn of the homesick Spanish refugees. May it tomorrow become a song of peace and hope for them."

IV. ADVENT AND CHRISTMAS

133. Cantique de Noël

Music: Adolphe Adam (1803–1856)
Words: Placide Cappeau (1808–1877)
Choral setting: Albert Lindström (1853–1935)

1. Mi-nuit, chré-tiens, c'est l'heu-re so-len-nel-le Où l'Hom-me Dieu des-cen-dit jus-qu'à nous. Pour ef-fa-cer la ta-che o-ri-gi-nel-le, Et de son Père ar-rê-ter le cour-roux. Le monde en-tier tres-sail-le d'es-pé-ran-ce À cet-te nuit qui lui donne un Sau-veur.

2. Le Ré-demp-teur a bri-sé toute en-tra-ve, La Terre est libre et le Ciel est ou-vert. Il voit un frère où n'é-tait qu'un es-cla-ve, L'a-mour u-nit ceux qu'en-chaî-nait le fer. Qui lui di-ra no-tre re-con-nais-san-ce, C'est pour nous tous qu'il naît, qu'il souffre et meurt.

3. De no-tre foi que la lu-mière ar-den-te Nous gui-de tous au ber-ceau de l'en-fant. Comme au-tre-fois une é-toi-le bril-lan-te Y con-dui-sit les chefs de l'O-ri-ent. Le Roi des Rois naît dans une hum-ble crè-che; Puis-sants du jour, fiers de vo-tre gran-deur. À vo-tre or-gueil c'est de là qu'un Dieu prê-che; Cour-

Peu-ple, à ge-noux, at-tends ta dé-li-vran-ce. No-
Peu-ple, de-bout! Chan-te ta dé-li-vran-ce. No-
À vo-tre or-gueil c'est de là qu'un Dieu prê-che; Cour-

IV. ADVENT AND CHRISTMAS

English lyrics:

1. O Holy Night! The stars are brightly shining,
   It is the night of the dear Saviour's birth.
   Long lay the world in sin and error pining.
   Till He appeared and the Spirit felt its worth.
   A thrill of hope the weary world rejoices,
   For yonder breaks a new and glorious morn.
   Fall on your knees! Oh, hear the angel voices!
   O night divine, the night when Christ was born;
   O night, O Holy Night , O night divine!

2. O night, O Holy Night , O night divine!
   Led by the light of faith serenely beaming,
   With glowing hearts by His cradle we stand.
   O'er the world a star is sweetly gleaming,
   Now come the wisemen from out of the Orient land.
   The King of kings lay thus lowly manger;
   In all our trials born to be our friends.
   He knows our need, our weakness is no stranger,
   Behold your King! Before him lowly bend!
   Behold your King! Before him lowly bend!

3. Truly He taught us to love one another,
   His law is love and His gospel is peace.
   Chains he shall break, for the slave is our brother.
   And in his name all oppression shall cease.
   Sweet hymns of joy in grateful chorus raise we,
   With all our hearts we praise His holy name.
   Christ is the Lord! Then ever, ever praise we,
   His power and glory ever more proclaim!
   His power and glory ever more proclaim!

English text by John Sullivan Dwight
(1812–1893)

⬇ Piano accompaniment available for download at
www.editionpeters.com/singalong

IV. ADVENT AND CHRISTMAS

134. Feliz Navidad

Words and music: José Feliciano (b 1945)

Piano accompaniment — Franziska Gohl

© J&H Publishing Company
Mit freundlicher Genehmigung von Chrysalis Music Holdings GmbH

IV. ADVENT AND CHRISTMAS

Rhythm accompaniment

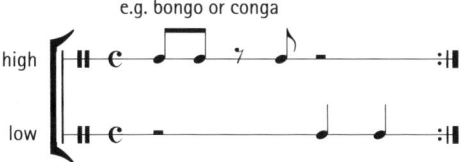

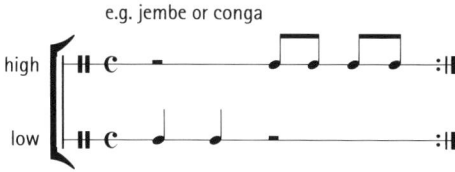

135. Noël, Noël 3-part canon

Words and music: Jan Holdstock

1. No-ël, No-ël! No-ël, No-ël! No-ël, No-ël! No-ël, No-ël!
2. Je-sus was born on Christ-mas Day. Long a-go and far a-way.
3. Bells in the steep-le ring-ing clear are wish-ing you a hap-py new year.

© Jan Holdstock

Piano accompaniment

Michael Gohl

*) also as introduction

IV. ADVENT AND CHRISTMAS

136. Jingle Bells

Words and music: James Lord Pierpont (1822–1893)
Choral setting: Markus Detterbeck

© Markus Detterbeck

IV. ADVENT AND CHRISTMAS

IV. ADVENT AND CHRISTMAS

3. Now the ground is white
   Go it while you're young,
   Take the girls tonight
   and sing this sleighing song;

   Just get a bobtailed bay
   Two forty as his speed
   Hitch him to an open sleigh
   And crack! You'll take the lead.

V. Gospel, Blues, Jazz

Hymn to Freedom

When ev'ry heart joins ev'ry heart and together
yearns for liberty, that's when we'll be free.
When ev'ry hand joins ev'ry hand and together
molds our destiny, that's when we'll be free.
Any hour, any day, the time soon will come
When men will live in dignity, that's when we'll be free.

Harriette Hamilton

Don't let the devil steal the beat from the Lord!
The Lord doesn't like us to act dead. If you feel it,
tap your feet a little – dance to the glory of the Lord!

Mahalia Jackson

V. GOSPEL, BLUES, JAZZ

137. A Loop Song

Words and music: Bertrand Gröger

*) Alternatively, this song can be performed by two (SA or AT) or three voices (SAB or ATB). The alto (main) part needs to be sung by ample forces supported by individual sopranos or tenors.

© 2014 by C. F. Peters

V. GOSPEL, BLUES, JAZZ

138. Everybody Sings Loop Song

Words and music: Bertrand Gröger

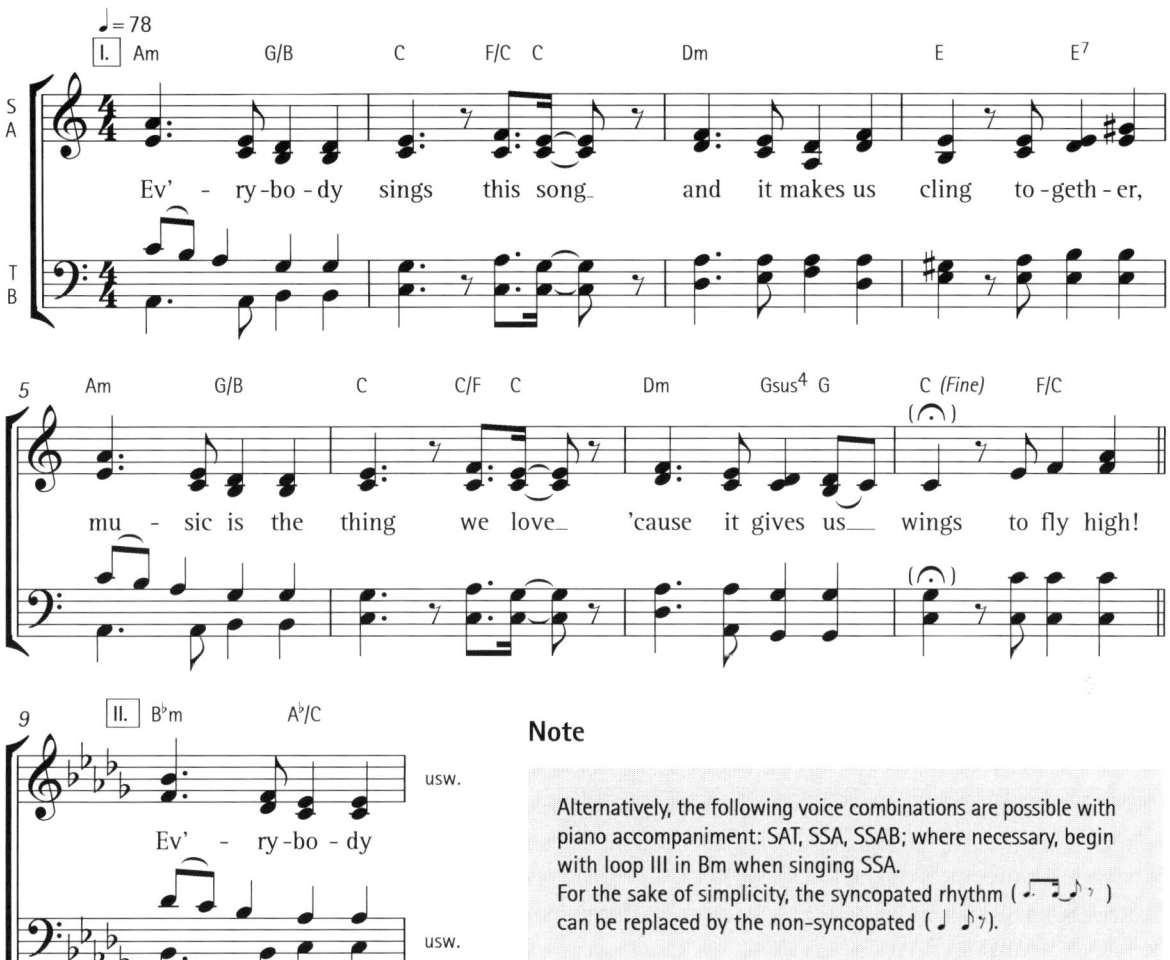

© 2014 by C. F. Peters

Note

Alternatively, the following voice combinations are possible with piano accompaniment: SAT, SSA, SSAB; where necessary, begin with loop III in Bm when singing SSA.
For the sake of simplicity, the syncopated rhythm can be replaced by the non-syncopated.

Chord-sheet:

	1	2	3	4	1	2	3	4	1	2	3	4	1	2	3	4
I.	Am		G/B		C		F/C	C	Dm				E		E^7	
	Am		G/B		C		F/C	C	Dm		G^{sus4}	G	C		F/C	
II.	B♭m		A♭/C		D♭		G♭/D♭	D♭	E♭m				F		F^7	
	B♭m		A♭/C		D♭		G♭/D♭	D♭	E♭m		A♭^{sus4}	A♭	D♭		G♭/D♭	
III.	Bm		A/C♯		D		G/D	D	Em				F♯		F♯^{7}	
	Bm		A/C♯		D		G/D	D	Em		A^{sus4}	A	D		G/D	
IV.	Cm		B♭/D		E♭		A♭/E♭	E♭	Fm				G		G^7	
	Cm		B♭/D		E♭		A♭/E♭	E♭	Fm		B♭^{sus4}	B♭	E♭		A♭/E♭	
V.	C♯m		B/D♯		E		A/E	E	F♯m				G♯		G♯^{7}	
	C♯m		B/D♯		E		A/E	E	F♯m		B^{sus4}	B	E		A/E	
VI.	Dm		C/E		F		B♭/F	F	Gm				A		A^7	
	Dm		C/E		F		B♭/F	F	Gm		C^{sus4}	C	F‖			

⬇ A video of the song performed with dance actions can be found at www.editionpeters.com/singalong

A further 44 loop songs by Bertrand Gröger are published by Schott (ED 20368)

V. GOSPEL, BLUES, JAZZ

139. If You're Happy

Words and melody: Helge Førde (b 1956)
Choral setting: Robert Sund (b 1942)

© With kind permission of SCHOTT MUSIC, Mainz

Piano accompaniment available for download at
www.editionpeters.com/singalong

V. GOSPEL, BLUES, JAZZ

140. Now Let Us Sing

Anonymous

V. GOSPEL, BLUES, JAZZ

141. C-Jam-Blues

Music: Duke Ellington / Barney Bigard
Arr.: Bertrand Gröger

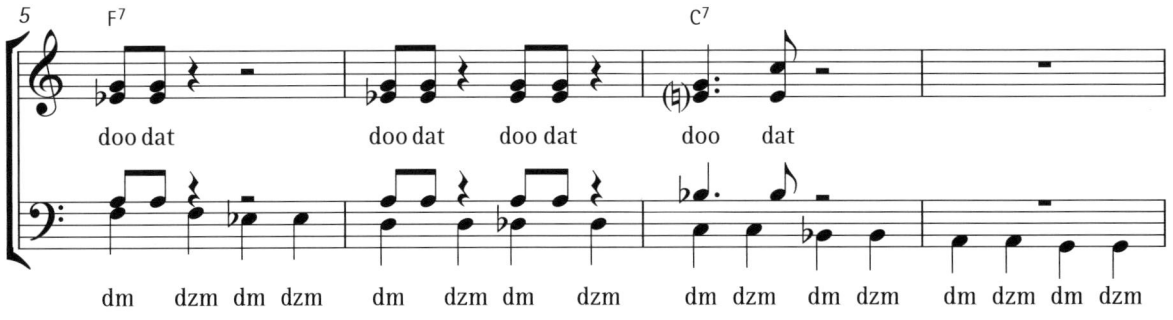
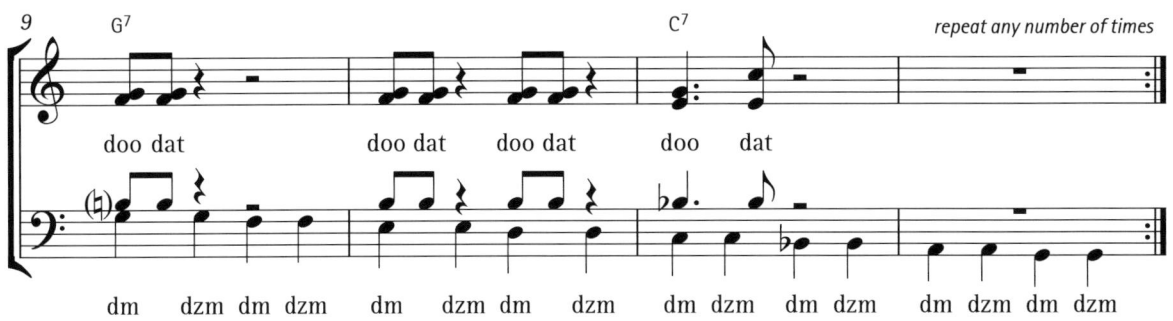

© Copyright 1942 (Renewed 1969) EMI Robbins Catalog Incorporated.
EMI United Partnership Limited.
All Rights Reserved. International Copyright Secured.

V. GOSPEL, BLUES, JAZZ

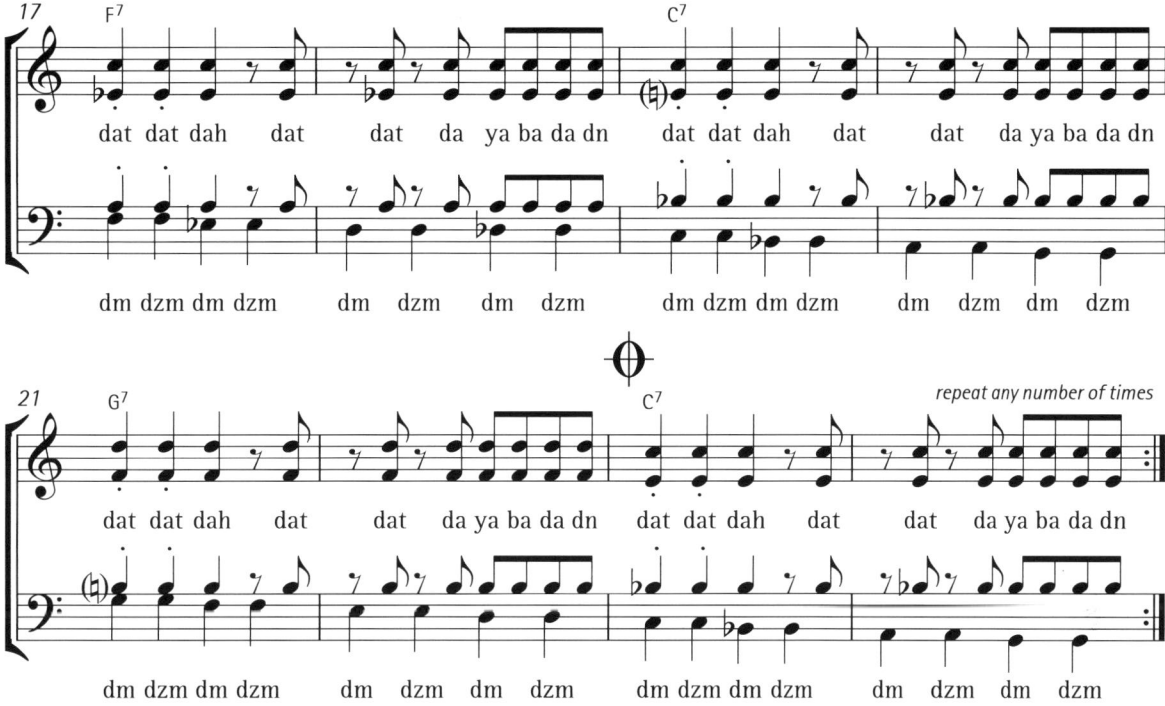

Possible piano accompaniment:

The l. h. plays the bass line an octave lower.

The r. h. plays fills in the SAT pauses.

Performance suggestion

1. B: theme
2. B+S: theme
3. B+S+A: theme
4. B+S+A+T: theme (repeat any number of times)
5. T: each singer to improvise individually (scat), SAB: theme
6. A+T: each singer to improvise individually (scat), SB: theme
7. S+A+T: each singer to improvise individually (scat), B: theme (repeat any number of times)
8. SATB: shout chorus
9. SATB: shout chorus + clap hands on 2 and 4

V. GOSPEL, BLUES, JAZZ

142. Give thanks

Traditional

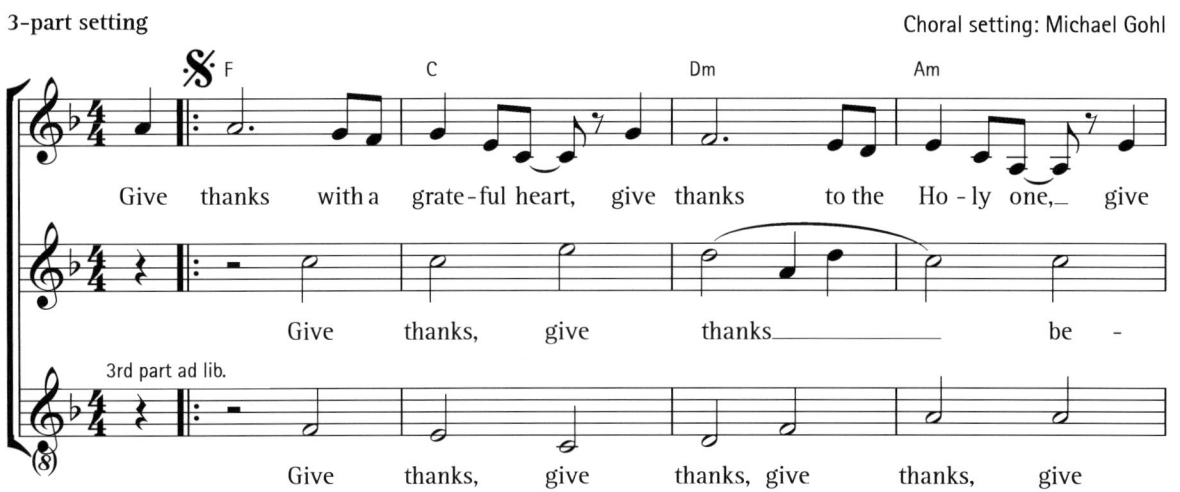

*) Only repeat the first part at the beginning of the song.

3-part setting

Choral setting: Michael Gohl

Performance suggestion

Sing once in unison and add the other parts the second time through.

V. GOSPEL, BLUES, JAZZ

© 1978 Integrity's Hosanna! Music adm. in D,A,CH by Gerth Medien, Asslar

*) Only repeat the first part at the beginning of the song.

V. GOSPEL, BLUES, JAZZ

143. Sister, Carry On

Words and music: Carolyn McDade

1. Sister, carry on,
   Sister, carry on.
   It may be rocky and it may be rough,
   but, Sister, carry on.

2. Sister, don't lose the dream,
   Sister, don't lose the dream.
   Don't sell out for no short time gain.
   Sister, don't lose the dream.

3. Sister, don't settle too soon,
   Sister, don't settle too soon.
   Til everybody's got their rights.
   Sister, don't settle too soon.

4. Sister, we share the way,
   Sister, we share the way.
   Heart to heart and hand to hand.
   Sister, we share the way.

5. Stand in solidarity,
   Stand in solidarity.
   Together bring a brand new day.
   Stand in solidarity.

6. Sister, carry on,
   Sister, carry on.
   It may be rocky and it may be rough, but,
   Sister, carry on.

Words and Music Copyright © 1992 Carolyn McDade. Reproduced by permission.

Sister, Carry On (SAA- or SATB-setting)

Words and music: Carolyn McDade
Arr.: Franziska Gohl (2015)

V. GOSPEL, BLUES, JAZZ

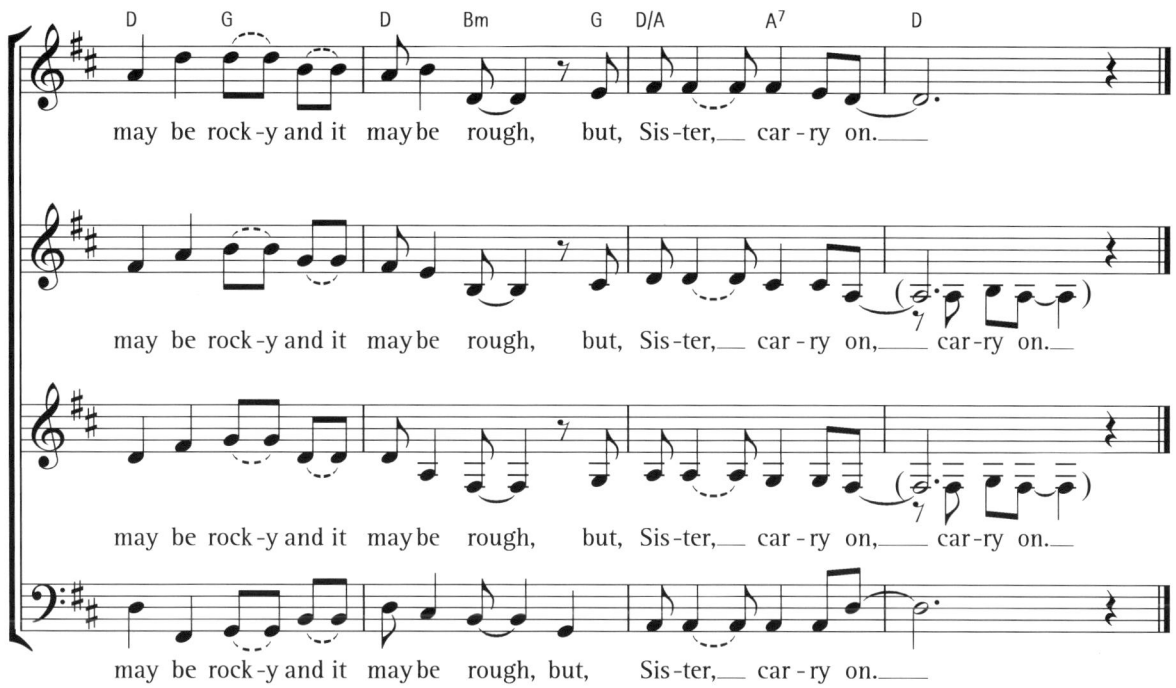

*) in the SAA-setting the bass part is replaced by the piano

Words and Music Copyright © 1992 Carolyn McDade. Reproduced by permission.

V. GOSPEL, BLUES, JAZZ

144. My Lord, What a Morning *)

Spiritual
Arr.: Michael Gohl

*) Also: My Lord, What a Mourning
**) Soprano solo ad lib. improvisando in second verse

© Arr. Verlag Schweizer Singbuch

V. GOSPEL, BLUES, JAZZ

⬇ A version of this arrangement for SSAA is available for download at **www.editionpeters.com/singalong**.
  Both versions can be sung at the same time.

V. GOSPEL, BLUES, JAZZ

145. I am His Child

Moses Hogan
(1957–2003)

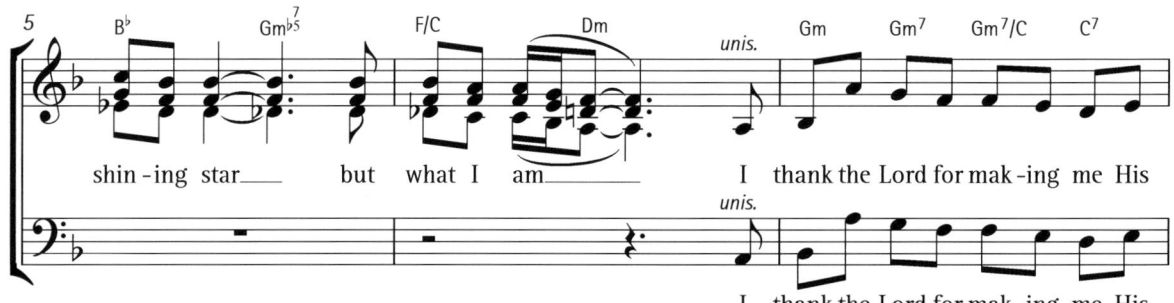
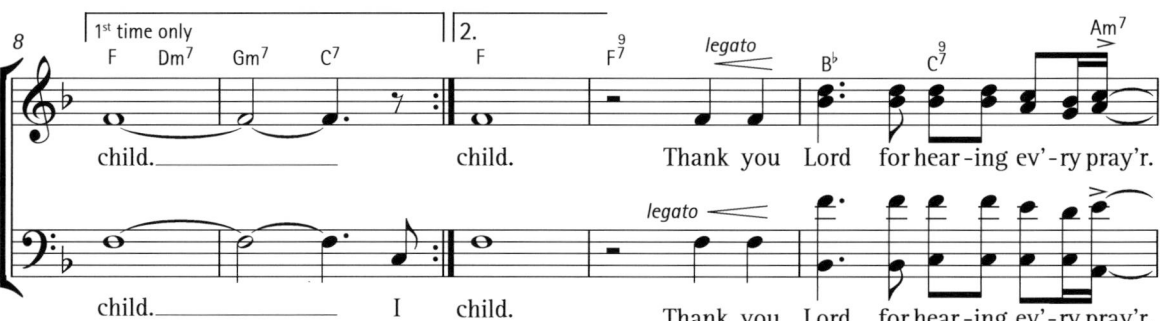

*) original version has piano part.

⬇ Piano accompaniment available for download at www.editionpeters.com/singalong

USED BY PERMISSION – Copyright © 1995, JEHMS, Inc., A Division of Alliance Music Publications, Inc.
P.O.Box 131977, Houston, Texas 77219-1977 International Copyright Secured. All Rights Reserved.

V. GOSPEL, BLUES, JAZZ

146. Hallelujah Gospel Theme

Words and music: Andraé Crouch

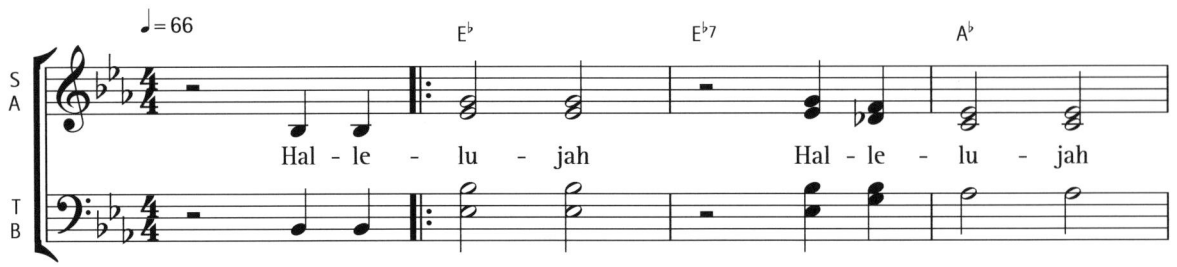
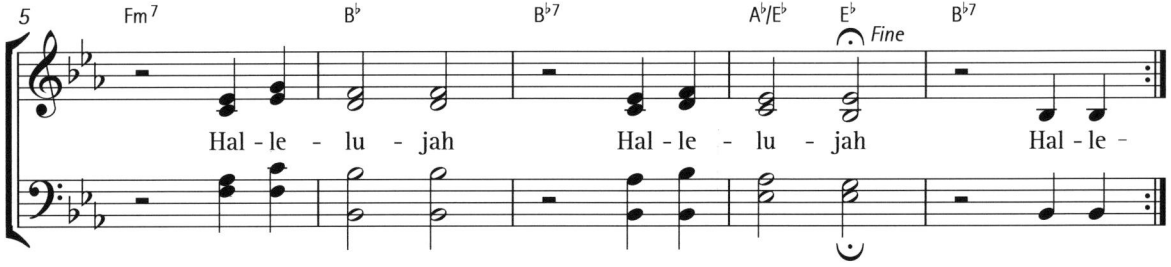

© Bud John Songs / Crouch Music
Adm. D, A, CH: Small Stone Media Germany GmbH, Köln

Performance suggestion

This vocal setting is intended as a basis for free improvisation by soloists. The high voice shown below is an example of improvisation of this sort.

The conductor is free to determine the structure and dynamics.

Descant ad. lib.

Michael Gohl

V. GOSPEL, BLUES, JAZZ

147. Hymn To Freedom

Words: Harriette Hamilton
Music: Oscar Peterson (1925-2007)

V. GOSPEL, BLUES, JAZZ

148. Hymn To Freedom (4-part setting)

Words: Harriette Hamilton
Music: Oscar Peterson
Choral setting: Paul Read

V. GOSPEL, BLUES, JAZZ

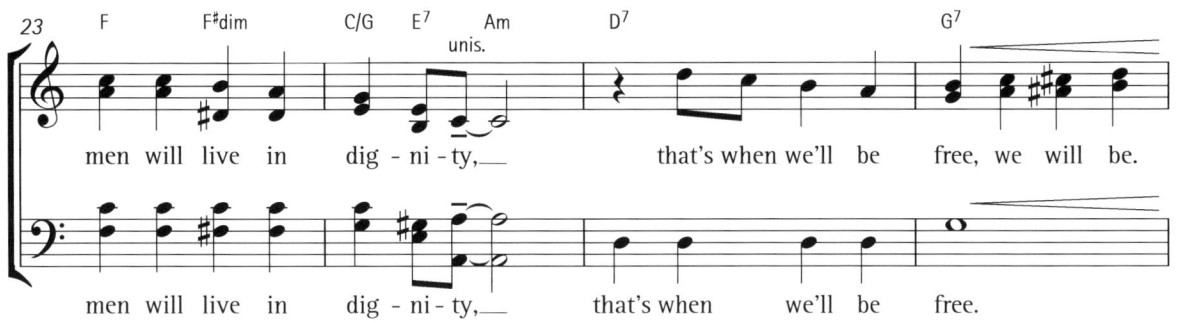
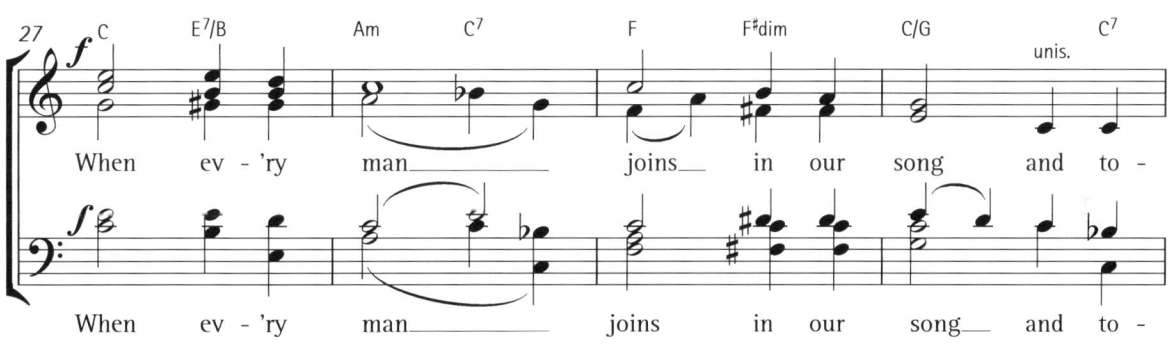
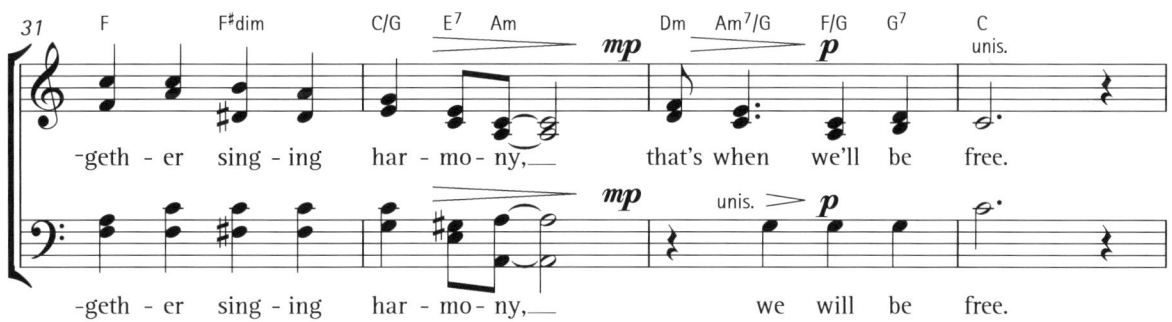
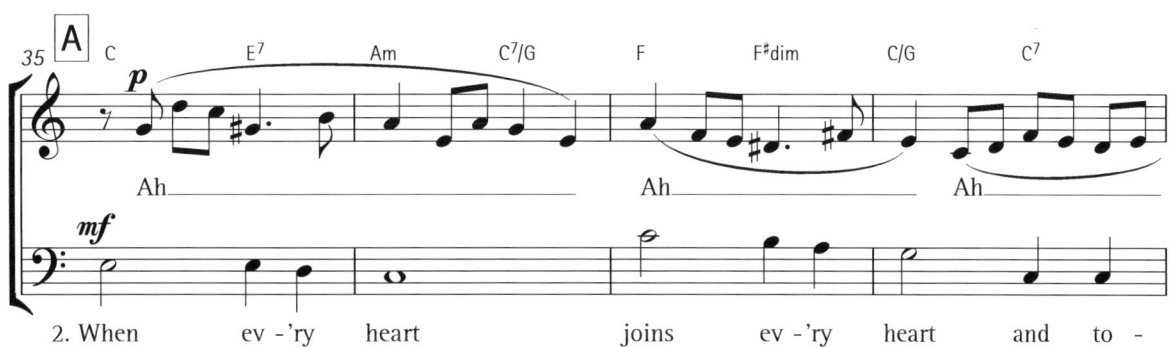

V. GOSPEL, BLUES, JAZZ

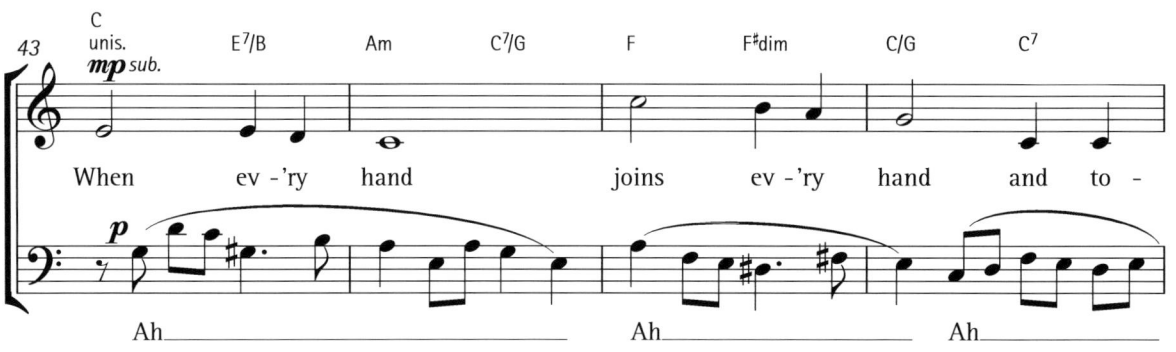

V. GOSPEL, BLUES, JAZZ

V. GOSPEL, BLUES, JAZZ

149. Yes, Lord, Yes

Andraé Crouch

Performance suggestion

This vocal setting can also be used as a basis for free improvisation by soloists.
(See note to "Hallelujah Gospel Theme", p. 184.)

© Zomba Enterprises Inc./Vaughn Street Music Adm. D, A, CH: Small Stone Media Germany GmbH, Köln

VI. Rock, Pop, Evergreen

With a smile on your face change the world.
With a Smile, Markus Detterbeck

Close your eyes and I'll kiss you, tomorrow I'll miss you ...
All my Loving, John Lennon & Paul McCartney

Isolation is not good for me.
Lemon Tree, Peter Freudenthaler & Volker Hinkel

Clap along, if you feel like a room without a roof ...
Happy, Pharrell Williams

VI. ROCK, POP, EVERGREEN

150. I am Sailing

Gavin Sutherland

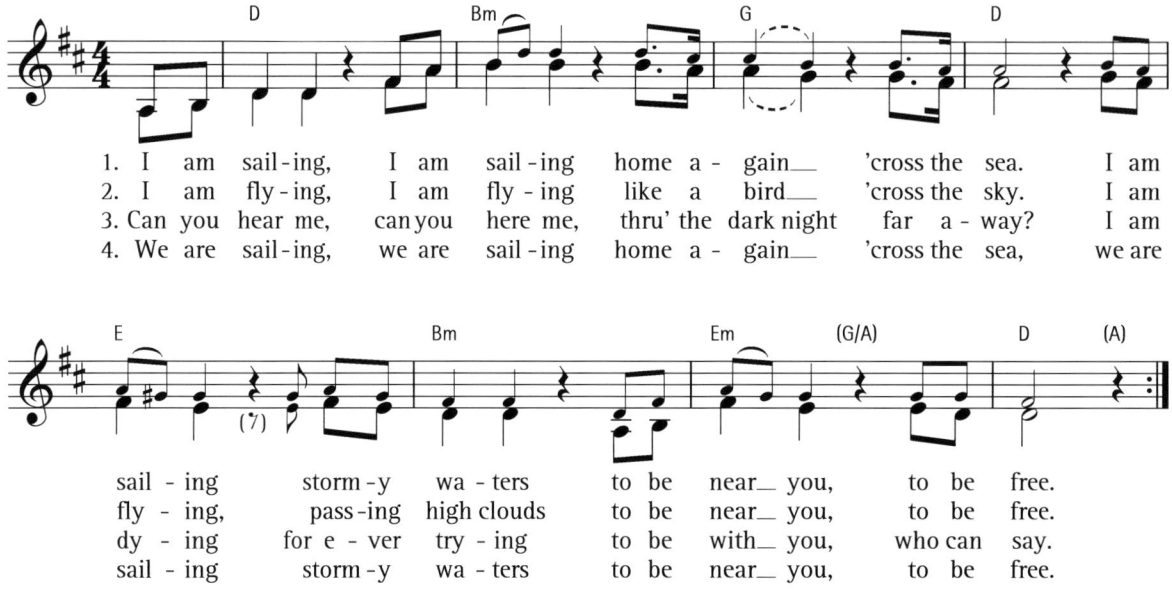

© Copyright 1972 Island Music Limited.
Universal/Island Music Limited.
All Rights Reserved. International Copyright Secured.

151. Love Me Tender

Elvis Presley / Vera Matson

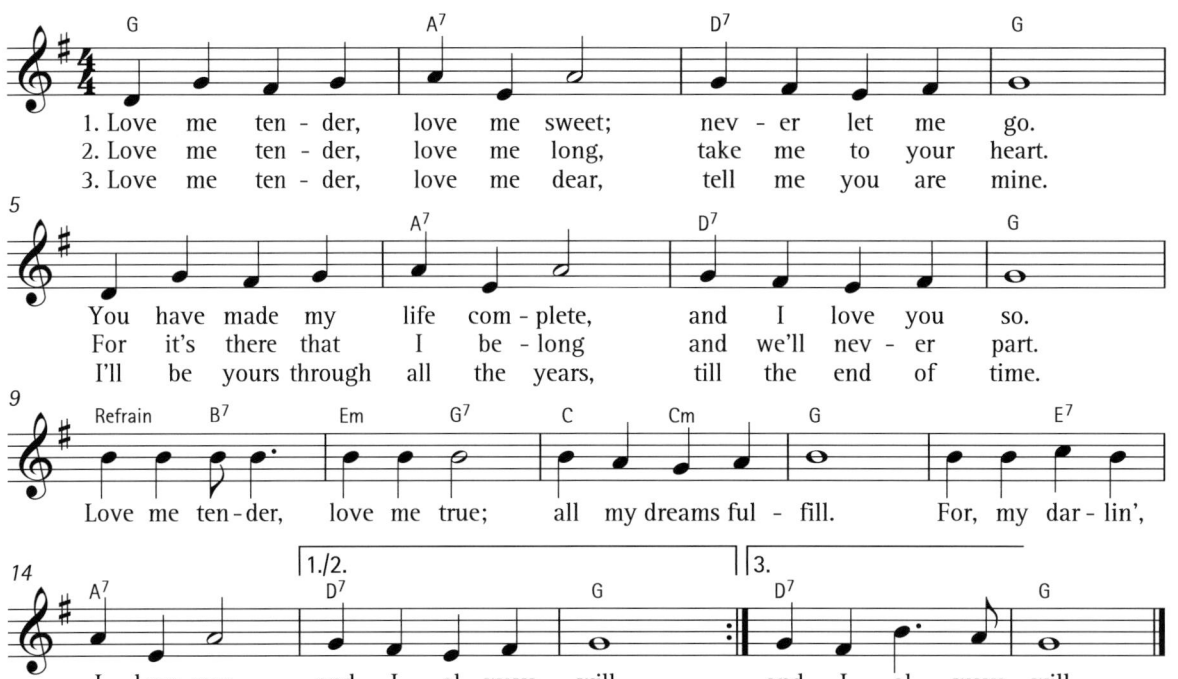

© Copyright 1956 Elvis Presley Music. All Rights Reserved. International Copyright Secured. Used by permission of Music Sales Limited.

VI. ROCK, POP, EVERGREEN

Love Me Tender 3-part setting

Elvis Presley / Vera Matson
Choral setting: Michael Gohl

"Love Me Tender" is a cover version of the song "Aura Lee", which dates from the time of the American Civil War (published 1864).

Aura Lee

1. As the blackbird in the spring
   'neath the willow tree
   sat an' piped I heard him sing,
   singing Aura Lee.
   Aura Lee, Aura Lee,
   maid with golden hair,
   sunshine came along with thee
   and swallows in the air.

2. In your blush the rose was born;
   Music, when you spake;
   Through thine azure eye the morn
   Sparkling seemed to break.
   Aura Lee, Aura Lee,
   Birds of crimson wing.
   Never song have sung to me
   As in that bright, sweet spring.

3. When the mistletoe was green,
   Midst the winter's snows,
   Sunshine in thy face was seen,
   Kissing lips of rose.
   Aura Lee, Aura Lee,
   Take my golden ring;
   Love and light return with thee,
   And swallows in the spring.

© Copyright 1956 Elvis Presley Music. All Rights Reserved. International Copyright Secured. Used by permission of Music Sales Limited.

VI. ROCK, POP, EVERGREEN

152. With a Smile

Words and music: Markus Detterbeck

© Helbling, Innsbruck-Esslingen-Bern/Belp

VI. ROCK, POP, EVERGREEN

153. Salsa Beach Band

Words and music: Markus Detterbeck

Today, the term "salsa" is often used to denote the type of dance music that used to be widely known as "Latin music". The voices in "Salsa Beach Band" replace the instruments typically found in a salsa band. The aim when performing the patterns vocally is to imitate the sound and playing style of the instruments in question. For example in the trumpet part, an emphasis should be placed on clean, crisp articulation.

Salsa Beach Band can also be sung as an accompaniment to song no. 49, *Un poquito cantas*.

© Helbling, Innsbruck-Esslingen-Bern/Belp

VI. ROCK, POP, EVERGREEN

154. Rock 'n' Roll Band

Words and music: Markus Detterbeck

VI. ROCK, POP, EVERGREEN

© Helbling, Innsbruck-Esslingen-Bern/Belp

Performance suggestion

The accompanying voices assume the role of the instruments typically found in a rock 'n' roll band. The main aim, when performing these patterns vocally, should therefore be to imitate the sound and feeling of such instruments. The tenor, for example, imitates the "rolling" character of a typical rock 'n' roll piano pattern. The "tsp" in the bass part imitates the hi-hat and should be articulated very crisply with the tip of the tongue at the front of the mouth.

These patterns offer scope for trying out new and interesting performance sequences. For example the bass starts and then the other instruments come in one after another. The voices can also be supplemented by real instruments.

155. Pata Pata

Music and words: Miriam Makeba, Jerry Ragovoy
Arr. and English words: Markus Detterbeck

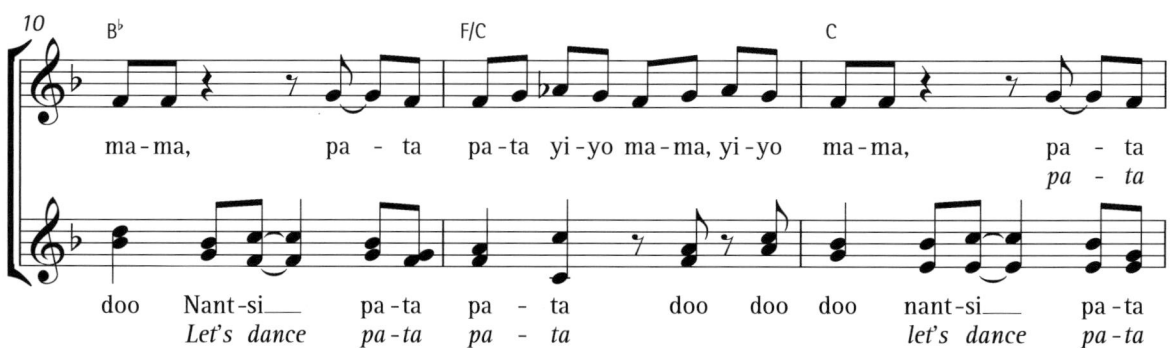

© 1967 Lovolar Music / Budde Songs, Inc. / Abekam Music
Rechte für D/A/CH: Rolf Budde Musikverlag GmbH, Berlin

VI. ROCK, POP, EVERGREEN

Performance suggestion

A small group of singers leads in with the accompanying pattern; the choir, as notated above, enters after seven bars.

VI. ROCK, POP, EVERGREEN

156. Hit the Road, Jack

Words and music: Percy Mayfield
Choral setting: Martin Carbow

VI. ROCK, POP, EVERGREEN

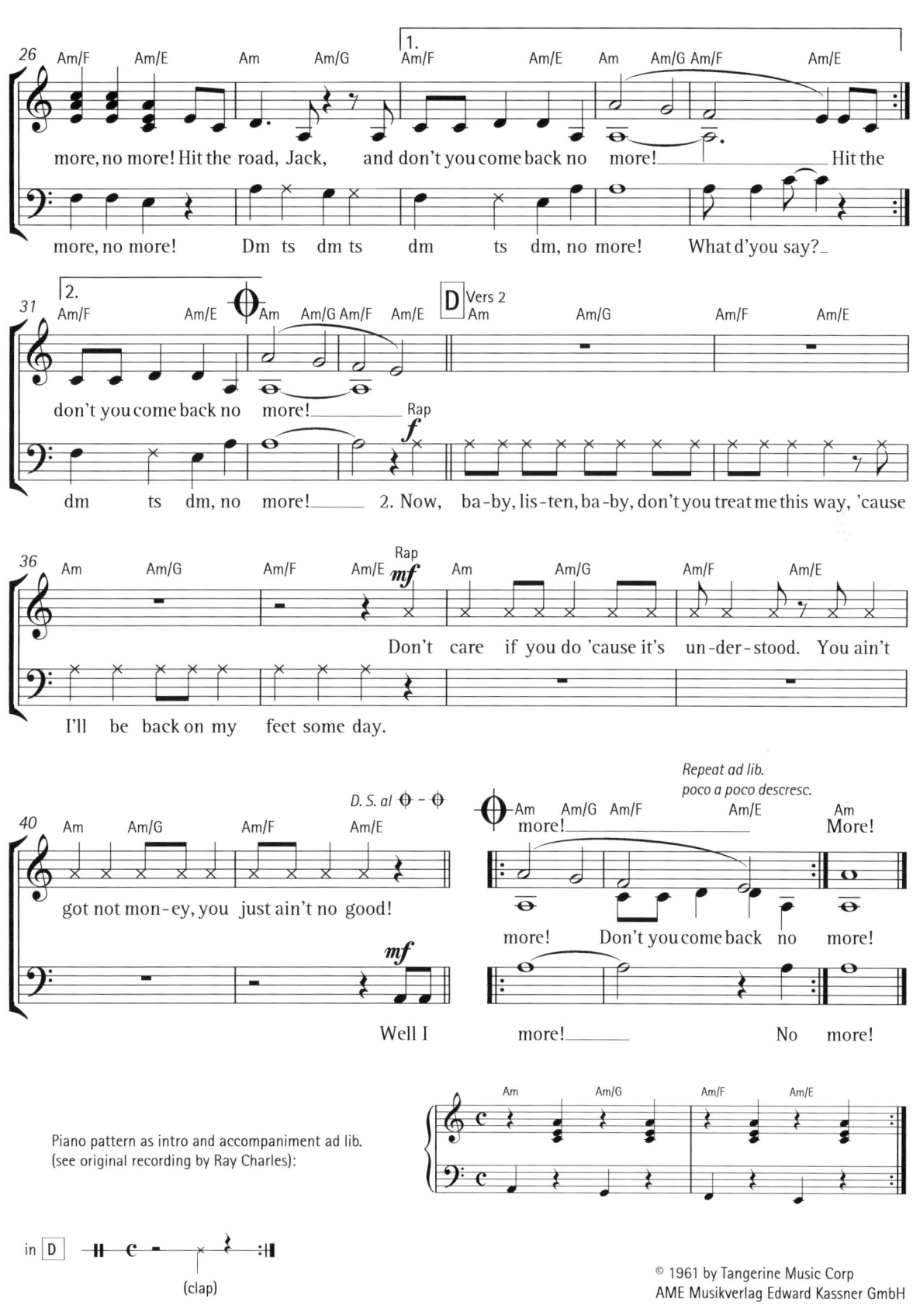

© 1961 by Tangerine Music Corp
AME Musikverlag Edward Kassner GmbH

VI. ROCK, POP, EVERGREEN

157. All my Loving

Words and Music: John Lennon and Paul McCartney
Choral setting: Teese Gohl

*) the accompanying parts can also be sung by high male voices

© Copyright 1963 Sony/ATV Music Publishing.
All Rights Reserved. International Copyright Secured.

VI. ROCK, POP, EVERGREEN

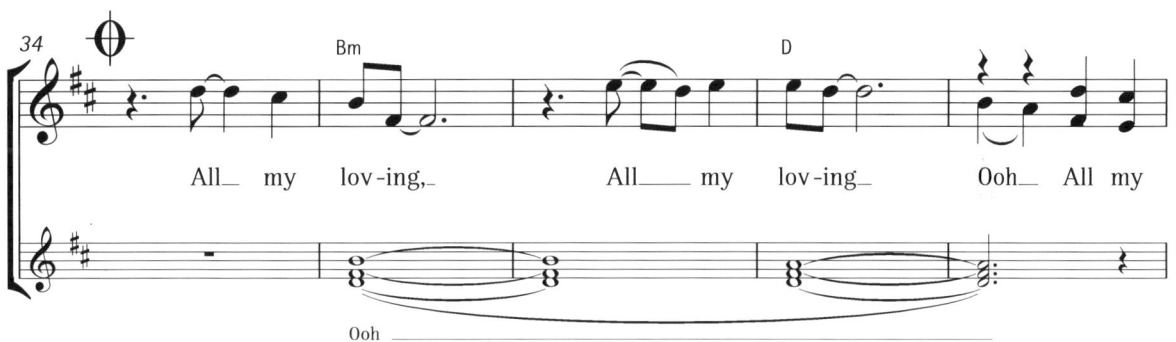

VI. ROCK, POP, EVERGREEN

158. Yesterday

Words and music: John Lennon and Paul McCartney
Arr.: Michael Gohl

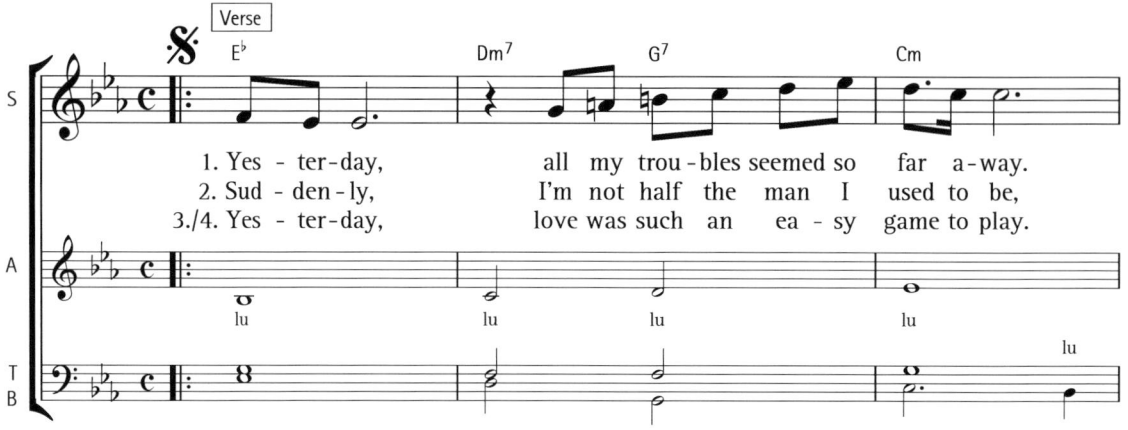

1. Yes-ter-day, all my trou-bles seemed so far a-way.
2. Sud-den-ly, I'm not half the man I used to be,
3./4. Yes-ter-day, love was such an ea-sy game to play.

Now it looks as tough they're here to stay. Oh I be-lieve in
there's a sha-dow hang-ing o-ver me. Oh yes-ter-day came
Now I need a place to hide a-way. Oh I be-lieve in

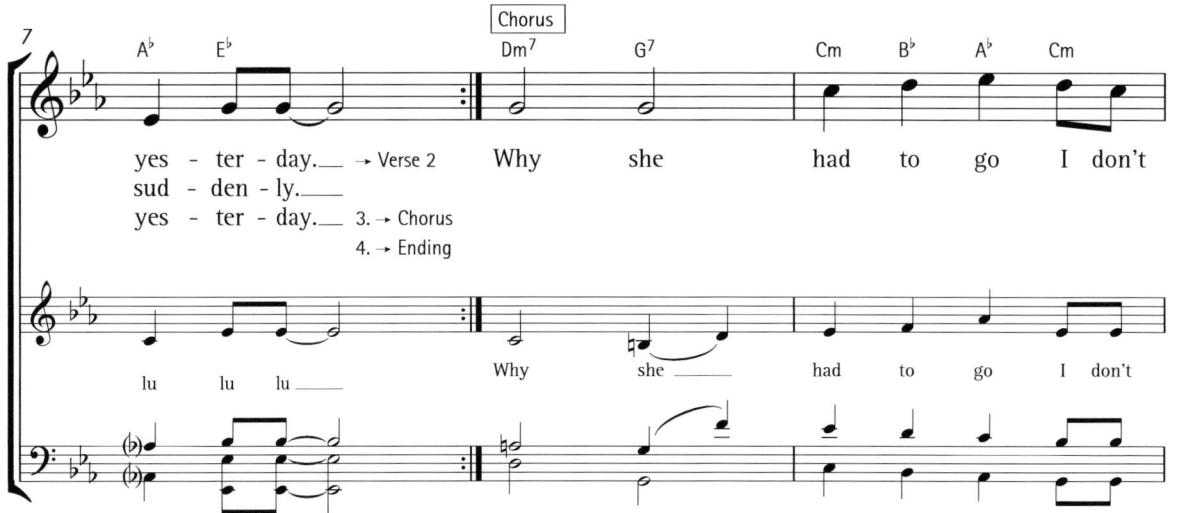

yes-ter-day. → Verse 2   Why she had to go I don't
sud-den-ly.
yes-ter-day. 3. → Chorus
             4. → Ending

© Copyright 1965 Sony/ATV Music Publishing. All Rights Reserved. International Copyright Secured.

VI. ROCK, POP, EVERGREEN

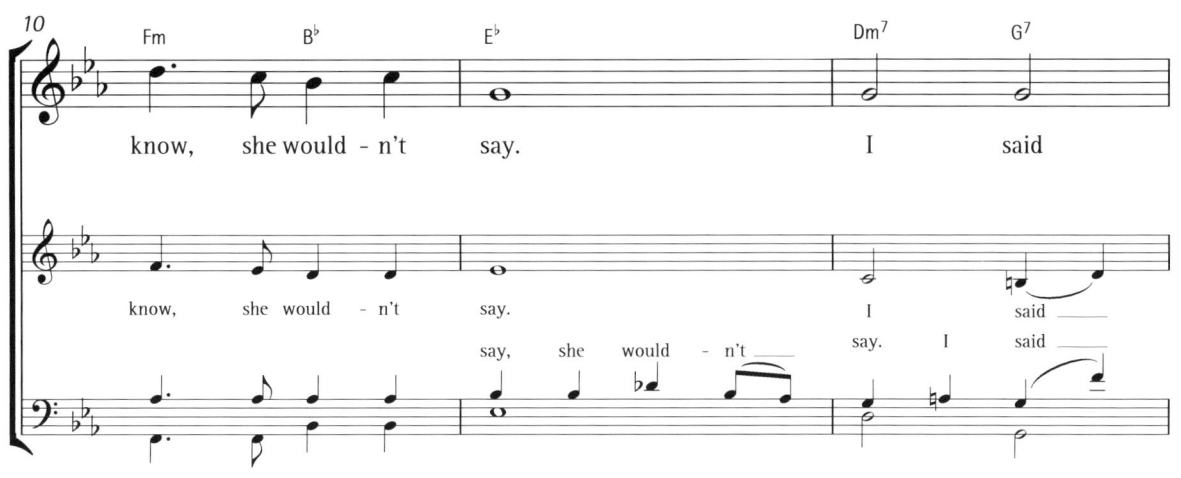
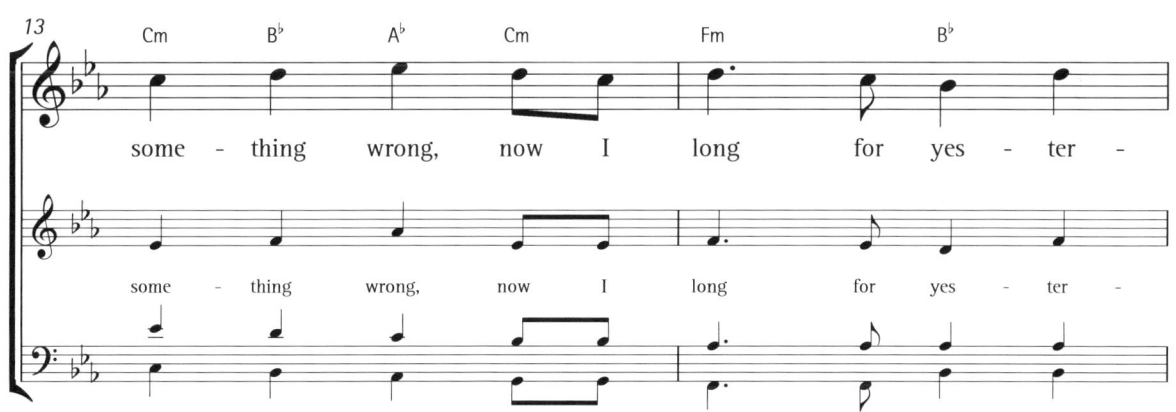
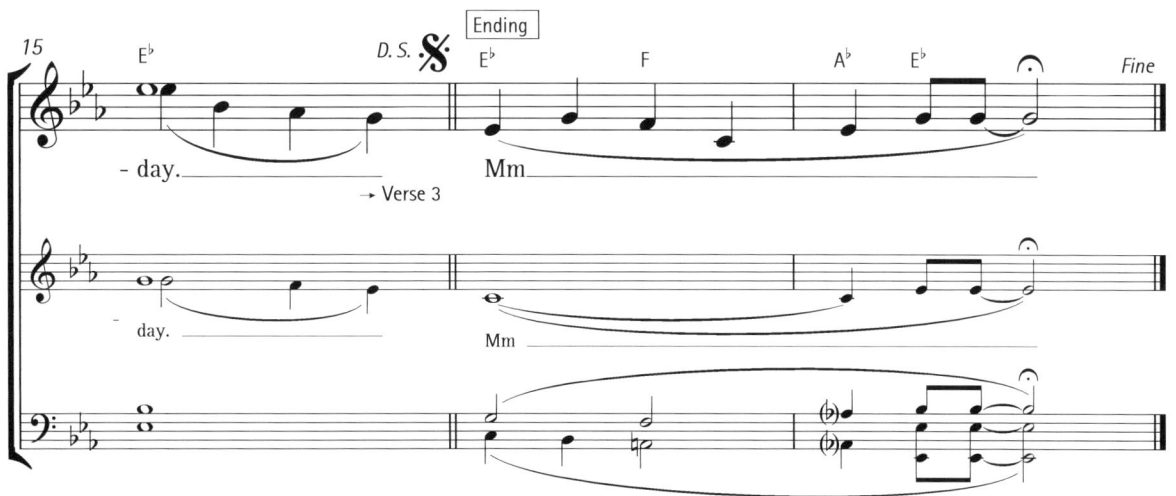

Sequence: verse 1 – verse 2 – chorus – verse 3 – chorus – verse 4 – ending

VI. ROCK, POP, EVERGREEN

159. Aunt Dinah has Blowed de Horn

Words and music: Scott Joplin
(1868–1917)

VI. ROCK, POP, EVERGREEN

160. Tears in Heaven

Words and music: Eric Clapton, Will Jennings
Arr.: John Høybye

© Copyright 1991 Blue Sky Rider Songs. Rondor Music (London) Limited/E C Music.
All Rights Reserved. International Copyright Secured.

VI. ROCK, POP, EVERGREEN

Sequence: A1 - B1 - A2 - B2 - C - A (instrumental solo) - B3 - A1 - B1

VI. ROCK, POP, EVERGREEN

161. That Lucky Old Sun

Music: Beasley Smith (1901-1968)
Words: Haven Gillespie
Choral setting: Robert Sund (b 1942)

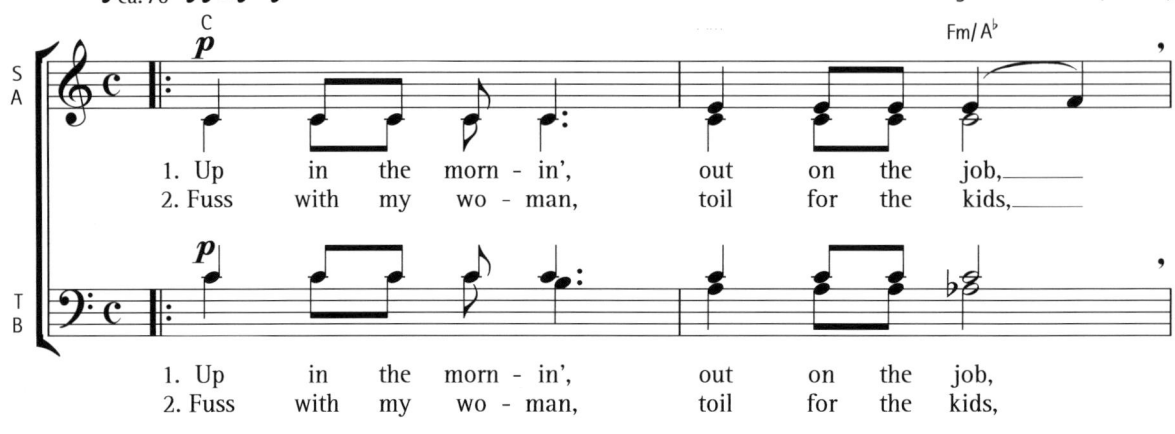
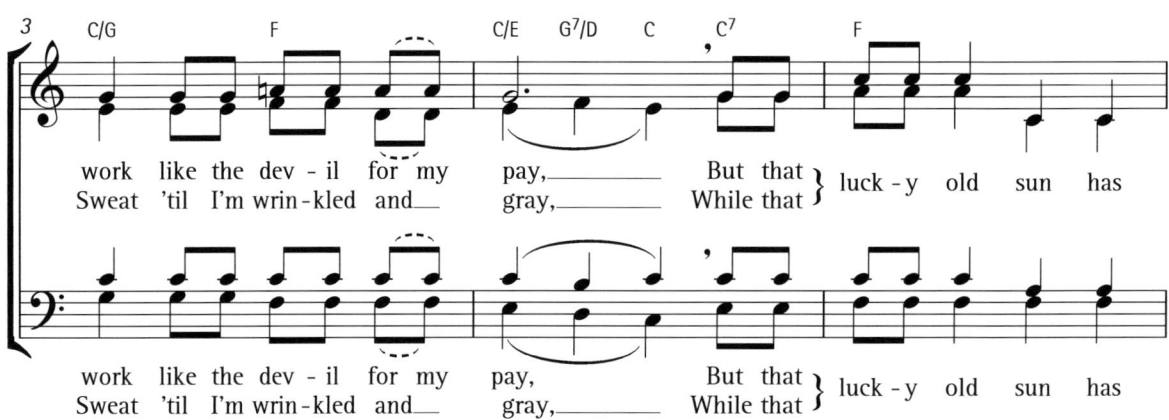

© Copyright 1949 (Renewed 1977) EMI Robbins Catalog Incorporated.
CPP/Belwin Incorporated.
All Rights Reserved. International Copyright Secured.

VI. ROCK, POP, EVERGREEN

VI. ROCK, POP, EVERGREEN

VI. ROCK, POP, EVERGREEN

162. Autumn Leaves

Music: Joseph Kosma
Original text: Jacques Prevert
English words: Johnny Mercer

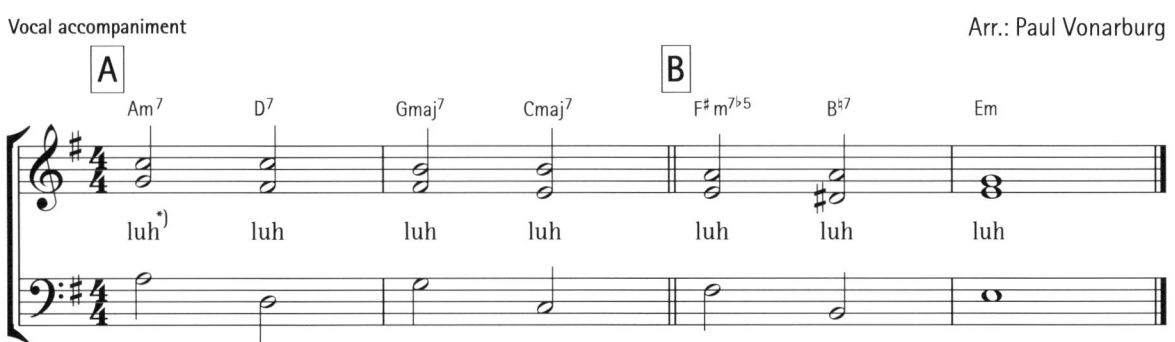

© 1947 by Enoch & Cie Editeurs, Paris
Für Deutschland und Österreich: Edition Marbot GmbH

Vocal accompaniment

Arr.: Paul Vonarburg

*) or hum

© Setting: Verlag Schweizer Singbuch

Sequence: A B - A B - B A - B B

VI. ROCK, POP, EVERGREEN

163. As Tears go by

Words and music: Mick Jagger, Keith Richards, Andrew Loog Oldham
Arr.: Walter Hoffmann

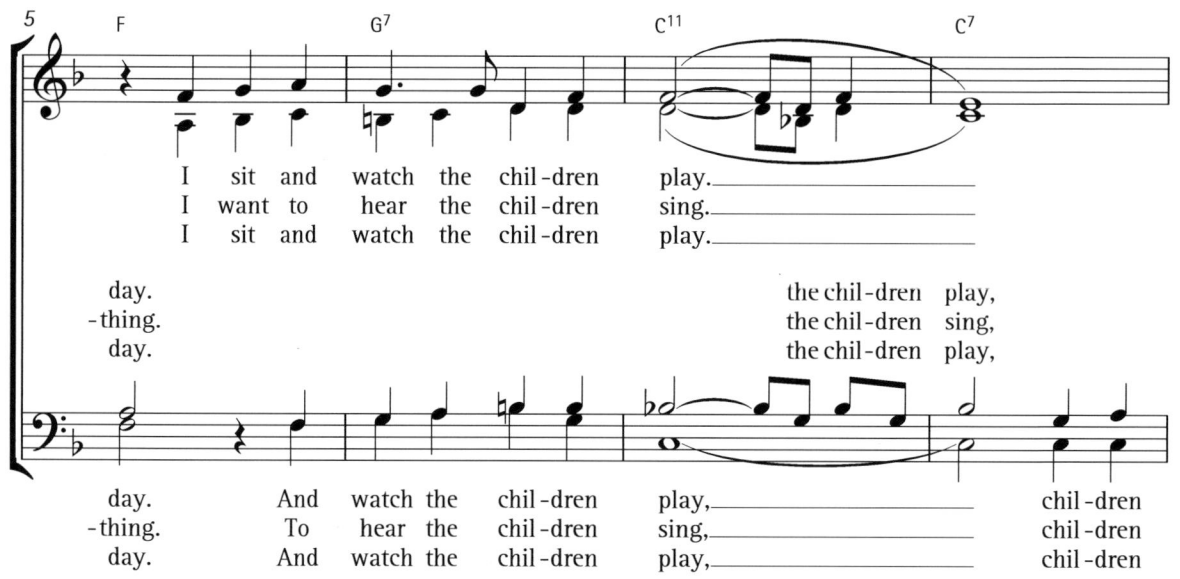

© 1964 ABKCO MUSIC, INC., 85 Fifth Avenue, New York, NY 10003
Used by Permission of ALFRED MUSIC. All Rights Reserved

VI. ROCK, POP, EVERGREEN

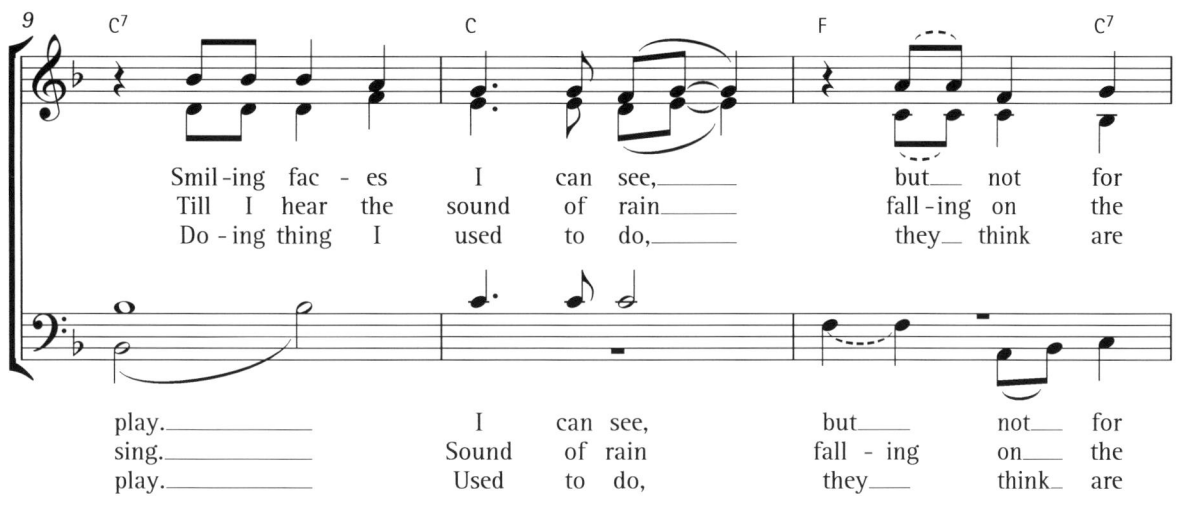
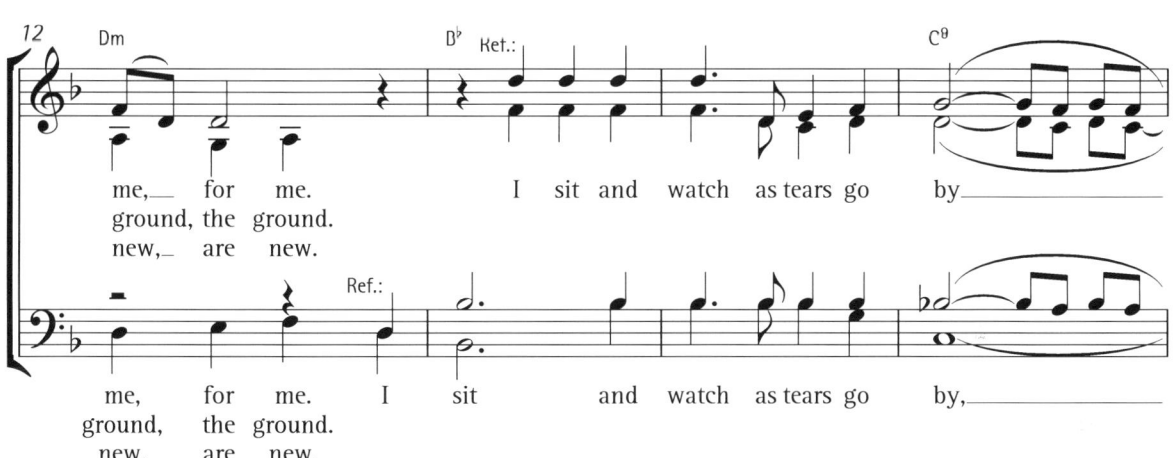

VI. ROCK, POP, EVERGREEN

164. Lemon Tree

Words and music:
Peter Freudenthaler, Volker Hinkel
Arr.: Markus Detterbeck

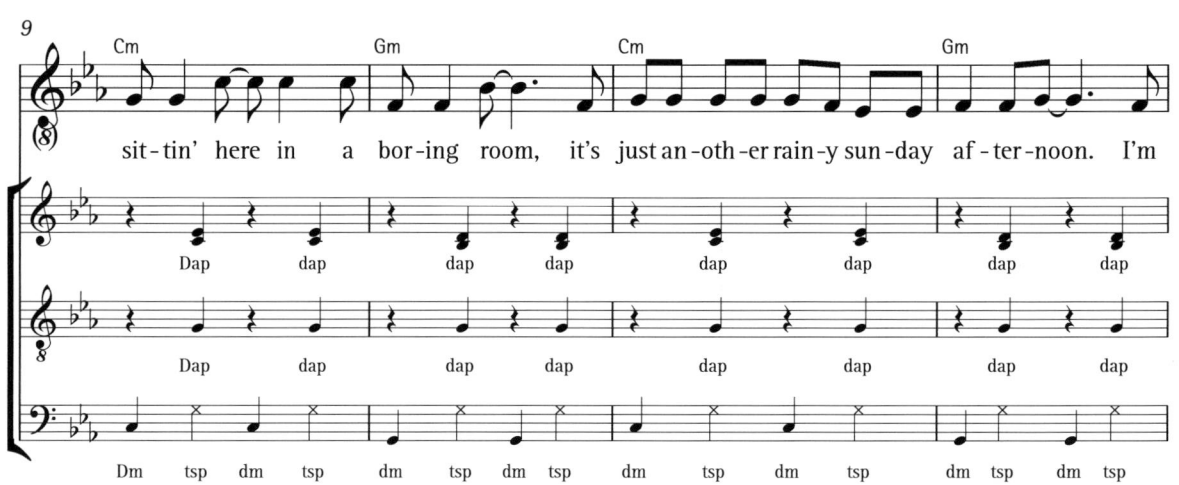

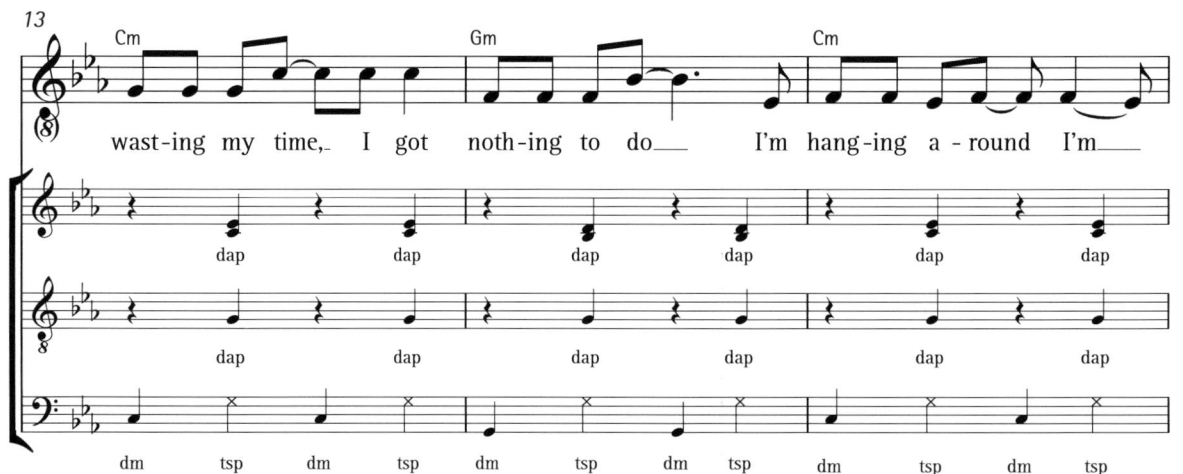

© EMI MMC Musikverlag GmbH

VI. ROCK, POP, EVERGREEN

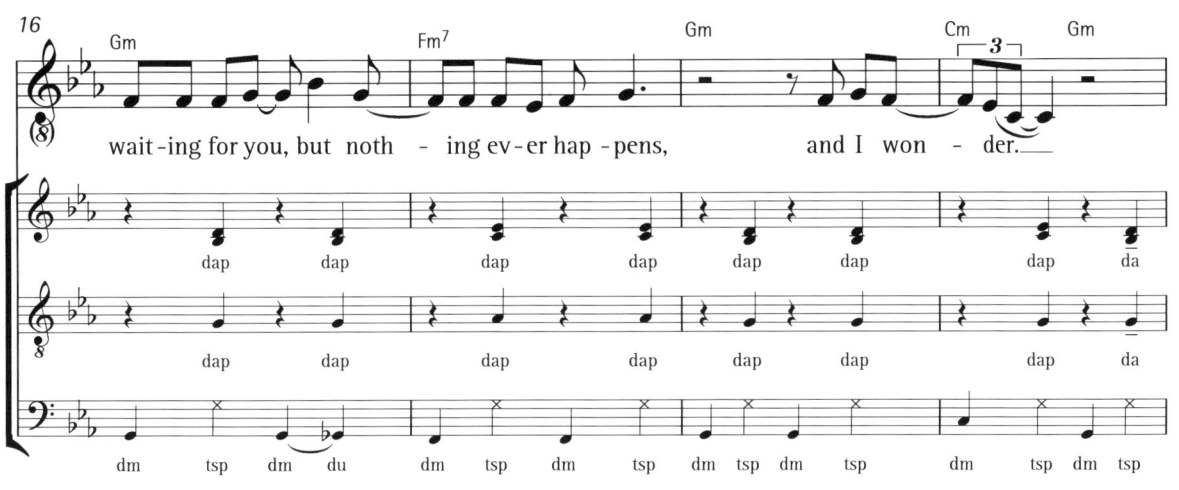
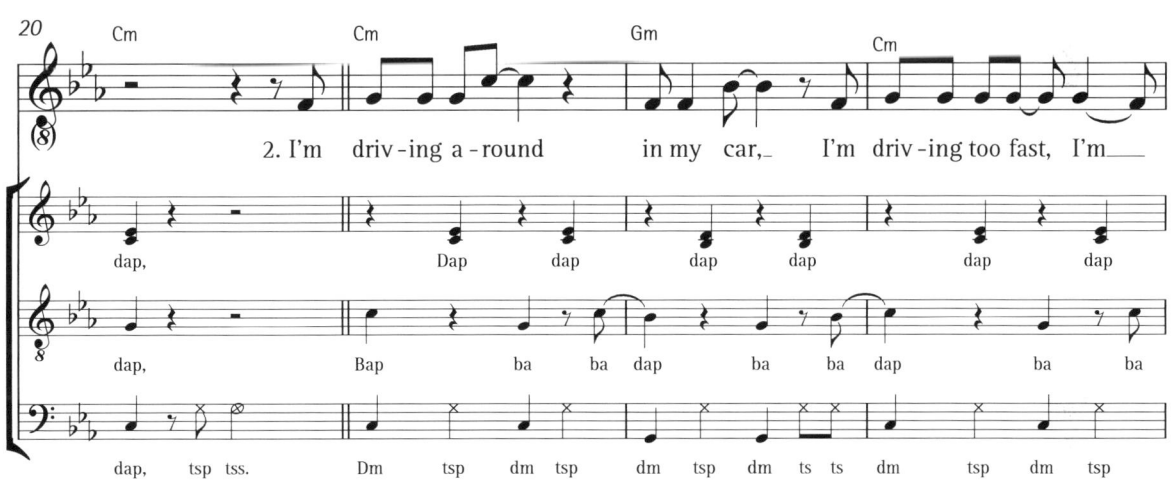

VI. ROCK, POP, EVERGREEN

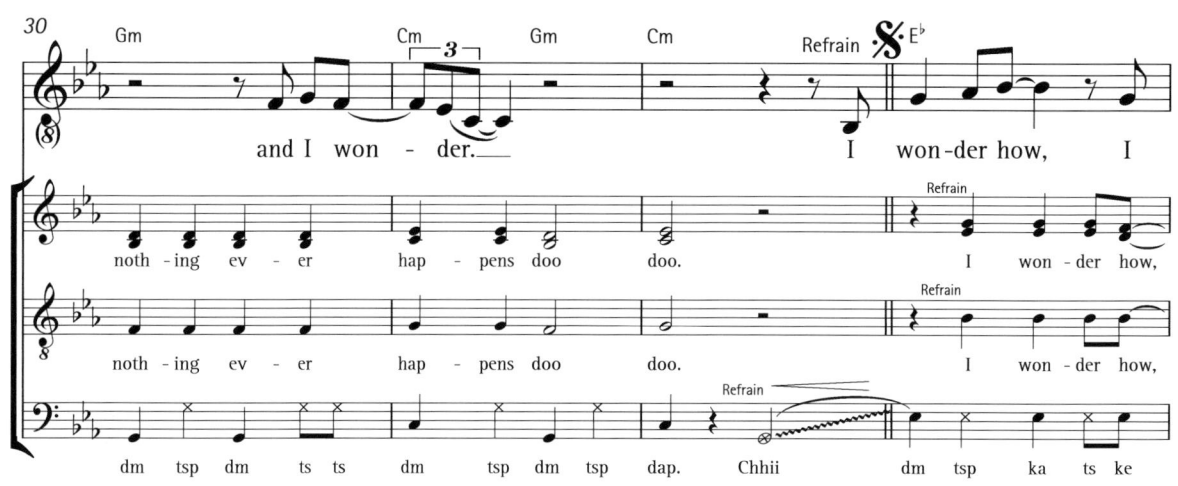
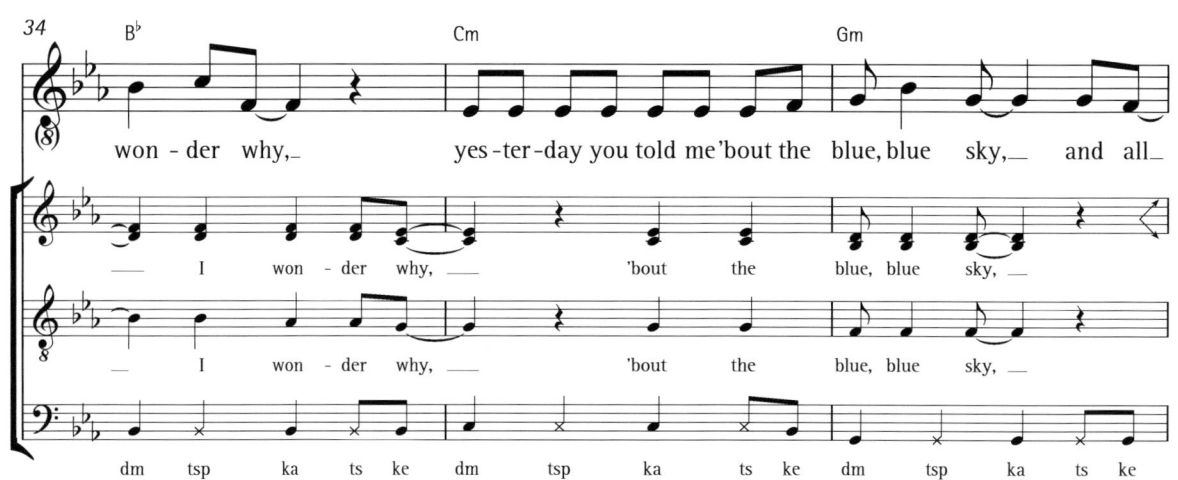

VI. ROCK, POP, EVERGREEN

VI. ROCK, POP, EVERGREEN

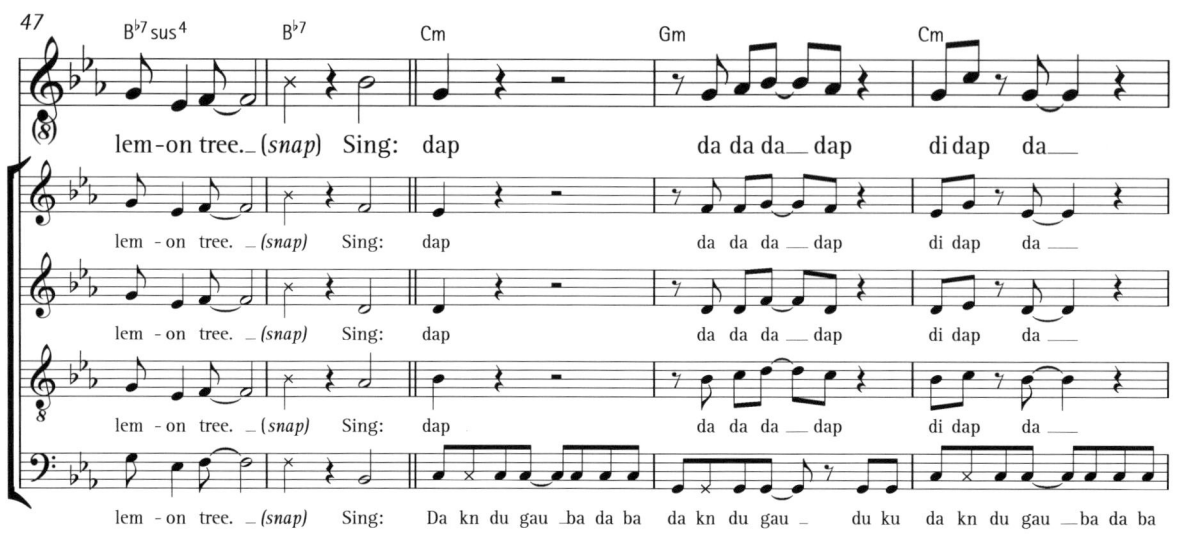

VI. ROCK, POP, EVERGREEN

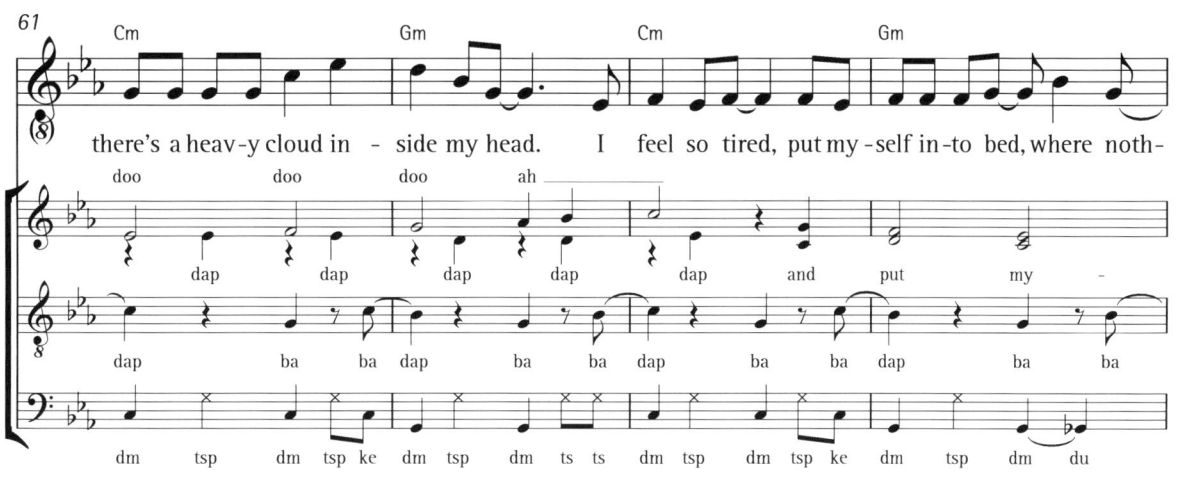

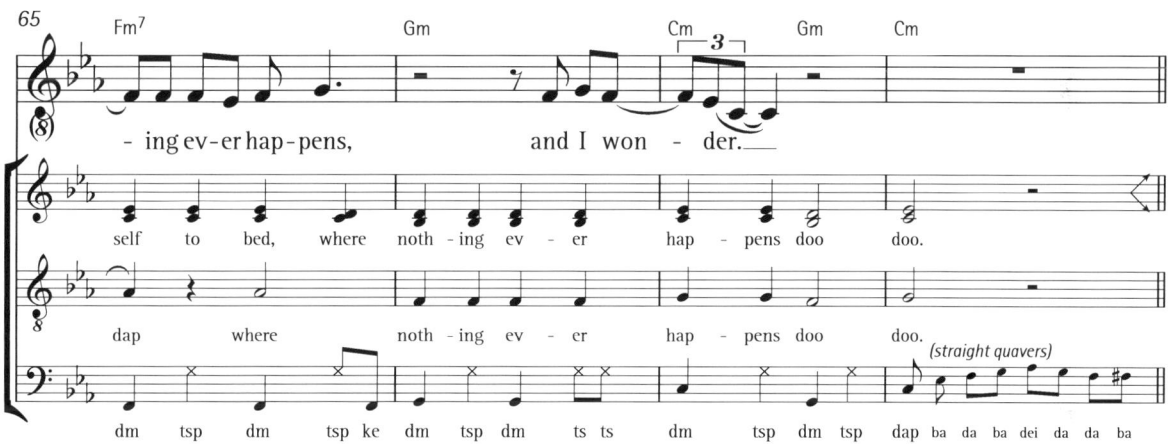

VI. ROCK, POP, EVERGREEN

VI. ROCK, POP, EVERGREEN

VI. ROCK, POP, EVERGREEN

165. Hallelujah, I Just Love Him (Her) So

Ray Charles (1932–2004)
Choral setting: Robert Sund (b 1942)

S + A: Let me tell you 'bout a boy I know, he is my baby and I love him so. Ev'ry morn-ing 'fore the sun gets up he brings me cof-fee in my favou-rite cup. That's why I know, yes I know, hal-le-lu-jah, I just love him (her) so.

T + B: When I'm a-lone and I have no friend I know she'll stay with me un-til the end. Ev'ry-bo-dy asks me how do I know, I look at them and say she told me so.

S + A: When I call him on the te-le-phone and tell him that I'm all a-lone, just be-fore I count from one to four I hear him (Four knocks) at my door.

T + B: In the ev'-ning when the sun goes down, when I'm a-lone and no one els's a-round,

© 1956 Unichappell Music Inc, USA; This arrangement © 2014 Unichappell Music Inc, USA; Warner/Chappell Music Ltd, London W6 8BS (for Europe excl. UK rights) Reproduced by permission of Faber Music Ltd; All Rights Reserved.

VI. ROCK, POP, EVERGREEN

VI. ROCK, POP, EVERGREEN

VI. ROCK, POP, EVERGREEN

166. Happy

Pharrell Williams
Arr.: Bertrand Gröger

VI. ROCK, POP, EVERGREEN

VI. ROCK, POP, EVERGREEN

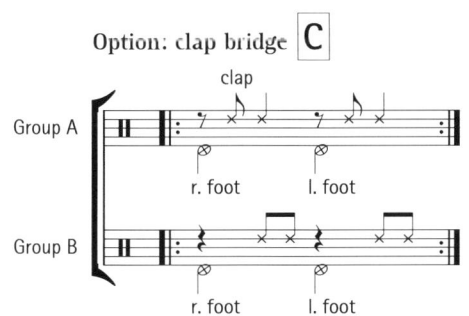

Performance tip

Sections B (chorus) and C (bridge) can be sung in any order.
In the original version there are also two verses (A):

1. It might seem crazy what I'm about to say.
   Sunshine she's here, you can take away.
   I'm a hot air balloon that could go to space
   with the air, like I don't care baby by the way

2. Here come bad news talking this and that – yeah.
   Give me all you got, don't hold back – yeah.
   Well, I should probably warn you I'll be just fine – yeah.
   No offense to you, don't waste your time. Here's why.

Sequence of the original:
A1 – B – A2 – B – C (clapping only) – C
(clapping and singing) – B (x2) – C – B (x3)

Voices can be omitted in the following order:
B (provided the performance is accompanied by piano), T, S2

Open Singing – Principles and Methodology

DIRECTING OPEN SINGING MEANS...

Singleitung
Singleitung (leading sing-along sessions) is more than choral conducting. However, the same rules apply to both when it comes to musical competence, the ability to communicate and conduct, and your methodology and didactic skills.

Imparting music
Open Singing can open singers up to new worlds of music, taking them deeper into the music and making them an active part of the musical experience.

Organization
Every minute is precious in Open Singing. Carefully conceived planning will smooth the way for making the most of the time given for music. Every successful plan begins with a clear vision, a solid credo, and strong fundamental values. These are needed to set detailed objectives and select constructive methods and practical steps. These general management principles have an impact on both the planning and the directing of Open Singing.

WHAT IS OPEN SINGING?

"Singing makes people happy!"
It is no longer common knowledge that communal singing is a pleasurable experience in many different ways. Singing together as a spontaneous manifestation of living is faced with extinction in our Western civilization of the 21st century. Even singing as part of life and survival – think of the countless work songs, love songs, battle hymns, songs of yearning for home and ritual songs – is becoming less and less a part of everyday experience. It is being replaced by the consumption of commercially produced music, especially pop songs.

This might be one reason why the topic of singing as a genuine element of expression for human mankind has now become a subject of scientific study in the frame of happiness research. The positive results are not surprising for insiders.

Within this scope, special importance has to be placed on Open Singing as the "rewarding" experience of doing something yourself instead of buying it.

The journey is the destination
Sing along! The call says it all: EVERYONE is invited to sing. In contrast to choral rehearsals and concerts, this is an "open" event. Open Singing is neither a choral rehearsal nor a choral concert in the strictest sense. The participants in traditional choirs must meet specific requirements. There is a "right way" and a "wrong way", and the concert is the long-term goal. On the other hand a choral concert is only "open" to the audience. Only the choral singers on the stage get to enjoy the experience of singing.

Compare this to Open Singing, which has nothing to do with the performance, of how the experience is presented to the audience. While singing, participants are both "rewarding" and "being rewarded". Open Singing is simultaneously the journey and the destination.

Beyond cult and ideology
Communal singing has the proven ability to fulfil purposes beyond the music and to endow meaning. It can socialize, encourage contemplation, train alertness, rouse, calm, embolden, stir up, politicize, ideologize, manipulate and much more.

Open Singing strives for more than that; it is a musical event. At its core are the singing as an existential expression of life on the one side and the song, the music, the content and the message behind each individual piece on the other. Led by a professional, Open Singing aims to provide both an intensive musical experience and personal experience of musical success.

Beyond ingratiation and animator clichés
Open Singing directors require strong presence and a lot of skill at communicating and generating enthusiasm. The heart of the event is not, however, focused on the director him or herself, nor on animation or choreography or the impressive performance of a pilot choir, but rather on the entire group of participants, the communal singing itself and the quality of the music thereby created. Animation, humour and entertaining moments must all serve the purpose of assisting the participants to succeed. The Open Singing director serves as a coach in this sense.

Beyond pedantry and claims to perfection

Open Singing is furthermore a pedagogical event. As such, there are a number of well-known stumbling blocks and pitfalls that emerge in the pedagogy. Pedantic preaching and inappropriate claims to perfection will quickly suffocate the genuine desire to sing and learn and strip away the meaning behind Open Singing.

Beyond fear and boredom – getting into the flow

It becomes possible to get into the "flow", as the experience is described by Mihaly Csikszentmihalyis, when a good balance is struck between demanding too little and too much. In Open Singing, there can be an enormous difference in the participant's abilities and expectations. That is why it is necessary to find the right balance and well-timed variation between simple and difficult tasks, between joyfully easy, playfully medium and occasionally hard challenges.

Good choral rehearsal and good choral concert

To a certain extent, Open Singing is both a successful "choral concert" and a good "choral rehearsal", an accomplished combination of enjoyment in singing while learning something new in a playful environment. There are some who anticipate being able to sing as many songs as possible – a "sing-along concert" –, while others are happy if they can be carried along for a while and lose themselves in the music and the atmosphere. The latter group tends to consist of older people, children and those who are forced to come along.

More importance needs to be placed on the entertaining aspect of a "concert" in Open Singing when the composition and therefore the expectations of the audience are manifold and difficult to predict. The participation of a good pilot choir and, if need be, of instrumentalists, as well as broad variety, humour, a varying tempo and musical/theatrical surprises are elements which are also considered in the dramaturgy of a concert.

The "choral rehearsal" facet in Open Singing: that is, the aspects of methodology and the conveyance of music, needs more attention when the setting suggests it – for example, titles such as "New songs for Advent and Christmas", "New songs for young and old", "Open Singing sessions", and "Weekly singing sessions in nursing homes". The participants rely on a professional director to help them sing and learn songs they wouldn't be able to sing or learn on their own.

More reward for more effort?

The fact that Open Singing is both rehearsal and concert in many ways also has an impact on the amount of preparation needed. It is greater, and there is no way around it. Both the director and any instrumentalists and singers need to have the music to be performed absolutely "concert ready". The director usually has to know everything by heart and be able to play along with the pieces.

And no matter how ideally the music has been prepared, it cannot simply be prettily presented one piece after another as in a concert. The director's work on the preparation, on the music conveyance and the methodology, can definitely be compared to the preparation for a finals lesson. The attendee's expectations are high and there is no second chance. The plan has to fit the situation, the communication has to "sparkle", and the inspiration needs to be there.

Does it make sense to add here that, at the end, one cannot expect adequate payment, much less enhanced professional prestige for the Singleitung or choral conducting other than "reward for the effort"?

No – the "reward" is far greater: a happy audience in which a different spark is ignited than is possible by simply listening to a concert. It is a more sustainable spark that can steadily grow.

OPEN SINGING – PRINCIPLES AND METHODOLOGY

SETTINGS

What is the setting? Who is the target audience?
Who organizes Open Singing? What can organizers expect and what visions and goals should they have? Are there specific requirements for the occasion? What target audience is addressed? Are there limitations, such as in the song choice or the infrastructure? Is the session truly "open" to everyone or is it appropriate to restrict who can participate? The clearer these classic "leadership issues" can be answered, the better the people responsible can plan and market the Open Singing session, as well as avoiding problems and averting failure.

Who communicates the invitation? What does the audience expect?
Every notice raises expectations. The less detail included in the invitation, the more room there is for individual expectations. The statement "for singing enthusiasts" raises different expectations than "for the whole family", "for beginners and late bloomers", or "for young and old". Depending on the organizers' intentions, it might be better not to simply call it "Open Singing", but rather "Open choir singing", "Open singing session" or "Open choral singing", for example.

Where will it take place?
The most important aspect when selecting the space where the Open Singing should take place is the visual and acoustic contact between the audience and the director. Communal singing presupposes that everyone can hear each other. It takes a space with good acoustics for the sounds to blend musically: the musical "we" in contrast to the "I". Poor acoustics, in which participants can only hear their own voice (like at outdoor concerts), prevent a genuine communal music experience, and might result in a sound which has more in common with the singing in a football crowd.

Singing outdoors is tempting, but the acoustics are poorly suited to the task. Walls and reflecting surfaces, building corners and roofs can create a somewhat musical space. Attention should be paid to the fact that, in addition to hearing the director and the instrumental accompaniment, participants need to hear themselves and their fellow contributors as a "choir".

The lighting is equally critical. While the director and the accompaniment (instrumentalists, pilot choir etc.) have to be easily visible, the participants cannot be sitting in the dark as in a concert. The light has to be at least sufficient to read the notes and the lyrics easily. Neglecting this seemingly trivial aspect can have a major influence on the success of Open Singing.

With a stage?
If you have more than a certain number of seat rows in the audience, it becomes indispensable to give the director and the pilot choir an elevated position. Groups of instrumentalists can more easily be placed on the ground level. If no stage is available, it is worth trying to arrange the seating diagonally and in a semi-circle around the director so that fewer seats are placed directly behind the ones in front.

With sheet music? With lyrics?
A fundamental decision to be taken is whether to hand out the songs with notes or just the lyrics. In Western culture, parallel to the decline in singing regularly, there has been a considerable reduction in the common knowledge of a repertoire of songs. However, many younger people know countless pop songs by heart.

Singing completely without notes and/or lyrics has one disadvantage; it limits the repertoire to either the most popular songs or to songs which can be learned from the beginning in a very short time. The latter is heavily dependent on the skills of the director; otherwise the Open Singing turns into a simple class. This book contains a number of easy songs and melodies which, with the right methodology, can be learnt and sung quickly.

There are techniques for directors that bring a group of people to sing together from a standing start without notes or already knowing the lyrics. The best known technique is the circle song (songs that are developed on the spot by a conductor by giving repetitive elements to different groups in the choir; the singers usually stand in a circle to hear each other better). Some examples of these are also printed in this book. They can be used to develop plenty of joy, self-confidence and musical energy.

The disadvantage of this technique is that the participants are entirely reliant on the director and the music learned is very hard to reproduce without him or her and outside of the space. A song sheet or at least a libretto is traditionally handed out in Open Singing sessions. This helps to achieve the goal to sing together and to spread the music.

For larger events and festivals, there is a longstanding tradition to publish entire songbooks. These tend to spread across the whole world through the participants and the choral directors and establish a basis for an international repertoire. It is also possible to project the songs and lyrics on a large screen. The disadvantage of this method, however, is that the participants cannot take the songs they sing home and so they will not be shared as much.

To encourage this sharing of the music, Edition Peters offers the option of individually tailoring a selection of songs printed in this book for specific occasions.

With musical accompaniment – piano and pilot choir?

A guiding principle of Open Singing is to "help participants succeed". This can be achieved more quickly if the space is filled with song and music from the beginning. The participants immediately feel uplifted and supported in the space. Therefore, it is recommended that Open Singing sessions are supported by at least a good piano accompaniment, even better by a pilot choir.

There are certainly situations and techniques that allow directors to stand in front of the participants and animate them to sing without a piano or other support. This is easier to do – provided this does not concern circle songs or instant composing – if the songs are known to the majority of the participants. Teaching new songs without piano accompaniment demands enormous aptitude if the director does not want to bore the audience or demand too much of participants.

Directors who are also virtuoso pianists can direct an Open Singing session from the piano on their own. This bears the risk, however, that their mobility, their contact with the audience, and the precise conducting will suffer. With the assistance of an experienced pianist, however, the director has more room for manoeuvre and can better follow the pulse of the participants. (See page 242 for more information on piano accompaniment.)

The pilot choir, or "support choir", is the best guarantee that Open Singing session will be successful. It can place the music in the space so that it is "ready for enjoyment", which is something the most talented director cannot do alone. Using a pilot choir spares several steps in the process and therefore clears several stumbling blocks as well. It acts as a role model, inspiration and "motor" at the same time.

Any choral grouping can serve as a pilot choir. It can even be a small vocal group, such as a quartet. The most important prerequisite is that the pilot choir really takes over the role model function, that is, that it masters the songs and fulfils the role of motivating and inspiring participants. It also has to be able to react flexibly to the instructions and occasional improvisations of the director.

In terms of organization, it is ideal if there is a pilot group nearby, or at least a choral group to show how the songs are sung. Quite often, choirs see this as a welcome change of pace or even as an opportunity to market themselves or gain more exposure. (See page 242 for more information on pilot choirs.)

There is also a successful tradition of including additional instrumentalists. Percussion, drums, solo instruments or an ensemble lend Open Singing an additional musical dimension. That "permission to sing ALONG", that rewarding feeling of being part of a greater musical whole, is reinforced even further. Many Open Singing sessions were in the past accompanied by a string quartet, a wind ensemble or a mixed ensemble. There are also examples of large Open Singing events accompanied by an orchestra or a big band.

Do not underestimate the additional work required to musically enrich the experience with additional instruments, whether it be preparing the arrangements and sheet music on the one hand, or the organization, funding, rehearsal and infrastructure on the other.

With electronic amplification?

The voice of the director or other speakers has to be easily heard and understood by all participants. If the number of participants is high and/or the space has poor acoustics, electronic amplification becomes mandatory. For greater mobility, it is preferable for directors to have a headset rather than a microphone with a stand. Directing Open Singing with a microphone in one hand demands a particularly adroit director.

Signs and signals

"Please open the songbook to page three. We will now sing the song *Halleluja* in the lower right!" Announcing and searching for the right notes is cumbersome and time-consuming. If the songs are numbered on the page or if songbooks with page numbers are available, then there is great advantage in using a number board. For large events, the practice of using a "number girl" or "number boy" has become tradition. A member of the pilot choir has all of the necessary page numbers or song numbers prepared in a folder and holds them high for all to see at a signal from the director. This can take place without comment while music – such as the prelude – is played or other comments are made.

OPEN SINGING – PRINCIPLES AND METHODOLOGY

CHECKLIST FOR SETTING UP THE SPACE

In open and variable spaces:
- Check and assess the acoustics and the visibility.
- Choose a position for the director, the piano, the pilot choir and/or the instrumentalists.
- Assess the height and breadth of the conductor's podium and/or the stage.
- Check the alignment of the audience to the director and the alignment of the seating if there is any.

In all spaces:
- Determine the ideal position for the director, pilot choir and/or the instrumentalists.
- Consider the ideal position and alignment of the audience. Consider any limitations which prevent the audience from spreading out too much.
- Create good lighting for the contributors (ability to read notes and lyrics).
- Light the stage (perhaps a spotlight on the director).
- Determine stage design: conductor's podium, placement of the piano, placement of the pilot choir (possibly a choir podium), placement of the instrumentalists.
- Amplification: microphone with stand or headset for director, amplification for the piano, amplification for the pilot choir and any soloists, amplification for the instrumentalists. Positioning of the mixer and the equipment.
- Plan a sufficiently large window of time for stage rehearsal and sound check.

REPERTOIRE AND DRAMATURGY

Music is nourishment
What kind of nourishment will be offered: a sumptuous buffet, a balanced meal, desserts only, fast food, heavy foods, or just bread and water? What does "bread and water" mean in terms of music? What music is "nourishment for the soul", "nourishment for the body", "for the heart" or "nourishment for the mind"? Is there music that nourishes all of these at the same time? What do we demand of the music? Does the music also have to serve as a drug, relaxant or stimulant?

The effect of music on people is hard to put your finger on. But this is right where the secret and the essence of the musical experience is hidden, as well as the motivation to make music ourselves and to participate in Open Singing.

It is therefore recommended to examine the songs and the music thoroughly to determine and to categorize it according to its impact, its "nourishment value" and to use this as the basis for organising a lively, balanced programme for a mixed audience. Depending on the choice of song and music, Open Singing will leave the participants feeling "well-fed", "stimulated", "stuffed", "hungry" or "eager for the next meal".

The provisions in the kitchen
Once the songs are chosen, perhaps also printed on a sheet or in a songbook, then the Open Singing director has to live with them the way a chef does with the provisions in the kitchen. Are important ingredients missing? Does the selection leave creative leeway? Does it cover the needs of the different participants? Is it suitable for good dramaturgy? Which musical aspects and criteria are served?

In this sense, the selection of songs in this book serves Open Singing directors as a kind of "pantry".

OPEN SINGING – PRINCIPLES AND METHODOLOGY

Examples of musical categories:
- Rhythm- and movement-oriented songs (metres, tempos, "grooves")
- Melody-oriented songs (single vocal part, with or without accompaniment)
- Sound- and harmony-oriented songs (hymns, multiple voices, homophony, polyphony)
- Lyric-oriented songs (strophic songs, songs from balladeers, tongue-twisters etc.)

Examples of song characteristics:
- intimacy – exuberance
- contemplation – proclamation
- tranquillity – movement
- sadness – merriment
- nature – society

Examples of musical genres:
- love songs
- spiritual songs
- hymns
- songs oriented toward seasons, annual festivals and religious holidays
- work songs
- dance tunes
- sentimental songs
- political songs
- songs of liberation

Examples of styles:
- folk songs from different cultures
- classical songs from different musical eras, sacred and secular
- blues, rock, pop and jazz songs
- gospels and spirituals
- swing and Latin songs
- rap, hip-hop and other current musical styles

The special seasoning – surprises

Artistic sensibility and musicality are demonstrated through the freedom to experiment and surprise, through the courage to do something unanticipated, especially through the subtle enrichment and elaboration of the music in the moment.

Amateurs in particular do not realize the beauty and depth of certain melodies and songs until they have been elaborated with vocals, instrumental accompaniment or improvisation. Many of the songs in this book are therefore prepared in such a way that they can easily be sung as a single melody or enriched with vocal arrangement, upper voices or with additional improvisations. The idea here is that the director assigns such supplementary tasks to individual singers or to the pilot choir, whilst the majority of the participants sing the simple version. A lovely moment of surprise can be created by waiting to add such elements to the song like a special seasoning once the audience is able to sing and "perform" the song.

Practical examples of "surprises"
- Canon *Dona nobis pacem*: once the participants can sing the canon, add the upper voice as the fourth follower.
- *All mein Gedanken*: have the participants sing the original version monophonically while the pilot choir sings the line from Brahms in between – as an intermezzo.
- *Noyana*: the participants only sing the melody. The pilot choir or a small singing group add the secondary voices.
- *Alleluia*: the participants sing the vocal phrase on the page while one or two soloists improvise alongside in the gospel style.
- *Evening Rise*: the participants hum the song while an instrument (e.g. a recorder) improvises alongside.

ACOUSTIC EXPERIMENTS AND IMPROVISATION

Sound clouds
The chosen song – generally a simple song for one voice – is sung phrase by phrase. When signaled to do so by the conductor, each singer begins the melody independently and at their own tempo and continues until the end of the designated phrase. The last note is held until all the singers have regrouped on it. The conductor closes out the note and leads in the next phrase. As a variation on this free sound cloud, the conductor determines which sections of singers or which areas of the audience to bring in when – for example, with an inviting gesture moving from the very left to the very right of the space, from the front to the back, from the gallery to the stalls, or with free movements throughout the space. This will give the sound cloud an additional spatial dimension.

Organ sound
This improvisational concept also involves dividing the song into phrases. The singers select a note from the indicated melodic phrase and confine themselves to it, holding it like an organ note. Everyone begins together, singing the melody up to the selected note, which is then held until the rest of the group reached the final note of the phrase. The conductor closes out the note in a musically meaningful manner (e.g. allowing it to fade away to nothing) and then leads in the next phrase.

Combination of **sound clouds** and **organ sound**: these two improvisational models can be combined and artistically embellished. Knut Nystedt has provided a masterly example in his version of the J. S. Bach chorale "Komm, süsser Tod" (p. 131).

Opening up "new" sound worlds
In Open Singing too, it can be liberating to break out of traditional diatonicism and conquer "new" sound worlds, and this can make the ear receptive to surprises. Many melodies and canons lend themselves to being sung simultaneously in different pitches and keys.
- Singing in parallel fourths and fifths: every song can in theory be sung in several pitches in parallel (see also *Canon Angelicus* below). Singing in parallel fourths and fifths is a first, simple step towards experimental singing and immediately creates a mediaeval atmosphere.
- Bringing canon entries closer together: many canons can be sung with much closer entries. The entry intervals are successively halved until a new voice begins on each note (e.g. No. 1 *All Praise*, No. 8/9 *Laudemus – Splendens*, No. 11 *Frühling voller Blüten ist*, No. 12 *Apollo*).

OPEN SINGING – PRINCIPLES AND METHODOLOGY

- Singing canons in parallel keys: each canon group begins a tone higher (or lower) and thus sings the canon in a higher (or lower) key. Other parallel keys can be appealing too.
- Canon Angelicus – Sanctus (p. 121): The composer and conductor Gunnar Eriksson (b 1936) has perhaps been the most creative of all Open Singing directors in his experimentation with songs and sounds. His suggestions have appeared in various publications and even go as far as overlaying different folk tunes. His sound experiment for the Canon Angelicus and Sanctus can be used as a model that can be applied to other songs as well.

Songs that lend themselves particularly well to acoustic experimentation:
No. 1 *All Praise to Thee*, No. 8 / 9 *Laudemus Virginem – Splendens Ceptigera*, No. 11 *Frühling voller Blüten ist*, No. 12 *Apollo*, No. 18 *Ding dong*, No. 25 *Ja dan duia*, No. 50 *Sakura*, No. 51 *Evening Rise*, No. 76 *Nocturne*, No. 81 *Gamla Moder Jord*, No. 96 *Der Mond ist aufgegangen*, No. 99 *All mein Gedanken*, No. 104 *Canon angelicus – Sanctus*.

Improvisation in the jazz-rock-pop tradition:
In some of the gospel songs, suggestions for improvisation have been offered as performance ideas. If, among the participants, there are singers with experience of improvisation in the jazz-rock-pop tradition, they will find no difficulty in enhancing many of the other songs with improvisations, thereby effecting a welcome musical "surprise". The songs can also serve as a basis for instrumental solos or spontaneous raps.

The following songs are particularly well suited to improvised solos:
No. 25 *Ja dan duia*, No. 26 / 27 *I like the flowers / Zwei Schritt nach links*, No. 32 *The Big Band*, No. 35 *Funky Goodbye*, No. 36 *Me and Jack*, No. 39 *Flying*, No. 40 *Sambabrasil*, No. 45 *A Summer's Over*, No. 51 *Evening Rise*, No. 56 *Janie Mama*, No. 66 *Noyana*, No. 67 *African Alleluja*, No. 81 *Gamla Moder Jord*, No. 112 *Alleluja*, No. 134 *Feliz Navidad*. All songs in the "Gospel, Blues, Jazz" chapter (No. 137-149). No. 152 *With a Smile*, No. 153 *Salsa Beach Band*, No. 154 *Rock 'n' Roll Band*, No. 162 *Autumn Leaves*, No. 165 *Hallelujah, I Just Love Him So*.

Canons
Singing canons grants the easiest access to multiple voices and to polyphony. The multiple voices lend the melodic elements an additional dimension and allow the communal acoustic space to unfurl. The polyphony – the dialogue between the different independent voices – effects the musical dialogue and thereby the "hearing" among the participants and creates a communal musical (acoustic) space. Classic polyphony is the greatest expression of the blending of multifaceted individuals ("I") with the harmonious whole ("we"). Singing canons is the fastest way to create a "choral experience".

Movement
Songs with movement, including with body percussion or with dance steps, lend an important dimension to communal singing. Beat and rhythm are the motor which keeps the music moving. Plato told us that "rhythm is the order in the movement". Rhythmic-musical movement loosens us up, centres us and energizes us. It brings our attention playfully to the body, to the body's coordination, and thereby to the here and now. At the same time, movement games create a humorous, socializing dynamic among the participants.

Discover something new
Healthy people of all ages are usually curious and eager to learn. Making music gives participants an occasion to "look beyond the ends of their noses" and take them to a place outside their usual comfort zones. The director of Open Singing can therefore occupy the role of a travel guide to unknown musical regions. These might be new compositions, new musical styles, unknown musical cultures, new acoustic spaces, special grooves, foreign languages, improvisations or musical experiments.

Dramaturgy

The director creates the overall impression of the event by building up moments of suspense, arranging contextual and musical references, contrasts, holds and climaxes, and playing with the rhythm (see p. 244) of the development stages. Was the programme well balanced with plenty of variety? Was a balance struck between easy and challenging? Which songs linger in the ear? Did you reach a broad range of participants?

Classic examples of the dramaturgical design of a piece or an evening-long musical event are infused in the large musical formats such as operas, oratorios and musicals, but also in solo concerts, symphonies, suites, etc.

Important dramaturgical design elements include:
- the introduction or overture
- the conclusion and any encore
- the order of songs by theme on the one hand and style on the other
- intensification and contrasts
- holds and various kinds of highlights (such as exuberance, intimacy (a solo, for example), emotion, virtuosity, hymnal grandeur, tonal unity, etc.)
- transitions which maintain or intensify the arc of suspense

Arrange transitions

A measure of the quality of a programme's dramaturgy is not only the quality of the individual parts but, equally important, the way in which these elements are bound together. Transitions can be planned into their component elements for the most part. However, their practical execution in the moment requires foresight, artistic intuition, an alert and flexible pilot choir (if available) and clear indicative gestures and instructions.

Elements of transition arrangement include:
- instrumental preludes, interludes and postludes
- attacca transitions with short or longer concertantes, any solo performances. These might even come from a different location in the space (contrast)
- scenic elements on the stage (e.g. change of position of the choir, new entrance onto the stage, etc.)
- comments and notes
- control of the applause
- lighting changes (if available)

METHODOLOGICAL ASPECTS

Basic attitude

Open Singing is usually short in duration and unique. The expectations are consequently high and the feeling of success has to engage quickly and still throughout. This is unlike with a normal choir, when there is more time available for everything and a choir can get accustomed to the particularities and even the inaccuracies of a choral director.

The following methodological tips therefore aim to create a music-filled, trusting atmosphere and therein effect rapid, playfully joyful learning and authentic music making. Rehearsals and Singleitung, however, are complex processes. Just as the cogs of a gear only work if they are placed in the right position and turn at the right speed, the methodological elements described below can only have a positive influence if they are deployed appropriately and at the right moment. "Seizing the moment" and the ability to quickly fulfil all expectations, is therefore an enormous challenge for the director of Open Singing.

One thing is certain, however; each method will only correspond to the learning behaviour of a subset of the participants. By varying the methods and manner of presentation, the director can give more participants the feeling of being addressed and they will stay "on board". In case of doubt, though, remember that musical flow and playful challenge are more inviting than fussily serving up each note on a silver platter.

Singleitung is more than conducting

Conducting is only a small though very important part of the set of skills required of a good director. Directors mobilize significantly more resources for guiding and organizing an event than conductors and pull the strings, even if they are not standing in front conducting. Singleitung begins with planning and covers programme organization, moderation, animation and methodology, all the way to management delegation completely in the background. Direction means taking on complete responsibility for the event without always being in the centre of it. The musical contributors (pianist, soloist groups, pilot choir) are the extended arm of the director. The manner in which they are deployed is an important component of the Singleitung. There also has to be good contact between them and the audience.

Hearing and understanding the audience
"We used to think a good school is one in which the students understand the teacher. Now we know that a good school is one in which the teacher understands the students." (Michael Feiten / Elsbeth Stern) In Open Singing, too, contact and communication cannot be a one-way street heading from the director to the audience. The director must see, hear and sense the audience as much as the other way round. It is important to emphasize this aspect when considering the setting and preparing the programme. It is not possible to create the same mutual contact in a 70-metre-long cathedral or a large public outdoor space as in a music room or a concert venue. Note: Roman amphitheatres proved the point that optimal visual and acoustic contact can be made with thousands of people. This prompted the French choir movement À coeur joie to regularly hold Open Singing events with nearly 5,000 participants in the antique amphitheatres at Vaison la Romaine in southern France (see picture on p.15).

Knowing, mastering and being the song
Directors who have to read the notes from the page cannot access their full faculties nor can they give 100% of themselves to the audience and the accompanists. At best, "knowing" a song is enough to select it. "Mastering" the song refers to mastery of all of its facets by heart. However, complete identification with the song is required for conveying the music. In the same way that a gifted storyteller is able to bring a story to life, conveyors of music resurrect a song in their very being. They "become the song".

Effecting attention not demanding it
Many choral directors demand attention. Good pedagogues effect and control it, deploying a style of Singleitung which effects attention and interest through skilful dramaturgy and methodology rather than through requests, The guiding principle is "effect attention with and through music".

Control interest – guide attention
Happy, healthy people chat – especially when they come expectantly for Open Singing. They look forward to the music and to singing. Music that resounds unexpectedly from the stage, a choir which strikes up the first song as it enters, usually draws the attention of the chatting audience immediately and the interest is greater than if a speaker steps onto the stage and politely asks for quiet. When a song ends and the pianist improvises a seamless transition into the next song, while a child simultaneously steps forward and begins the next song as a solo, the flow and the musical tension is better preserved than if there is applause (for whom?) and the director announces the next song, gives the page number and explains the special features of the song, etc.

Avoid missteps
"Success" and "failure" are always a matter of benchmarks and expectations. The feeling of having done "something wrong" in a choir depends heavily on the type of task and the expectations of the choir director. An exaggerated but illuminating maxim for choir directors is "It's always the fault of the choir director!" To understand it better, replace "fault" with "responsibility". Naturally, the choir director is not "responsible" for everything that happens in the choir, whether positive or negative. Rather, choir directors plan, lead, decide every tiny detail from one second to the next, give direction, and communicate with their voices, their bodies and their gestures. Every action of the choir director triggers an immediate and inevitable reaction in the contributors, to which the choir director must in turn react. And in this regard, "no reaction" is also a reaction. Choir directors are therefore only "at fault" or responsible for their own conduct and their reactions to the situation. It is their own conduct which leads the participants either to succeed or to fail – or to have the feeling of success or failure.

Successful directors of Open Singing therefore estimate the potential of attendees as well as much as possible, recognizing their heterogeneity and remaining open to any and all reactions, adjusting the tasks accordingly. The goal is to help participants experience and maintain a steady string of small "successes". This effects the desired sense of achievement and the targeted "joy" and lets the music thrive and "lift".

Celebrate successes
A look or a thumbs-up signal to the addressed party is enough in this respect. The authentic positive reaction, the "positive affirmation" or "reinforcement" of the tiniest success and progress – "I heard it!" – works like fertiliser in the learning process. There is definitely no room in this category for the impersonal and overused "Good!" or "Good, but!" which has been passed down through generations.

Nevertheless, it is the task of Open Singing directors to recognize many individuals, make a quick moment of contact with them and signal that their achievement was heard, even in a large group of contributors.

Playful learning – failing with relish

Laughing is like oil in the process of learning. The concept of "homo ludens", playing man, formulated in the 30s by Johan Huizinga, has been confirmed in many ways. It is well known among those who study the learning process that learning in a free, trusting environment, playful attempts and "failing with relish", driven by "intrinsic motivation" and "belief in one's own self-efficacy" (Albert Bandura) – "I can do it!" – are more effective than "cramming". Making music always has a playful, sometimes even athletic or artistic dimension, too. Children are proud when they can perform a complicated hand-clapping movement game or a tongue-twister faster than the person who teaches them to do it.

These kinds of elements are present in many songs. Some examples include: the hand movements in *Ding dong*; the "ribeli, rabeli, räbeli, robeli, böll" in *Alpenrumba*; and the complex variant 3 in *Lai-la*. Canons and more demanding music are also sometimes collectively "derailed". The general outbreak of jocularity that happens when something goes wrong, or there is a moment of chaos, eases tensions and creates common solidarity. In this respect, Open Singing directors' ability to occasionally laugh at themselves is also important. This is why "humour" is also part of the heading of the first chapter.

Singing instead of speaking

Music only takes place when it can be heard. Speaking is a music killer of the highest order. The participants are primarily there to sing. It need not even be an obstacle if the director is not particularly adept in the language of the participants. A successful Open Singing can be done with few words, capable gestures and other methodological means. There are singing leadership methods which are used completely wordlessly. These are indispensable when the amplification system stops working.

Showing instead of telling

The living "role model" naturally whets listeners' appetite to imitate it. The audience also receives far more information from the presentation of artistry by this "role model" than can be communicated through wordy explanations. In Open Singing, showing how to do something has to become a "musical treat", even if it is nothing more than an interval, a rhythmic pattern or a refinement of language. In this way, there are constantly little musical experiences in Open Singing which represent both a treat, inspiration, and an invitation to join in.

Boosting the powerhouse

Every group has its powerhouse. If the powerhouse falters, the whole team falters. Here, "boosting" means recognizing and reinforcing the abilities of the individuals who make up the powerhouse and continually challenging them to stay at their level. The task of the director is to discover and strengthen them. Directors do not do this obviously, but rather with generally reinforcing comments that everyone can interpret as they will.

Sometimes the principle of "one for all" serves this purpose. When directors address one person or group of people in the audience, the others also feel addressed, even if they are not directly concerned. For example, "The man in the back right is doing this series of steps wonderfully. Just copy him!" and "Have you heard how wonderful the sound coming down from the balcony is?" and "If my ears don't deceive me, there are quite a few experienced choral singers in our audience! Who is one of them? – Thanks for helping us!".

It is also important to take opportunities for direct contact with children, to reinforce them and occasionally give them special tasks or bring them onto the stage. When children are happy, their parents are, too.

Many of the songs included in this collection contain "fuel for the powerhouse" in the form of ad lib. voices, subsidiary or supplementary parts or opportunities for improvisation.

Offer support – individualize

The musical experience becomes more intense when directors offer support and easier alternatives for the slower learners and those who need help – instead of adjusting the general difficulty of the songs or the learning tempo to the slower learners. Some "ad libs" for slower learners include:
- Have them sing the melody while others sing the choral arrangement.
- Hum the melody or sing the vowels while others sing the lyrics (which might be in a foreign language).
- Only have everyone sing the refrain.
- Teach everyone a simple accompanying ostinato and then have individuals sing the main voices or improvise.
- Prominently support the secondary voices with choristers or instruments (e.g. using the amplification system).

Never say "No!"

Recognizing what is wrong does not actually mean identifying what is right. One seldom achieves the desired result by avoiding the undesired. Learning research has proved what attentive teachers have not failed to notice: It takes as enormous amount of thought and control to avoid one behaviour ("Don't shout!") in order to achieve the desired behaviour ("Form an O

OPEN SINGING – PRINCIPLES AND METHODOLOGY

with your mouths!"). The rule for Open Singing is: "Show, don't tell!" and "Assist, don't correct!". The participants are open for new things, they want to learn and love humour, but they do not want to be reprimanded. Phrases such as "Who else has already discovered the rest?" are better than "Please don't sing into the rest!" and "Who can sing so quietly that their neighbour can barely hear them?" beats "It's still too loud!"

Never say "Once again!"
Learning means having to repeat. But not every repetition is learning. It is well known that people cannot do exactly the same thing twice. Every repetition is, perforce, "worse" or "better". In this sense, "repetition" is not a possibility. "Repeat" comes from "re-petere", an active verb: "to strive after again", "to ask for again", "to beseech again". Every learning activity, including so-called repetition, done without alert attentiveness, interest and a clear goal before one's eyes is a waste of time and, in the end, tiring and frustrating for learners. Moreover, "blind" repetition merely cements every imprecise behaviour. Consequently, avoid the repetitive, blunt, inattentive attempt to do the same thing once again. The well known guiding principle for this is, "No repetition without new instruction or inspiration". Instead, strive each time for new quality, a new technical precision, or a new facet of expression.

Assisting instead of lecturing
If something sounds "wrong", it is not usually necessary to point it out. It is more organic to use the call-and-response method and "ride on the beat" (see p. 241) right afterwards to let participants experience the "right music". This lets them discover the differences themselves and correct their own mistakes. Directors can rely on the fact that many will have noticed their errors the first time and will be thankful for the second chance without having to interrupt the proceedings.

Consciously choose the level of communication
Open Singing directors make their own jobs harder and complicate the learning process for the participants when they do not consciously choose the level of communication, change it too rapidly or mix it accidentally. Should the audience "listen" closely, "watch" closely, "sing from the page" or "think about the instructions"? Changing too quickly confuses them and obstructs the learning effect.

The most important levels of communication are:
- listening, to store the music and sing it themselves
- watching, to follow the signals, store the movements and perform them themselves
- reading, to execute the notes
- accepting, memorizing and executing oral instructions

Through alert recognition, directors have to determine what the participants have processed and implemented before taking the next step and changing the level of communication.

When is "good" good enough?
Open Singing has different objectives and consequently different musical quality criteria from a choral rehearsal or choral concert. The goal of "good enough" is achieved when the essence of the music, of the song, has been made audible and has come alive, when the song "touches" and "moves". Depending on the song, the essence might be more in terms of the rhythm, the melody or the tone. When working on a canon with groove and movement, little time will be spent on the correct pronunciation, whereas the sound of the language in a foreign language song will be essential. The melody and the lyrics are more essential than the secondary parts in a new folksong. In contrast, the polyphony is decisive in an African choral song. When determining whether the goal of a piece has been achieved in Open Singing, the overall sound, the mood of the audience, and the emotional reaction of the participants serve as more objective quality criteria than they do for choral singing. It is okay to take a relaxed view of the auditory results in Open Singing. Success is measured in whether the participants want more.

PRACTICAL METHODOLOGICAL ELEMENTS

Riding on the beat
One of the most important techniques for introducing songs and rehearsing, which is also one of the most challenging for directors, is "riding on the beat". In this technique, the song is divided into small, coherent, easily understood musical units, be they sections of the melody, rhythms or lyrical units. A basic beat and a certain phrase length underlie the proceedings. The director communicates these musical units to the participants in a call-and-response manner. The musical units are then gradually put together to reveal the entire song. The attraction of this technique lies in the fact that learning takes place in a playful, joyful manner even while music is created and "grooved" throughout the entire learning process without interruption. This technique can be employed regardless

of whether the unit is a rhythm, a lyrical phrase, a melody or a four-part polyphonic phrase.

"Pulling the emergency brake"...

will be fined!" – unless it saves lives: for example, the heartbeat of Open Singing. Open Singing should only be interrupted to create curious, interested attentiveness or to allow for a laugh. In other cases, it is only discouraging and tiresome.

The piano as the heartbeat of the music

A good piano accompaniment breathes life into the song. It is better to go without piano accompaniment than to have one that hinders the flow of the music or the Singleitung.
The piano accompaniment
- plays the music first to open the audience to the character and style of the song, as well as any melody and choral setting
- carries the song rhythmically and harmonically
- supports individual parts
- improvises transitions
- enriches and enlivens the song through inspired additions and counterparts
- plays interludes during which the director can make comments and give instructions
- improvises accompanying patterns during movement games
- and much more besides.

Ideally, pianists at the side of the directors know the songs so well that they can be constantly attentive to the singing leader and observe and react flexibly to instructions, signals and conducting. They master the various styles of the chosen songs and can improvise well where necessary. Directors for their part, give the pianist precise guidance, know their strengths and weaknesses and work with them conscientiously and productively so that the two together can create a harmonious entity.

Chorister or pilot choir – source of inspiration and driving force

Choristers and pilot choirs are both a source of inspiration and a driving force. They also make it possible to employ manifold techniques to maintain the musical flow and simplify the learning process. The "development of a polyphonic part-song with notes" is deliniated here to represent some of the many options available.

- The pilot choir hums or sings the lyrics of the polyphonic composition.
- When repeated, the audience is invited to hum the song together with the pilot choir as well as they can in multiple voices. Those who find it too hard can simply listen.
- In the next run-through, a soprano soloist or a group of sopranos sings the soprano part of the song with lyrics into a microphone. The sopranos in the audience are invited to sing along to the melody with lyrics. The other parts continue to hum – with the support of the pilot choir or the piano. The soprano part is thereby amplified in the space and easily audible as a concert-ready role model.
- In the next run-through, which happens without a break, the alto soloist sings her part into the microphone to support the altos while the others hum their parts.
- Once all of the parts have been sung individually with amplification in this manner, everyone sings the song in their part with lyrics and, perhaps, hums together once again at the end.
- By doing it this way, the song is sung polyphonically several times back-to-back and all participants have the chance to learn their parts according to their abilities. The faster learners need not wait and the slower learners have several opportunities to learn their part while humming, even as the polyphony evolves further and further. Thanks to the presence of the pilot choir, the participants do not merely rehearse but actually make music, "give a concert" in fact, so that even passive participants can enjoy the offering.

Rejuvenation

There is always a risk of plummeting into a mood of swaying and nostalgia when the first tones of a widely known song are played. The alertness, self-perception and attentive listening immediately wane and the participants lean back into their individual comfort zones. They begin only to sing and stop making music. Making music, however, means to create something by listening to each other. Singing within our comfort zones is still musically uplifting when the ear and creative drive remain alert. These can be stimulated by artistic impulses from the director.

Some examples include:
- The song is first presented in a surprising musical version, e.g. sung solo in a child's voice or in a good choral arrangement.
- An inspiring piano part is used to pave the way for the entry of the song, which is then not only accompanied but also enriched by the piano.
- The director gives interesting notes on the background of the song or the meaning of the lyrics.

- The Singleitung triggers the making of differentiated music by, for example, shaping the tempo, the dynamic or the articulation, exposing the "primal force" of the song and initiating "magical moments".

Signs and signals

Signs and signals replace words and maintain the musical flow. They supplement or replace the notes. Signs using the hands, arms or the entire body (e.g. going down on bended knee) are only effective if they are clearly visible and unmistakable in their meaning. The larger the audience, the more precise and larger these signs must be. Signs and signals can certainly be augmented and combined with words or even song. Signs become signals when directors consciously select them for an instruction and always use them the same way. They only work when they
- are large enough and clearly visible,
- are used consistently,
- are employed at just the right moment.

A typical signal is the raised thumb for "1st verse", "begin", "1st voice" and two fingers for "2nd verse", "second part" or "2nd voice". The most widely used signal is the one for "attention": one arm held up loosely with the index finger pointing while the other arm continues to conduct. It has the effect of preparing the participants for a new instruction while they sing. Boards and items can also be used as signs and signals.

A classic example of the useful employment of signs is the canon *Dona nobis pacem*. Many people may know the song by heart but they always have the same uncertainties: bar 3 is easily confused with bar 7, and the third part of the canon is sung instead of the second. The differences between these parts is obvious and can therefore be indicated with signals. "stay open", "sing from top to bottom" and "sing from bottom to top". It is most effective when these three melody movements are shown each time simultaneously for all three voices.

Effective conducting

Clear conducting is a "power tool" and can accomplish surprisingly musical communal success in Open Singing. The recommended technique – herein called "effective conducting" – does not arise from the prescribed form or tradition, but rather from the question of whether and how effectively the movements affect the singers and the event. The guiding principle is "As little as possible – as much as necessary!" Effective conducting can bring about musical miracles in Open Singing. They can turn simple melodies and modules into quite complex pieces. Some examples include: *Alles verrinnt*, or the canons *Da pacem Domine*, *Hotaru koi* and *O-re-mi*. The cornerstones of effective conducting are explained in more detail in the planned volume about the direction of Open Singing (Edition Peters, in preparation):
- the inviting gesture
- the inhalation gesture
- large, calm movement
- the clear distinction between signal, entry and keeping time
- the right timing of signs and signals

Great conductors use this type of conducting naturally without losing the classic beat forms.

Variants in canon division

The classical method of dividing canons into groups in the auditorium is to do it spatially. There are various other and more creative divisions, however, which will intermix the contributors differently and achieve an exciting dynamic among the participants. With large audiences, it is also important to divide the groups so that the voices are also mixed. Suggestions for different kinds of canon division which yield a good intermixing in the audience include:
- Certain chair rows (e.g. A = row 1, 5, 9 et seq. B = rows 2, 6, 10 et seq. C = rows 3, 7, 11 et seq. D = rows 4, 8, 12 et seq.)
- Everyone whose birthday is in January to March / April to June / July to September / October to December.
- Everyone whose birthday is on the 1st–9th / 10th–19th / 20th to the last day of the month.
- Everyone born on a day that is an even or odd number.

Other options are: division by zodiac sign, by hair or eye colour, by age (note: make sure to assess the group's abilities correctly first). The greatest degree of independence and, at the same time, the best intermixing among the participants is to do "no dividing up at all". The accompanying instruction is "Everyone sings a different voice than they hear their neighbour singing" or "Everyone sings the vocal part they hear the least of".

Rhythmizing

This is a term used in pedagogy, where practitioners speak of rhythmizing an instruction sequence, a lesson, a day. The term does not refer to the content or methods, but rather, in the widest sense, to "tension and relaxation", to stretching a single lesson phase out in time, but also to the selection of levels on which the learners are addressed (e. g. "head, heart or hand") and the intensity of attention and concentration demanded of them. In contrast to "dramaturgy", which is related to rhythmization, the latter can only be programmed to a limited extent because in the end it has to be shaped in dialogue with the learners.

OPEN SINGING – PRINCIPLES AND METHODOLOGY

The art of rhythmization in Open Singing presupposes that directors
- perceive the audience at all times and correctly assesses its state of mind and its potential,
- have an expansive repertoire of music-methodological reaction options,
- always have their eye on the dramaturgical arc and the timing of the occasion.

> **Elements of rhythmization include:**
> - focussing on details or on the whole
> - increasing or slowing the tempo
> - intensifying or relaxing the concentration and attentiveness
> - switching between having to listen and being challenged oneself
> - switching between challenging and easy, and between the known and unknown
> - switching between intimacy and exuberance, between serious and joyful and between other characteristics of the music and lyrics.

SELF-REFLECTION AND VIDEO RECORDINGS

The craft of directing and conducting cannot be learned from a book. The courage to gain practical experience and advice from seasoned third parties is indispensable. Exact self-observation and self-reflection, however, are the most effective means of quickly developing direction skills. The best teachers for directors are regular video recordings of one's own work. In making such recordings, it is critical that the camera be pointed at the director during the key moments. However, the audience should also be recorded at regular intervals. Two cameras working in parallel are ideal.

Answering the following question will help you assess your performance:
- Am I easy to see and hear?
- Do I understand my instructions and the significance of the movements?
- Do the instructions sound the way I imagined they would?
- Do the movements look the way I intended?
- Do I appreciate my voice and the inflection of my comments?
- Does the audience's reaction match what I observed at the time?
- Does the audience sound the way I perceived at the time?
- Do I discover audience reactions which I missed during the sessione?
- Do the dramaturgy and the rhythmization match the occasion?
- Do I discover that I have unconscious and unnecessary behaviours?
- How effective are the accompanists (pianist, pilot choir etc.) at making music?
- Would I like to sing under this direction?
- What do I have to, or would I like to, change?
- What steps do I take to do so?

One recommended way to augment self-observation is to ask participants and other persons, be they specialists or the organizer, to give you feedback. These outside evaluations are generally a refreshing way of rounding off self-evaluation.

Assessing the success of your Open Singing:
- How many minutes did your participants actually spend singing, dancing, moving, speaking?
- How many songs and movements will they happily sing and show to their friends and family at home?
- How many new songs did they encounter, and how many of these are they eager to work on further?
- What do the participants remember/talk about most? Ideally, they will primarily think about the musical experiences they shared, rather than technical aspects such as the quality of the Singleitung or the performance of the pilot choir.

Appendix I: Alphabetical Index of Titles
(titles and incipits)

A

A Loop Song	170
A Summer's Over	51
A White Rainbow	82
African Alleluja	80
Ah ya zein	81
Alas, my love, you do me wrong	100
All mein Gedanken, die ich hab	113
All mein Gedanken, die ich hab (SATB)	114
All my Loving	202
All Praise to Thee	14
All through the Night	98
Alleluja (Trad.)	129
Alpen-Rumba	46
Alpen-Rumba Vocal percussion	47
Alta Trinità Beata	127
An Irish Blessing	146
An Irish Blessing (SATB)	147
And did those feet	152
Apollo	20
Are you sleeping	31
Arirang	65
Arirang (SATB)	66
As Tears Go By	214
Aunt Dinah has Blowed de Horn	206
Autumn Comes	99
Autumn Leaves	213
Ayelevi	27

B

Bonne nuit, cher enfant	143
Branle du Quercy	28
Breath Soft, Ye Winds	134
Bruder Jakob	31
Buenas noches mi amor	143

C

Calypso	39
Canon angelicus – Sanctus	121
Cantique de Noël	162
Çayeli'nden öteye	87
Chlungi Halunki	46
C-Jam-Blues	174
Come Ye Sons of Art	129
Csendes álmot, jó éjt	143

D

Da pacem Introitus	118
Da pacem, Domine (M. Franck)	16
Da pacem, Domine (P. Petersen)	16
Das erste Gebot der Kunst	54
Der Hasbâcher	109
Der Mond ist aufgegangen	110
Der Mond ist aufgegangen (SATB)	111
Dindirindin	144
Ding dong	26
Dito	35
Dobrú noć	90
Dona nobis pacem, 3-part canon	19
Dorme, dorme	143
Du fragsch mi, wär i bi	112

E

El cant dels ocells	160
El haderech	84
En veure despuntar	160
Evening Rise	58
Evening Rise (SSAATB)	58
Everybody Sings	171

F

Feliz Navidad	164
Flikkain polska	93
Flying	44
Frà Martino, campanaro	31
Frère Jacques	31
Freue dich, Welt	154
Frühling voller Blüten ist	19
Fruit canon	38
Funky Goodbye	40

G

Gabon maiteño	143
Gamla Moder Jord	94
Give It Up!	21
Give thanks	176
Glory, Glory	14
Goedenavond, goede nacht	143
Goli goggoli!!!	48
Good Morning (Evening)	24
Goodbye	23
Greensleeves	100
Guten Abend, gut' Nacht	142

H

Hail! Blessed Virgin Mary	157
Halleluja (K. Lafferty)	155
Hallelujah Gospel Theme	184
Hallelujah, I Just Love Him (Her) So	224
Happy (Ph. Williams)	227
Hark! The Herald Angels Sing	156
Heigh-Ho! Anybody home?	30
Hejo, spann den Wagen an	30
Hello (F. Fluri), 3-part canon	22
Hey, our mother, wake up	94
Hine ma tov u'manayim	30
Hit The Road, Jack	200
Hotaru Koi	37
Hue Gim Go	63
Hymn to Freedom	185
Hymn to Freedom (SATB)	186

I

I Am His Child	182
I am Sailing	192
I am the god of Harmony	20
I Like The Flowers	33
I may not be all that you are	182
Ich bin der Gott der Musika	20
If You're Happy	172
Immortal Bach	131
Istanbul Kasap Havası	86

J

Jaakoo kulta	31
Ja dan duia	32
Jahreszeiten-Kanon	19
Janie Mama	63
Jasmin Flower	64
Jerusalem	152
Jingle Bells	166
Join Along in East and West	50
Joy To The World	154
Jubilate (Praetorius)	17
Jubilate Deo	17

K

Keshet l'vana	82
Kom!	96
Komm, süsser Tod	131

APPENDIX I: ALPHABETICAL INDEX OF TITLES

L

La Bamba	62
La Nuit	136
Lahko noc, otrok moj	143
Lai-la	25
Laudemus Virginem	18
Leijoo	92
Leka nosht i lek sun	143
Lemon Tree	216
Let me fish off cape St. Mary's	60
Let us kiss and say goodbye	40
Levon hetki nyt lyö	143
Lili eder bat	102
L'on a fait fair' un navir'	106
Look at the birds	44
Loop Song	170
Love Me Tender	192
Lullaby and good night	143

M

Magnificat (Taizé)	122
Makumaná	36
Mango mango	38
Martinillo	*31*
May the Road rise to meet you	146
Me and Jack	42
Mester Jakob	31
Minoi, Minoi	70
Miserere mei Domine	120
Mo Li Hua	64
Move On!	34
Mu Süda, Ärka Üles	91
My every thought that I possess	113
My Lord, What a Morning	180

N

Nada te turbe (Taizé)	123
Nginesi Ponono	78
Nimba kalimba	36
Ninna nanna, mio ben	143
Nocturne	89
Noël, Noël	165
Now Let Us Sing	173
Noyana	79
Nun ruhen alle Wälder	126

O

O Little Town of Bethlehem	158
O Nuit!	136
Olson III	132
O-re-mi	72

P

Pata Pata	198
Peste dealuri, pe-un nor	143
Pique la baleine	106
Polska efter Jon-Sebastian	52
Porompom pón (Porompompero)	101

Q

Quare dormis, o Iacobe	31

R

Regocijad, Jesús nació	154
Réunis Aujourd'hui	15
Ritsch, ratsch fidirullala	108
Robinson	29
Rock 'n' Roll Band	196

S

Sag, wo schläfst du?	94
Sakura	57
Salsa Beach Band	195
Sambabrasil	45
Samiotissa	84
Sanctus, Sanctus	121
Sangena	75
Sankta Lucia	105
Santa Lucia	104
Schläft ein Lied	110
Seasons Canon	19
Shenandoah	61
Si ya hamba	74
Singt dem Herren	17
Sister, Carry On	178
Sov på min arm	89
Splendens Ceptigera	18
Spring	43
Stabat Mater (Kodály)	130
Step to the left	33
Što mi e milo	85
Sul mare luccica	104
Sweet and low	140
Szel lo zúg távol	150

T

Tábortűznél	150
Taga del i öst och väst	50
Tears in Heaven	208
Tebe pojem	124
That Lucky Old Sun	210
The Big Band (J. Fischer)	37
The First Commandment of Art	54
The River She is Flowing	116
Tiliseb	88
Tuonane Paradiso	145

U

Uinu vaikselt, mu lind	143
Un poquito cantas	56
Una mattina	107
Up in the mornin'	210

V

Va, pensiero	148
Vader Jacob	31
Vanitas Vanitatum	43
Vem kan segla förutan vind	95
Veni Creator Spiritus	128
Vent, vrais, vent du matin	30
Von guten Mächten	54

W

Wach auf, mein Herz, und singe	91
We are marching in the light of God	74
We shuv nezea	84
Wer hat an der Uhr gedreht?	40
When ev'ry heart joins ev'ry heart	185
While the moon her watch is keeping	98
With a Smile	194
Would you know my name	208

Y

Yakop usta	31
Yes, Lord, Yes	190
Yesterday	204

Z

Zwei Schritt nach links	33

Appendix II: Index of titles by categories

HOW TO APPROACH THE SONG CATEGORIES

The following division of songs into specific categories is designed to help the directors plan "sing along" events. If a song is not included in a particular category, this does not necessarily mean it is unsuited to that category. The intention is rather that the songs in any given category should be particularly well suited to it:

- The category **especially for children** can be useful when compiling a programme exclusively or predominantly for children (for example in schools), whereas the category **especially for families** starts from the premise that an event with a wide mix of ages will develop a different dynamic and allow a wider range of songs to be included.

- The category **especially for young people** is also intended for events predominantly for or with youngsters. However, this category contains more than just easily accessible, lively songs, as it is the editors' experience that under expert direction, young people quickly become receptive to more demanding music, such as simple polyphony. On the other hand, many "grown-ups" enjoy singing easily accessible, lively songs! Directors of good children's and young people's choirs, on the other hand, will find suitable repertoire in this book under the category **for experienced choral singers** and/or **for equal voices**.

- The categories **especially for newcomers and late starters** and for **singing without music** are not without challenges as the methodological skills of the director play a decisive role with these target groups. Fundamentally, however, these categories contain songs that are easy to learn and to sing, either because the melody and words are catchy or because the editors assume that the melody and/or words are already reasonably well known.

- The category **especially for experienced choral singers** is intended for singers that have no problem reading music and no fear of polyphony or experimentation.

- Moments of contemplation are called for in all sorts of situations. Anniversaries, births, weddings, funerals and so on can be occasions for singing with other people. In addition, many of the songs in this book are suitable for Advent and Christmas even if they are not included in Chapter IV. The category **for contemplation and/or Advent** is designed to cater for such occasions.

APPENDIX II: INDEX OF TITLES BY CATEGORIES

No. chapter/title	Adults	Young people	Children	Families	Newcomers/late starters	Equal voices	Movement	Contemplation/Christmas	Singing without sheet music	Experienced choral singers
I. CANONS, HUMOUR, MOVEMENT										
1. All Praise to Thee (Th. Tallis), 4–8 part canon	•	•	•	•	•	•		•		
2. Glory, Glory (M. Gohl), 3-part canon	•	•		•		•		•		•
3. Réunis Aujourd'hui (C. Geoffray), 3-part canon	•					•				•
4. Da pacem, Domine (M. Franck), 4-part canon	•					•		•	•	•
5. Da pacem, Domine (P. Petersen), 3 canons	•					•		•	•	•
6. Jubilate Deo (M. Praetorius), 5-part canon	•	•			•	•		•		•
7. Jubilate (M. Praetorius), 6-part canon	•	•			•	•		•		•
8. Laudemus Virginem, 3-part canon	•									
9. Splendens Ceptigera, 3-part canon	•				•	•		•		•
10. Dona nobis pacem, 3-part canon	•	•	•	•	•			•	•	•
11. Jahreszeiten-Kanon (P. Dubs), 4-part canon	•	•	•	•	•	•				
12. Apollo (M. Gohl), 4-part canon	•	•				•	•		•	
13. Give It Up! (M. Gohl), 5-part canon	•	•	•	•		•	•		•	•
14. Hello (F. Fluri), 3-part canon	•	•	•	•	•				•	•
15. Goodbye (F. Fluri), 4-part canon	•	•				•			•	•
16. Good Morning (R. Sund), 5-part canon	•	•		•	•					•
17. Lai-la (Czech folk tune, M. Gohl)	•	•	•	•	•	•	•		•	•
18. Ding dong (M. Gohl), 4-part canon	•	•			•	•	•		•	•
19. Ayelevi (Trad. Ghana)	•	•	•	•	•		•	•	•	
20. Branle du Quercy (French dance music)	•	•	•	•	•		•		•	
21. Robinson (German children's song, M. Frey)	•		•	•	•					
22. Heigh-Ho! Anybody home?, 3-part canon		•		•	•				•	
23. Hine ma tov u'manayim, 2-part canon	•	•	•	•	•	•			•	
24. Frère Jacques, 4-part canon			•	•	•				•	
25. Ja dan duia (S. Perkiö), 8-part canon	•	•	•	•	•				•	
26. I Like The Flowers, 3-part canon	•	•	•	•	•				•	
27. Zwei Schritt nach links, 4-part canon	•		•	•	•	•	•		•	
28. Move On! (Barkani / Natzchan), 6-part canon	•	•		•			•		•	
29. Dito (J. Siegrist), 3-part canon	•	•	•	•	•		•		•	•

APPENDIX II: INDEX OF TITLES BY CATEGORIES

No. chapter/title	Adults	Young people	Children	Families	Newcomers/late starters	Equal voices	Movement	Contemplation/Christmas	Singing without sheet music	Experienced choral singers
30. Makumaná (J. Debón), 4-part canon	•	•	•	•	•	•	•		•	
31. Hotaru Koi (Trad. Japan), 3-32-part canon	•	•	•			•			•	•
32. The Big Band (J. Fischer), 3-6-part canon	•	•			•	•				•
33. Fruit canon, 3-part canon		•	•	•	•	•	•		•	
34. Calypso (J. Holdstock), 3-part canon		•	•	•	•	•			•	
35. Funky Goodbye (M. Detterbeck)	•	•			•	•			•	
36. Me and Jack (J. Rathbone)	•	•			•				•	
37. Vanitas Vanitatum (J. P. Sweelinck), 4-part canon	•	•				•		•		•
38. Spring (Th. Gummesson), 3-part canon	•	•		•	•	•			•	
39. Flying (A. Simmons), 3-part canon	•	•				•				•
40. Sambabrasil (Th. Gummesson), 3-part canon	•	•	•	•	•	•			•	
41. Alpen-Rumba (U. Führe), 3-part canon	•	•	•		•	•	•		•	•
42. Alpen-Rumba Vocal percussion (M. Gohl)	•	•								•
43. Goli goggoli!!! (W. Buchenberg)		•	•	•			•	•		
44. Taga del i öst och väst (G. Eriksson), circle song	•	•			•	•			•	•
45. A Summer's Over (G. Christensen), 3-part canon	•	•				•				•
46. Polska efter Jon-Sebastian (G. M Hägg)	•	•								•
47. The First Commandment of Art (J. Haydn), canon	•	•								•
48. Von guten Mächten (M. Gohl), 4-part canon	•	•	•	•	•	•		•	•	•

II. AROUND THE WORLD

No. chapter/title	Adults	Young people	Children	Families	Newcomers/late starters	Equal voices	Movement	Contemplation/Christmas	Singing without sheet music	Experienced choral singers
49. Un poquito cantas (Trad. South America)	•	•			•	•	•		•	
50. Sakura (Trad. Japan; H. Willisegger)	•	•				•				•
51. Evening rise (Indian folk song)	•	•	•	•	•	•		•	•	
52. Evening rise (SSAATB, arr. M. Ansohn)	•					•		•		•
53. Let me fish off cape St. Mary's (Kelland / Loomer)	•	•				•				•
54. Shenandoah (Trad. USA)	•	•	•	•	•					
55. La Bamba (Trad. Mexico)	•	•	•	•	•					
56. Janie Mama (Trad. Caribbean), 4-part canon	•	•	•	•		•			•	
57. Hue Gim Go (Trad. Taiwan)	•		•	•		•				•

No. chapter/title	Adults	Young people	Children	Families	Newcomers/late starters	Equal voices	Movement	Contemplation/Christmas	Singing without sheet music	Experienced choral singers
58. Mo Li Hua (Chinese folk song)	•	•		•	•	•			•	
59. Arirang (Korean folk song)	•	•	•	•	•	•			•	
60. Arirang (SATB, arr. Young Jo Lee)	•									•
61. Minoi, Minoi (Trad. Samoan, arr. C. Marshall)	•	•	•	•	•	•	•		•	
62. O-re-mi (Trad. Nigeria, arr. M. Brewer)	•	•	•	•	•	•				•
63. Si ya hamba (Trad. South Africa, arr. F. Gohl)	•	•	•	•	•	•			•	
64. Sangena (Trad. Zulu, arr. Prof. M. Khumalo)	•	•		•	•	•			•	•
65. Nginesi Ponono (Trad. South Africa, arr. M. Gohl)	•	•	•	•	•		•		•	•
66. Noyana (Trad. South Africa, arr. F. Gohl)	•	•	•	•	•	•		•	•	•
67. African Alleluja (M. Detterbeck)	•	•				•		•		•
68. Ah ya zein (Trad. Arabic, arr. H. Willisegger)	•	•		•	•	•			•	
69. Keshet l'vana / A White Rainbow (J. Hadar)	•	•			•					•
70. Samiotissa (Greece, Island Samos)	•								•	
71. El haderech (Trad. Israel, arr. M. Gohl)	•	•	•	•			•			
72. Što mi e milo (Trad. Macedonia)	•	•				•				•
73. Istanbul Kasap Havası (Trad. Turkish-Greek)	•	•		•	•	•	•		•	
74. Çayeli'nden öteye (Trad. Turkish, arr. M. Başman)	•	•	•	•	•	•	•		•	•
75. Tiliseb (from Estonia, L. Virkhaus)			•		•			•	•	
76. Nocturne (E. Taube / A. Öhrwall)	•									
77. Dobrú noć (Trad. Czech, arr. Van den Borre)	•									•
78. Mu Süda, Ärka Üles (from Estonia, C. Kreek)	•	•			•	•		•		
79. Leijoo (Trad. Lapland, S. Valvanne)	•	•			•	•			•	•
80. Flikkain polska (Trad. Finland, K. A. Pöllanen)	•					•				•
81. Gamla Moder Jord (Trad. Sweden; M. Detterbeck)	•					•	•			•
82. Vem kan segla förutan vind (arr. G. Eriksson)	•	•								•
83. Kom! (M. Åslund)	•									•
84. All through the Night (Trad. Wales, M. Goldring)	•									•
85. Autumn Comes (Trad. England, arr. A. Merusch)	•	•		•		•			•	
86. Greensleeves (Trad. England / Scotland)	•	•		•	•	•				
87. Porompom pón / El Porompompero (Trad. Spain)	•			•	•	•			•	

APPENDIX II: INDEX OF TITLES BY CATEGORIES

No. chapter/title	Adults	Young people	Children	Families	Newcomers/late starters	Equal voices	Movement	Contemplation/Christmas	Singing without sheet music	Experienced choral singers
88. Lili eder bat (Basque Country, arr. J. Busto)	•									•
89. Santa Lucia (Trad. Italy)	•	•				•				
90. Sankta Lucia (SAB, arr. C.-B. Agnestig)	•			•		•				•
91. Pique la baleine (P. Denain / L. Guilloré)	•	•								•
92. Una mattina (Trad. Italy)	•	•		•		•				•
93. Ritsch, ratsch fidirullala (Trad. Swiss, M. Gohl)	•	•	•	•		•			•	
94. Der Hasbâcher (Trad. Austria)	•	•	•	•					•	•
95. Schläft ein Lied (M. Gohl / J. von Eichendorff)	•	•	•	•		•			•	
96. Der Mond ist aufgegangen (J. A. P. Schulz)	•	•	•	•		•				
97. Der Mond ist aufgegangen (SATB, A. Seifert)	•									•
98. Du fragsch mi, wär i bi (Trad. Switzerland)	•	•	•	•	•	•				•
99. All mein Gedanken, die ich hab (arr. M. Gohl)	•	•		•		•			•	
100. All mein Gedanken, die ich hab (SATB, J. Brahms)	•									•
101. The River She is Flowing (Trad. Indian, arr. M. Gohl)	•		•	•		•	•		•	

III. CLASSICAL AND SACRED

No. chapter/title	Adults	Young people	Children	Families	Newcomers/late starters	Equal voices	Movement	Contemplation/Christmas	Singing without sheet music	Experienced choral singers
102. Da pacem Introitus (arr. B. Kinzler)	•					•		•		•
103. Miserere mei Domine (J. P. Sweelinck / M. Gohl)	•					•		•		•
104. Canon angelicus – Sanctus	•							•		•
105. Magnificat (Taizé, J. Berthier)	•	•		•		•		•	•	•
106. Nada te turbe (Taizé, J. Berthier)	•	•		•				•	•	•
107. Tebe pojem (St. St. Mokranjak)	•							•		•
108. Nun ruhen alle Wälder (H. Isaac / J. S. Bach)	•							•		•
109. Alta Trinità Beata (Italian lauda, anonymous)	•							•		•
110. Veni Creator Spiritus (P. Esterházy)	•			•				•	•	•
111. Come Ye Sons of Art (H. Purcell)	•									•
112. Alleluja (Trad., W. Gohl)	•	•		•				•		•
113. Stabat Mater (Z. Kodály, arr. I. Sulyok)	•							•		•
114. Immortal Bach (J. S. Bach, arr. K. Nystedt)	•	•						•		•
115. Olson III (T. Riley)	•	•					•			•

No. chapter/title	Adults	Young people	Children	Families	Newcomers/late starters	Equal voices	Movement	Contemplation/Christmas	Singing without sheet music	Experienced choral singers
116. Breath Soft, Ye Winds (W. Paxton)	•									•
117. La Nuit (J. Ph. Rameau, arr. J. Noyon)	•	•		•						•
118. Sweet and low (J. Barnby)	•									•
119. Guten Abend, gut' Nacht (J. Brahms)	•			•	•	•				•
120. Dindirindin (Cancionero de Palacio)	•									•
121. Tuonane Paradiso (Trad. Tansania, arr. A. Schmid)	•	•	•	•				•	•	
122. An Irish Blessing (Trad. Irland, J. E. Moore Jr.)	•	•		•		•		•	•	•
123. An Irish Blessing (SATB, J. E. Moore Jr.)	•							•		•
124. Va, pensiero (from "Nabucco", G. Verdi)	•	•								•
125. Tábortűznél (L. Bárdos)	•									•
126. Jerusalem (C. H. H. Parry)	•	•		•						•

IV. ADVENT AND CHRISTMAS

No. chapter/title	Adults	Young people	Children	Families	Newcomers/late starters	Equal voices	Movement	Contemplation/Christmas	Singing without sheet music	Experienced choral singers
127. Joy To The World (G. F. Händel, arr. B. Fritschi)	•	•	•	•	•	•		•		
128. Halleluia (Karen Lafferty), 2-part canon	•	•	•	•	•	•		•	•	
129. Hark! The Herald Angels Sing (W. H. Cummings)	•			•	•			•	•	
130. Hail! Blessed Virgin Mary (Ch. Wood)	•							•		•
131. O Little Town of Bethlehem (17th century)	•			•				•		•
132. El cant dels ocells (arr. O. Martorell)	•									•
133. Cantique de Noël (A. Adam, arr. A. Lindström)	•			•				•		•
134. Feliz Navidad (J. Felicianol)	•	•	•	•	•	•		•	•	
135. Noël, Noël (J. Holdstock), 3-part canon	•	•	•	•				•	•	
136. Jingle Bells (J. L. Pierpont, arr. M. Detterbeck)	•							•		•

V. GOSPEL, BLUES, JAZZ

No. chapter/title	Adults	Young people	Children	Families	Newcomers/late starters	Equal voices	Movement	Contemplation/Christmas	Singing without sheet music	Experienced choral singers
137. A Loop Song (B. Gröger)		•	•		•				•	•
138. Everybody Sings (B. Gröger)		•	•		•	•			•	•
139. If You're Happy (H. Førde, arr. R. Sund)	•	•	•		•	•			•	•
140. Now Let Us Sing (anonymous)	•	•			•	•			•	•
141. C-Jam-Blues (D. Ellington, arr. B. Gröger)	•	•			•	•			•	•

APPENDIX II: INDEX OF TITLES BY CATEGORIES

No. chapter/title	Adults	Young people	Children	Families	Newcomers/late starters	Equal voices	Movement	Contemplation/Christmas	Singing without sheet music	Experienced choral singers
142. Give thanks (H. Smith, arr. M. Gohl)	•	•	•	•	•	•		•	•	
143. Sister, Carry On (C. McDade, arr. F. Gohl)	•	•			•	•		•	•	•
144. My Lord, What a Morning (arr. M. Gohl)	•					•		•		•
145. I Am His Child (M. Hogan)	•					•		•		•
146. Hallelujah Gospel Theme (A. Crouch)	•	•		•		•		•	•	•
147. Hymn to Freedom (O. Peterson)	•	•		•				•	•	
148. Hymn to Freedom (SATB, arr. P. Read)	•							•		•
149. Yes, Lord, Yes (A. Crouch)	•	•		•	•				•	•

VI. ROCK, POP, EVERGREEN

No. chapter/title	Adults	Young people	Children	Families	Newcomers/late starters	Equal voices	Movement	Contemplation/Christmas	Singing without sheet music	Experienced choral singers
150. I am Sailing (G. Sutherland)	•	•	•	•	•	•			•	
151. Love Me Tender Love Me Tender (Presley / Matson, arr. M. Gohl)	•	•		•	•	•			•	
152. With a Smile (M. Detterbeck)	•	•								•
153. Salsa Beach Band (M. Detterbeck)	•	•							•	•
154. Rock 'n' Roll Band (M. Detterbeck)	•	•		•						•
155. Pata Pata (M. Makeba, arr. M. Detterbeck)	•	•				•			•	
156. Hit The Road, Jack (P. Mayfield, arr. M. Carbow)	•									•
157. All my Loving (Lennon/McCartney, arr. T. Gohl)	•	•		•	•					
158. Yesterday (Lennon/McCartney, arr. M. Gohl)	•	•		•	•				•	
159. Aunt Dinah has Blowed de Horn (S. Joplin)	•									•
160. Tears in Heaven (Clapton/Jennings, arr. J. Høybye)	•	•		•						•
161. That Lucky Old Sun (arr. R. Sund)	•	•								•
162. Autumn Leaves (J. Kosma / J. Mercer)	•	•		•	•	•			•	
163. As Tears Go By (arr. W. Hoffmann)	•	•		•	•	•			•	•
164. Lemon Tree (arr. M. Detterbeck)	•	•	•	•	•	•				
165. Hallelujah, I Just Love Him (Her) So (arr. R. Sund)	•	•			•	•				
166. Happy (Ph. Williams, arr. B. Gröger)	•	•			•				•	•

The Editors

MICHAEL GOHL

© Walter Pfäffli

Michael Gohl is a conductor and music pedagogue from Zurich. For more than 25 years he has been directing Open Singing sessions all over the world – in every possible setting and on every imaginable scale, including international choir festivals such as Europa Cantat, the World Symposium of Choral Music, Les Choralies and Zimriya Israel. Michael Gohl is an internationally sought-after workshop leader and choral competition juror. He teaches at the Zurich University of the Arts, is principal of Musikschule Zollikon and has co-edited numerous songbooks and music-teaching materials. A special focus of his work is on youth development and music education. He has won a number of awards with his youth choir Jugendchor Zürich and has moderated some two hundred orchestral concerts given by well-known orchestras including the Zurich Tonhalle Orchestra, the Stuttgart Philharmonic and the Munich Philharmonic.

Michael Gohl was introduced to the Open Singing tradition by his father Willi Gohl (a founding member of the EFYC) during his youth, starting in 1967 with Europa Cantat, whose open singing sessions were conducted by Gottfried Wolters, César Geoffray, Uriol Martorell and Willi Gohl. As a professional clarinettist and pilot choir singer, he has subsequently contributed to dozens of "Singt mit!" (Sing Along!) events and radio broadcasts.

JAN SCHUMACHER

Professor of Choral Conducting at the University of Church Music in Rottenburg and conductor of Camerata Musica Limburg and the choir of TU Darmstadt, Jan Schumacher studied school music, German language and literature and choral conducting in Mainz and Frankfurt. Even as a child and youth, Jan Schumacher (who received his early musical training as a member of the Limburg Cathedral Boys' Choir and the youth choir of the state of Rhineland-Palatinate) was fascinated by the act of singing with other people, and this fascination remains the driving force behind his varied musical activities today. With his choirs he is developing a broad repertoire that extends from Gregorian chant to contemporary music and jazz, from the symphony orchestra to the big band and also includes vocal and electronic improvisation.

Jan Schumacher holds seminars for singers and conductors in numerous European countries as well as Iceland, Turkey, Argentina, Venezuela and the USA. He has co-edited various choral albums including *Reine Männersache*, published by Edition Peters. As Vice President and Chair of the Music Commission of the European Choral Association – Europa Cantat, he is charged with the enviable task of promoting choral music through the fostering of international exchanges between singers, conductors and composers.